FEMALE REVOLT

Female Revolt

WOMEN'S MOVEMENTS IN
WORLD AND HISTORICAL PERSPECTIVE

Janet Saltzman Chafetz
Anthony Gary Dworkin
University of Houston—University Park

with the assistance of Stephanie Swanson

Rowman & Allanheld
PUBLISHERS

ROWMAN & ALLANHELD

Published in the United States of America in 1986
by Rowman & Allanheld, Publishers
(a division of Littlefield, Adams & Company)
81 Adams Drive, Totowa, New Jersey 07512

Library of Congress Cataloging-in-Publication Data

Chafetz, Janet Saltzman.
  Female revolt.

  Bibliography: p. 225
  Includes index.
  1. Feminism—History. 2. Feminism—Cross cultural
studies. 3. Women's rights—History. I. Dworkin,
Anthony Gary. II. Swanson, Stephanie. III. Title.
HQ1121.C45 1986   305.4'2'09   85-22141
ISBN 0-8476-7392-8
ISBN 0-8476-7359-6 (pbk.)

86 87 88 / 10 9 8 7 6 5 4 3 2 1
Printed in the United States of America

Contents

Tables and Figures

Tables

Figure

Preface and Acknowledgments

In recent years women's movements have been the subject of considerable scholarly interest. Despite the quantity of available studies, several fundamental theoretical and comparative questions concerning women and social movements are still unanswered in the literature. This book is our attempt to delineate and address these questions.

In 1984 Janet Chafetz published *Sex and Advantage*, which is concerned with the factors that explain the degree to which females are categorically disadvantaged relative to males. In preparation of that book, she became aware that women have seldom, collectively, revolted against structured sex inequality despite the pervasiveness in time and space of considerable female disadvantage. A theory is needed to explain the lack of women's movements or at least to delineate the conditions that did lead to the rare instances of this form of revolt.

About the same time the *Western Sociological Review* requested manuscripts dealing with the linkages between macro and micro processes, especially issues relevant to the disadvantaged, including women. The authors share an interest in the topic of women as a minority (see Dworkin and Dworkin 1982): Chafetz from a macro structural, Dworkin from a micro social psychological perspective. Our article in that journal is revised and expanded here as chapter 3.

A number of general theoretical approaches to social movements exist in the literature, including ones that have appeared recently (see chapter 3). Yet an examination of the rather substantial literature pertaining to feminist movements discloses history, not theory. Typically described are a plethora of phenomena and changes during the decade prior to the reemergence of American feminism with little attempt to establish their causal linkages. Chapter 2 reviews these explanations.

Another impetus for writing this book is the nonexistence of a comprehensive study of women's movements across time and space. Most analyses concentrate on the United States at the turn of the century or at the present, or on the nineteenth-century movement in Great Britain. Discussions of other movements, while available, are widely scattered. Comparative studies of women's movements are confined to a few cases and rarely involve analyses of different historical eras or from different parts of the world. Consequently, causal theories are virtually impossible, since idiosyncratic factors cannot be distinguished from universal ones on the basis of only a few case studies. Chapters 4 and 5 rectify this shortcoming in their presentation of data on 32 first-wave and 16 second-wave movements. Chapter 6 is a partial test of the theory developed in chapter 3, using these 48 cases as a sample.

Chapter 1 was originally intended to present an overview of the various ways women, historically, have revolted, with the exception of women's movements. But Stephanie Swanson, our extraordinarily enthusiastic and dedicated research assistant, provided so much material that chapter 1 grew into a major analysis. Nowhere else are so many varied expressions of female revolt discussed as a coherent unit. It provides insight into the active role of women in revolting against their own oppressions and those of others. Ms. Swanson's research went well beyond what can be expected from a graduate student, and extended long after the stipend that funded her work had expired.

The Center for Public Policy at the College of Social Sciences, University of Houston, provided funds for the research. We are also grateful to the sociology department for providing summer funds for our assistant's work. We wish to thank our colleague Sol Tannenbaum for his generous assistance in translating some of the West German census reports. Finally, our departmental secretaries Lonnie Anderson and Brenda Gibson cheerfully typed and retyped much of the manuscript, for which we thank them heartily.

FEMALE REVOLT

1 Forms of Female Revolt

Since at least the emergence of settled agrarian societies, and in many instances in more technologically simple societies as well, females as a category have been disadvantaged relative to males in most times and places (Blumberg 1978; Chafetz 1984; Martin and Voorhies 1975; Nielsen 1978; O'Kelly 1980). While the degree and specific manifestations of sex stratification have varied considerably (Chafetz 1984, chap. 1), women's relative access to the scarce values of their societies has been markedly inferior to that of their male class peers in nearly all agrarian, pastoral, and industrial societies, as well as some horticultural and foraging.

Despite the worldwide historical prevalence of female disadvantage, only occasionally have women openly and collectively revolted against their deprivations. In fact, it is safe to assume that many females in any given society have not even been cognizant of the fact that, on the basis of their sex alone, they are systematically disadvantaged. This book represents an attempt to understand the circumstances under which large numbers of women have become aware of their collective deprivation, defined it as illegitimate, and organized in an effort to change the structure of society. Stated otherwise, if female disadvantage is so pervasive across time and space, what explains the emergence of women's movements in specific places in specific eras?

Women's movements have been rare in history, and have occurred only in the last century. Other forms of female revolt have occurred in many times and places, however. Substantial numbers of women have engaged in a variety of forms of individual and collective behavior in response to strains either unique to their sex or particularly felt by members of their sex. In a later chapter we shall address the variables which explain the emergence of women's movements. At this point we will examine a variety of forms of female revolt other than explicitly women's movements. In earlier historical epochs, female revolts did not become full-fledged women's movements since a sufficiently large number of women had not yet come to the recognition of the commonality of their plight, not because they were treated better.

The distinction between a women's movement and all other forms of female revolt lies in several phenomena. First, the focus of activity in women's movements is consciously oriented to some disadvantages that are unique to the female sex. The first and essentially only priority is to rectify female disadvantage. Women's movements involve the coordinated activities of groups, utilizing networks of communication, and engaging in sustained activities over a number of years. Such movements vary in terms of the scope of their ideology. Some challenge the full range of social institutions and definitions. We shall call them feminist. Others challenge only a limited range of institutions and tend not to question the basic societal definitions of appropriate gender roles. These we will refer to as ameliorative. Some of the forms of female revolt presented in this chapter approach our definition of ameliorative women's movements. However, even these failed explicitly to define the gender role or sex stratification systems as fundamentally illegitimate. By this we mean that they did not question social definitions and stereotypes of proper feminine and masculine behavior or institutionalized forms of sexual inequality.

INDIVIDUAL-LEVEL REVOLT

In virtually all times and places a number of women have, as individuals, manifested behavior that could be interpreted as some form of revolt against restrictions and inequities based upon their sex. At the mildest level is negative sex stereotyping, the practice of which members of both sexes engage, especially directed against members of the other sex. Such stereotypes may reflect a rudimentary understanding that women's problems with men are rooted in phenomena that transcend individual personalities and relationships. However, if this is the only expression of revolt, it will serve as little more than a very temporary catharsis, having virtually no ramifications for social structure or for women's behavior. Indeed, as a result, the existing gender role and stratification systems may be bolstered, as hostilities are harmlessly dissipated.

Some observers have concluded that much of the individual female behavior stigmatized by others as deviant are manifestations of revolt, albeit often unconscious, against gender-based inequities (Schur 1984: 8–9), for instance, lesbianism, many behaviors defined as the manifestion of mental illness when expressed by females, and those who refuse to conform to any number of feminine gender role expectations, resulting in stigmatization as "tomboys," "bitches," "unfeminine," or any number of other unflattering labels.

From this perspective, by rejecting males as sexual partners, lesbians reject gender restrictions implicit in heterosexual relationships (Bunch 1975; Chafetz, Beck, Sampson, West, and Jones 1976). For instance, Brooks (1981: 31) asked a lesbian sample what aspects of heterosexual relations are most unattractive. Over half (55 percent) responded, "assumption of male dominance," and one quarter (26 percent) cited "women's role expectations." These findings are mirrored in more qualitative data presented by Ponse (1978) and by Chafetz, Beck Sampson, West, and Jones (1976: chap. 7).

Likewise, psychiatric definitions of what constitutes mental illness for females, going back at least to Freud, are viewed by many as, at least in part, an attempt by male professionals to exercise control over nonconforming women (Chesler 1972; Smith 1975). Citing Goffman (1972), Schur contended

> that mental illness designating is likely to occur when those persons with whom an individual is regularly interacting conclude that he or she is "not prepared to keep his place." This notion seems particularly germane to the situation of women in our society. Given the numerous restrictions placed on female behavior, women are highly vulnerable to being deemed out of "place.". . . male domination of the formal processes of psychiatric diagnosis adds further to this vulnerability [1984: 197–98].

Helping professionals (social workers, psychologists, and psychiatrists) have defined mental health in terms that differentiate the two sexes, but are the same for a mentally healthy male and adult. By definition, a "healthy woman" could not be a "healthy adult" (Broverman, Broverman, Clarkson, Rosenkrantz, and Vogel 1970, 1972). Revolt against the feminine role, then, might lead to traits of mental health in an adult, but were likely to be labeled as illness on the basis of a woman's sex.

In virtually every era and place, some females have refused to conform to at least some gender role expectations and thus have been stigmatized as deviant or peculiar (if not sick) by their families and communities. For example, Veevers interviewed wives who were voluntarily childfree, a major form of female deviance almost everywhere that can be interpreted as revolt against the restrictions motherhood places on most women. She found that "all the wives interviewed feel that they are . . . stigmatized . . . including such unfavorable traits as being abnormal, selfish, immoral, irresponsible, immature, unhappy, unfulfilled, and nonfeminine" (1974: 505). Schur commented on the fact that voluntarily unwed motherhood is often viewed as "a 'willful' violation of maternity and motherhood norms," and as such is defined "as constituting an even more serious 'offense' than simply being 'caught' in an unwanted pregnancy" (1984: p . 87). Accidentally transgressing the norm of premarital virginity and "legitimate" motherhood is defined as deviant, but a result of loss of control. Willful transgression implies revolt and is thus more harshly stigmatized, inasmuch as it constitutes a double threat to the status quo.

One final example of individual-level female revolt concerns juvenile delinquency. Male delinquents are overwhelmingly guilty of acts that are criminally illegal, regardless of the perpetrator's age. Crimes against property and persons characterize their behavior. Girls, however, are most often adjudicated delinquent on the basis of status offenses specific to being minors. Such girls are defined as "ungovernable," which typically means that they are sexually active, as well as possible truants or runaways, and in general that their parents have lost control over their behavior. In short, it means that such girls are rebelling against the feminine role requirements of docility, obedience, and chastity. Boys manifesting such behavior, and especially precocious sexual activity, are rarely adjudicated delinquent on that basis alone. Despite the more serious offenses characterizing male delinquency, females are more frequently incarcerated and generally treated more harshly by the juvenile justice system (Chesney-Lind 1974, 1978; Sarri 1976).

Individual level, female revolt against the sex stratification and gender role systems of their societies is apparent everywhere in a variety of guises, only a few of which have we touched on here. However, typically, as long as female revolt is expressed as individual-level deviance, social control mechanisms available within the community are sufficient to stigmatize and punish transgressors, discourage most others from imitating them, and ensure that there are no general, social change ramifications of their behavior. In other words, change in the sociocultural system of sex inequality does not result from individual revolt. We now turn to those forms of female revolt which have been collective in nature but which do not meet the criteria of a women's movement.

WITCHCRAFT

Witchcraft has existed at least since recorded history began (Taylor 1974:1), and has been predominantly, if not overwhelmingly, female. This topic constitutes a bridge between our discussion of individual-level revolt and our subsequent discussions of various forms of collective female revolt, inasmuch as witchcraft has been both individual and collective in its manifestations. The witch coven and Black Sabbath Satan worship services of medieval and early modern Europe (see Lederer 1968:204), as well as collective societies of witches in some African tribes, represent the organized aspect; the thousands, possibly millions of both self-proclaimed and merely accused witches in colonial New England, medieval, and early modern Europe, and elsewhere, the individual aspect. The scope of this discussion is not to examine (1) what prompted the massive persecution of witches in particular times and places, (2) why the pervasive belief in witches has existed, (3) the social functions of witchcraft or of its persecution, or (4) any of the other related issues which have spawned a substantial literature on the topic of witches. We are more narrowly concerned with witchcraft as a manifestation of female revolt.

Witchcraft, or magic used for evil purposes, has generally been defined as either exclusively or predominatly female (although Gray (1979) disputed this). Cavendish (1979:35) noted this for classicial Greece and Rome. Russell (1972:280; see also Briffault 1963; Parrinder 1963:191) stated that in many parts of Africa and some regions of India witches are usually female. Indeed, Parrinder (1963:191) also found that female magic in many parts of Africa is always defined as evil, whereas males use magic for both good and bad purposes. In his review of magic in tribal societies, Briffault observed: "When magic comes to be exercised by organized male priesthoods, the illicit practice of the art by women is regarded as presumably malignant in intention. The magic woman who is no longer a priestess must necessarily be a witch" (1963:287).

Yet Russell noted (1972:279; see also Monter 1976:26) that in fifteenth century Europe, accused witches were about equally distributed between the sexes, but witch-hunts were not very pervasive. The massive European witch-hunts began early in the sixteenth century and ended rather abruptly in most places in the closing decades of the seventeenth; the latter decades also witnessed the New England witch trials. It was during this era that the identification of "witch" with "female" occurred most explicitly in the West (Monter 1976:21). Although men were sometimes suspected, it was almost always as individuals, rarely as part of a group (Russell 1972:279; Monter 1976:26), and such men were often closely related to a woman so stigmatized. This change occurred as a direct result of the publication of a book commissioned by Pope Innocent VIII, *Melleus Maleficarum (The hammer against witches)*, written by two Dominican inquisitors between 1487 and 1520. It was a highly detailed account of the supposed habits and practices of witches, which explicitly and more "clearly and vigorously than its predecessors," linked these practices with femaleness (Monter 1976:25; Carmody 1979:126). Between 1487 and 1669 it went through thirty editions in France and the German and Italian states (Hoch-Smith 1978:246).

The outcome of this linkage is only too apparent in the figures cited in Table 1.1. Not less than 70 percent, and as many as 92 percent of those accused in various European locales were female. Both Catholic and Protestant areas are equally represented in this data. Monter (1976:116–17) cited figures for Geneva that indicated that 76 percent of the accused were female from 1537 to 1662, but in the year of the worst persecution, 1571–72, 90 out of 99 accused witches were female. Sebald (1978:132) discussed the German region of Franconia, where the ratio of females to males was 10:1. In speaking of England from 1564 to 1663, Currie (1968:27) noted that only 16 out of 204 people executed as witches were male. Of the 31 people tried and executed for witchcraft in 1692 in Salem,

Table 1.1   Proportion of Accused Witches in Various European Locales Who Were Female

	Dates	Percent Female	Total Number Accused[a]
Jura, Switzerland	1539–1683	77	1,375
Castilian Inquisition	1540–1685	71	456
Essex County, England	1560–1675	92	290
Namur, Belgium	1509–1646	92	366
Dept. du Nord, France	1542–1679	81	260
Ostrobothnia, Finland	1665–1684	78	152
Saarland, Germany	1575–1632	72	439
Solothurn, Switzerland	1541–1720	82	137
Southwest Germany	1562–1684	82	1,288
Venetian Inquisition	1552–1722	78	549

[a]Numbers recomputed by authors
Source: Taken from Monter (1976:119).

Massachusetts, 24 or 77 percent were female (Sebald 1978:164). Koehler found 73 percent female when considering all those accused during the Massachusetts witch trials of 1692–93 (1980:391). Taylor's data on colonial Connecticut showed that from 1647 to 1786, 37 people were tried as witches, 75 percent of whom were female (1974:156–57). Considering all of New England from 1620 to 1699, of 311 accused witches, 74 percent were female (computed from Koehler 1980: 474–491). Many of the males accused were victims of guilt by association; half of the 56 males accused during the 1692–93 Massachusetts trials were close relatives of females who had been accused earlier. Rarely, however, was a female accused by association with a male (Koehler 1980:390).

Every scholar who has studied witchcraft in Europe and New England has recognized that both self-proclaimed and accused witches were not only usually female, but also tended to be elderly and disproportionately unmarried, especially widowed. They were mostly, although not exclusively, drawn from the poorest socioeconomic classes. Monter (1976:80) discussed the persecutions in Toul, in Lorraine Province, France, where, of 53 women arrested between 1584 and 1623, 29 were widowed and 12 never-married, for a total of 77 percent unmarried. In the Geneva trials of 1571–72, 50 percent of the women were widowed, 16 percent single, and almost all were poor (1976:116–18). Noting that during the early modern era, a substantial number of women never married, Monter (1976:122) concluded that their proportion among accused witches reflected their proportion of the general population. Nevertheless, widows were everywhere disproportionately high in their representation among the accused. He concluded that since widows are generally old, it is unclear whether their persecution stemmed from age or from marital status (1976:121–22). In several different locales around Europe for which data are available, the median age of witch suspects was 60, and this in an age when women were considered old in their 40s (1976:123). Sebald (1978:43) noted the same marital and age phenomena in speaking of Franconian witch trials. Briffault (1963:284) found that in tribal societies as well, witches tend to be old. Colonial New England, too, persecuted primarily the elderly (over age 50); as many as 75 percent of the accused in some places were in that age group (Koehler 1980:276). The poor were accused as well (1980:281). Among all accused witches in New England during the years 1620–99, only 58 percent were married at the time (computed from Koehler 1980:474–91).

In all places where people believe in witches, at least some of those said to be witches define themselves as such and purposely engage in practices which, by community consensus, are supposed to be indicative of witchcraft. Many, if not most, scholars have viewed such women as involved in a form of revolt, and men have responded with social control efforts through witch-hunts, even if they do not explicitly use such terminology. In speaking of African societies, Parrinder wrote that "women . . . find some escape from male domination in witch associations, and witch-hunts put them back in their place" (1963:60). Such witch-hunts, in turn, have been conducted by secret societies of men, the prime purpose of which is to protect males by combating female power as it is expressed in witchcraft. Briffault (1963:285; see also Hoch-Smith 1978) argued that in tribal societies, women use witchcraft as a "substitute for physical force" to reinforce their authority. Hoch-Smith (1978:249) pointed out that sometimes males, such as those of the Yoruba tribe in Nigeria, respond by placating the self-styled witches, but they also use them as scapegoats during periodic witch-hunts. The last organized witch-hunt among the Yoruba occurred as recently as the early 1950s (1978:266).

In speaking of colonial New England, Koehler remarked that some women "may have become witches because they wanted to possess the more direct power Satan offered them" (1980:278). He continued:

> Witchcraft became . . . proof of the female potency which women could hardly enjoy or assert in Calvinism. The discontented women demonstrated such potency by denying the centers of the ideal women's existence: submission before the husband and childbearing. Disqualifying herself from the restraints of the feminine role, and in fact inverting it, the witch began life anew [1980:279].

Confessed women's testimony showed that "they were far from loving their husbands and children," that they lacked "wifely deference," and that they were "cantankerous" (Koehler 1980:279). Moreover, confessed New England witches often directed their evil magic against children, which suggests that witches were "combatting the proper maternal role" (1980:280). In general, Koehler said of the self-avowed witches, "These women detested their ordained feminine roles of submission and maternity, and they inspired a great deal of fear" (1980:293). So, for New England women, witchcraft was an "avenue for female resistance" (1980:294).

When we turn to Europe, we find the same phenomenon. In his discussion of Franconia, Sebald said of self-proclaimed witches in general (i.e., not specifically female ones): "Witchcraft can be rightly called *justice magic* . . . . It was an equalizer exerting control over all statuses. Magic could be used to retaliate against tyrants" (1978:178, 184). Of course, poor women, and especially the elderly and the widowed, were the most powerless of the powerless, for whom magic must have appeared the only avenue for redressing grievances against the more powerful. In his analysis of European witches generally, Monter argued:

> People who rely on magical means of revenge are primarily those who are incapable of using the more normal or socially approved means of revenge such as physical violence (very common in early modern European villages) or recourse to law courts. Older women . . . had only magical revenge—or at least society assumed they had magical means of revenge, which amounted to the same thing in terms of . . . legal consequences [1976:124]

Cavendish echoed this with his assertion that for self-defined witches, its "great attraction all through the centuries has been as a road to power and success unattainable by ordinary approaches" (1979:161; also 119). In a similar vein, feminist Elizabeth Janeway wrote that "the witch role permits the woman to imagine that she can exercise some sort of power, even if it is evil power" (1971:129). Lederer proclaimed of medieval witchcraft that it was a "veritable feminine revolution . . . aimed at destroying . . . a patriarchal dictatorship" (1968:205). In short, deprived of other means of rebellion against the disadvantages and restrictions inherent in the female role, some women have turned to magic to gain power, in the process provoking the fear of males and, indeed, of their entire communities. It is little wonder, then, that witchcraft has been everywhere so heavily represented by females, and that the old, the unmarried, and the poor have been so disproportionately found among self-proclaimed witches.

What of those who have been merely accused of witchcraft and have not taken upon themselves such a definition? In what way has the existence of hundreds of thousands, maybe even millions, of such victims manifested female revolt? Basically, the same can be said of these women as was mentioned earlier with reference to mental illness: that the designation of the term *witch* has been a powerful social control mechanism used to punish those people, especially female, who failed to conform.

> Generalizations about the witch's behavior proclaim the opposite of respectful conduct, condemn such behavior, and by so doing assert the proper cultural values. The witch establishes an image of what people should *not* be . . . . In essence, thus, the image of the witch made a contribution to the maintenance of social order [Sebald 1978:182].

Indeed, Szasz (1961:205, 304) argued that the contemporary labeling of people as "mentally ill" is almost the exact counterpart of the medieval label of "witch," both of which function to help preserve the status quo. Conrad and Schneider, citing Szasz, made essentially the same point. They stated that in fifteenth- and sixteenth-century Europe, "anyone who showed psychological, behavioral, or physical deviation was labeled a witch or sorcerer" (1980:42–43).

Although the accusers might be either sex, those who tried witches in Europe and North America, or persecuted them in Africa or classical Rome and Greece, were virtually all male officials—lay or ecclesiastic (Lederer 1968:199). One can speculate that their fear of females who deviated from prescribed roles has been particularly great relative to many kinds of male nonconformity and that female revolt has been defined as especially threatening to the status quo. Speaking of European witch trials generally, Garrett wrote:

> When a woman failed to maintain her reputation because of inappropriate female behavior, she faced not ostracism—that was practically impossible in the village or the packed urban neighborhood—but distrust, animosity, and even fear . . . . Years of distrust and suspicion might culminate in accusations of witchcraft . . . [1977:466].

Monter explained European witchcraft accusations in terms of "projections of patriarchal social fears onto atypical women, those who lived apart from direct male control of husbands or fathers" (1976:124). Cavendish,in speaking of classical Greece and Rome, talked of the witch figure as a "wildly exaggerated stereotype of the woman who does not stay dutifully at home, obedient to her menfolk" (1979:35).

"Vulgar" speech, or indeed "any unconventionality in a woman's sexual attitudes or behavior" (Koehler 1980:272) could arouse suspicion of witchcraft in colonial New England. Accused witches often showed such traits as "impatience . . . a desire to command, malice, and vengefulness," or simply failure to behave like a "proper lady" (1980:277). Koehler went on to point out that a woman was "either a proper lady, struggling to live up to a stereotyped ideal; or a whore or witch, undermining modesty and the reputed joys of submissive maternity." Given the "intangible quality of the witch's offense," any "abnormal" female could be stigmatized as such, perhaps especially rebellious women in a society "which viewed independent-minded women with suspicion and alarm" (1980:293–94). Koehler cited an estimate that two thirds of accused New England witches were guilty of either rebellion against authority figures (parents, husband, or magistrates) or of adultery (1980:404). Those who had openly flouted the ideal feminine role received quick convictions. For instance, the first person to be hanged during the Salem witch-hunt had been three times marrried but "would not be dominated" by any of her husbands. She operated an unlicensed tavern where people played illegal games, and she dressed "provocatively" (1980:404). During these witch-hunts, many petitions were signed to save the more traditional women who were also accused; "no one . . . argued on behalf of the nontraditional women accused" (1980:406). Perhaps the most famous New England woman convicted of witchcraft was Anne Hutchinson. Her "crime" was to demand equality with men as an interpreter of divine writ (1980:282). Dorothy Waugh was denounced as a witch in 1660 "for attempting to speak at Sabbath services" (1980:288).

Quaker women were especially likely to be branded as witches by Puritans in the early 1660s. "The extraordinary assertiveness of Quaker women had helped to create a Puritan state of mind which inextricably linked Quakerism with witchcraft" (Koehler 1980:289). In fact, as we shall discuss in a later section, women were often overrepresented in dissident religious movements such as Quakerism and the various heresies of medieval Europe. Russell claimed that

> The fact that women made their presence felt in orthodox reform, heresy, and witchcraft . . . to a greater extent than anywhere else in medieval society suggests that they felt deprived, not of wealth, but of the dignity and worth they deserved as human beings. In turn, the activity of women disturbed, even frightened, the male establishment . . . who had every intention of keeping women in their place [1972:282].

Perhaps the most famous accused witch was Joan of Arc. Janeway commented: "Joan of Arc . . . was accused of witchcraft by the English because they couldn't deny her power, for she had beaten them in the field, but they couldn't permit themselves to think that such a defeat by a woman was normal. It had to be magical" [1971:127].

Janeway (1971:128) also discussed a contemporary case of witchcraft accusations in the Mysore region of India. Socioeconomic changes created a new class of female moneylenders, as the region shifted into a money economy. The few moneylenders of earlier times were rich male landlords who prevented borrowers from going bankrupt. The women were not as effective and their "driven clients" as a result reacted by accusing them of witchcraft. Not their greed, but their violation of the traditional feminine role was the basis of the accusations, according to Janeway (ibid.). Likewise, in Africa "where females gain authority in male-dominated societies . . . male suspicion and resentment are focused in the concept of witchcraft, with attitudes, practices, and roles that are strikingly similar to those of the European Middle Ages" (Hoch-Smith 1978:248). Hoch-Smith documents this assertion with particular attention to the Nupe and the Yoruba, in both of which cultures women are very successful in business and very independent, yet face accusations and persecutions as witches.

A number of practices appear to be ascribed to witches almost universally. For our purposes, a few are especially interesting. Almost everywhere witches have been accused of intending harm to children, of aborting pregnant women, and of interfering with fertility, reflecting a widespread fear and/or the reality of revolt against the maternal role. In this vein, midwives in medieval Europe were especially liable to be accused of witchcraft (Ehrenreich and English 1973; Forbes 1966:117–130; Lederer 1968:200–201). Koehler reports that of 79 suspected witches in pre-1692 New England, 40.5 percent of the women, but only 16.7 percent of the men were accused of harming children (1980:280). Another characteristic almost universally attributed to witches is bizarre or "unnatural" sexual behavior, and related to this, the use of castrated penises and stolen semen in their rituals or concoctions. While a variety of psychological explanations have been adduced in the literature to explain this set of beliefs, we think it manifests, at least in part, a sexualized expression of a more general fear of female independence from male control.

We end this discusson of witches with a brief look at some of the "victims" of witchcraft: the "possessed." In many places, a substantial proportion of those who accused others of witchcraft were females, often girls, whose own bizzare behavior was interpreted as the result of a witch's malice. In the Salem witch trials, most of the possessed were adolescent girls; indeed, it was they who began the phenomenon. Koehler (1980:394–96) argued that their behavior represented an unconscious rebellion against the restrictions on their freedoms that, as young females, they suffered. They attacked authority figures because it was the only form of rebellion available to them. Through the mechanism of a "fit" they could engage in otherwise forbidden behavior such as dancing, singing, drinking alcohol, fantasizing about sex, and criticizing their elders—even including ministers. "The choice of victims [i.e., those accused of witchcraft], many of them eccentrics, suggests that the bewitched females were most discomforted by those women who had acted upon their own inner needs to ignore or defy the ideal feminine sex role" (1980:398). Monter also noted that the "possessed" who accused others of witchcraft in Europe were primarily women and children, "society's weakest elements" (1976:139). Citing examples in Africa and Apulia, Italy, Garrett (1977:467) argued that claiming to be possessed grants special privileges or license to women in male-dominated societies. "It provides one of the few socially sanctioned outlets for frustration and powerlessness, one of the few legitimate means of protest against husbands and other men who dominate the afflicted women" (1977:468).

Women throughout history have revolted against the disadvantages and restrictions placed upon members of their sex in male-dominated societies by becoming witches, either individually or as part of a collectivity. They have revolted, albeit less consciously, by becoming the "victims" of witches. And finally, many who rebelled have been stigmatized as witches, with the not rare consequence of forfeiting their lives. For the self-proclaimed it has brought some measure of power and independence when no other opportunities have existed to do so. However, for most who have been involved, a terrible cost has been paid over the millennia. In the final analysis, this form of revolt can only last as long as people continue to believe in magic, as the witch's "power" is not really demonstrable apart from such a belief system. In the West, this meant that the era of the eighteenth-century Enlightenment all but spelled the end of this form of female revolt, and its persecution, although it continues to exist in some parts of the world today.

DISSIDENT RELIGIOUS MOVEMENTS

In discussing witches, we noted in passing that in both Europe and colonial New England women were often associated with dissident religious groups, such as Quakerism and a variety of medieval heresies. Furthermore, such association often resulted in accusations of witchcraft (Koehler 1980; Russell 1972). Even in the absence of persecution as witches, heretics were often persecuted simply as heretics, where the power of an established religion enabled such a practice. In this section we focus specifically on women's role in some Christian religious movements—both medieval heresies in Catholic Europe and dissident Protestant groups in North America.

There is ample documentation of the fact that during most of its history, Christian theology and practice (like that of the other world religions) have been very misogynistic (e.g., see Miller and Swift 1977: chap. 5; Pagels 1976; Ruether 1973). The Protestant Reformation did little to change the fifteeen-hundred-year-old Christian (i.e., Roman Catholic) view of women as inferior, potentially evil if uncontrolled, polluted, subordinate, and without any right to authoritative roles in religious institutions. Calvinists and Lutherans joined Roman Catholics in punishing women who deviated from their prescribed "place," by persecuting them as witches. Indeed, there is little in the literature to distinguish the basic Reformation religions from Catholicism in terms of their views toward, or treatment of, women. It is against this general backdrop that women's role in dissident religious movements can be understood as yet another form of female revolt, not fundamentally different from the kind of revolt manifested by self-proclaimed witches (Russell 1972).

The late Middle Ages witnessed a profusion of heresies, or religious movements defined by the established Catholic church as propounding erroneous, devil-inspired doctrines and practices. Contemporary observers at that time, as well as some recent scholars, have noted the disproportionate number of women attracted to these movements. Pagels (1976:300; see also Wakefield 1974:74) cited a medieval bishop's complaint that women in particular seem attracted to heretical groups, and especially those in which prayers were offered to the Mother and in which women could become priests. Lerner (1972:229) noted that a disproportionate number of the Free Spirit heretics of the thirteenth and fourteenth centuries were female, while Russell (1972:281) claimed that women were "prominent among heretics" of all kinds in medieval Europe. Wakefield (1974:74) and Strayer (1971:32,37) spoke of the high proportion of women, especially of the nobility, among the Cathars and, to a lesser extent, the Waldenses, both major heresies that flourished in the twelfth and thirteenth centuries.

Despite such recognition, and a vast historical literature concerning medieval heresies, there are only fragmentary references to the general role of women (as distinct from specific biographical accounts) in this phenomenon. These scattered references all concur in the view that the heresies in which women were highly active defined and treated their sex better than did the established church of Rome. Wakefield stated that "in Catharist teaching, in contrast to . . . medieval Christian thought, women were not regarded as by nature inferior to men." Indeed, "some female Cathars enjoyed positions of prestige and authority" (1974:74). In a more detailed analysis of the Cathars, who were also called Albingensians, Strayer stated:

> It is noteworthy that women could be accepted as members of the "perfect," which may help to explain why Catharism was so attractive to many women . . . . To be one of the "perfect" gave a woman a higher status in the Cathar Church than she could ever attain in its Catholic rival [1971:32].

The Cathars flourished in France from the mid-twelfth until the early thirteenth centuries, when they were brutally supressed by a papal army. They had minimal hierarchy, their ministers being the "perfects" just mentioned. A perfect publicly renounced the world, gave up all property, and wandered the country seeking to convert others (see also Russell 1972:282). According to Guttentag and Secord (1983:62), Albigensians despised marriage and children as well.

As for women's attachment to the Waldensian heresy, a movement contemporaneous with the Cathar and often confused with it by the common people, Strayer said of Waldo, the founder, "He saw no reason why women should not be allowed to preach as well as men. (Here again we find that unusual acceptance of the equality of women that seems to have had an especial appeal to the ladies)" (Strayer 1971:37). This group too was "savagely persecuted."

The Free Spirits, a thirteenth- and fourteenth-century, primarily German heresy, was also heavily comprised of females, about whom Lerner wrote:

> Women could not become priests, but Free-Spirit doctrine offered them something better than that: full union with divinity. A tract like *Schwester Katrei*, in which a woman rises to a position of distinct superiority to her learned male confessor, surely must have given a goal and sense of identification to numerous others [1972:230].

They too were persecuted by the church.

Noting that women of all classes, from the nobility to the poorest, participated in medieval heresies, Russell attributed this to "a quest for dignity and meaning" in a society where women were "faced with a lack of sympathy on the part of the orthodox establishment" (1972:282). Lerner cited a German source which claimed that "heretical doctrines . . . satisfied female yearnings for emancipation" (1972: 230, fn. 7).

The largest single female religious movement of medieval Europe was not really a heresy, although it was periodically treated as such by the church, and its members were therefore sometimes persecuted (Leff 1967:18). This was the Beguine movement, which began in the twelfth century and grew rapidly in the thirteenth, after which it was controlled and regulated carefully by the church and continued in existence, in truncated form, until the French Revolution. It was a general, northern European phenomenon that was most widespread in the urban areas of the Lowlands, France, and Germany (1967:18). The Beguines were female communes that were halfway between church-sponsored nunneries and lay life. There was a male counterpart, called Beghards, but they were never as numerous as the Beguines. The primary reason for their existence was the incapacity of regular, church-sponsored convents to accommodate the huge female demand for a communal, religious life. The substantial surplus of unmarried women for whom no marital partners were available (due to very high male mortality), plus the ever-present widows, combined with a very real, widespread religious fervor and the church's unwillingness to open new convents, to create this demand (McDonnell 1969). In addition, as Lerner noted, "to make matters worse, there was a scarcity of legitimate female vocations" (1972:230).

The women lived a communal, religiously focused and chaste life, but they engaged in ordinary, secular work, typically in the textile trades, to earn their subsistence. The movement began among aristocratic and patrician women in the twelfth and thirteenth centuries (Leff 1967:17; McDonnell 1969). By the fourteenth century most of the participants were from the lower classes, and the Beguines had become the poorhouses of many communities. The Beguines offered employment opportunities to the poor, and to the wealthy an alternative to marriage. Also, "one factor which persuaded women of gentle birth to embrace a rule or adopt the penitential life was the very narrowness of the sphere to which they were confined" (McDonnell 1969:85). Leff made essentially the same point by stating that for women, "it was . . . the only way to some kind of independent existence which had its own significance. As such it was an outlet from the confines of a man's world, as well as a vocation" (1967:17).

The church authorities viewed the Beguines as a problem. Although they were officially recognized and sanctioned by the church, they were not under its direct control, and therefore were essentially unregulated as to practice or theology. The church vacillated in its policies toward the Beguines, but by the fourteenth century there was a major move to bring them under the more strict and direct control of church authorities. This resulted in large measure from the widespread reality—and even more widespread perception—of heresy within the Beguine movement. Especially in the German states, the Free Spirit heresy and the Beguine movement became very closely intertwined (Leff 1967:315; McDonnell 1969), in reality as well as in the view of the church. Leff (1967:18) argued that it was the independence of the Beguines that led to their being defined and persecuted as heretics. Their demise as independent communes followed upon this persecution.

We now shift attention to the other side of the Atlantic, about two hundred years later, to seventeenth-century colonial New England. From the point of view of Puritans, there were a series of heresies in that century to which "women, in particular, were susceptible" (Koehler 1980:216). The first religious rebel was Roger Williams, whose heresy occurred in 1635–36 and whose followers were disproportionately female. Although he defined women as unfit for preaching or governing, his theology stressed freedom of conscience and the equal humility of all persons before God. Koehler (1980:217) felt that women were especially attracted to William's theology because they were freed from the constraint of depending entirely on their husbands and fathers for religious guidance.

The first major female revolt, however, came a year later when Anne Hutchinson became an outspoken leader of the Antinomian heresy in Boston. With her "powerful example of resistance, the distressed female of Massachusetts discovered how to channel their deeply felt frustrations into a viable theological form and to rebel openly against the spiritual and secular status quo" (Koehler 1980:218). The Antinomians believed that all power comes directly from God and thus men and women are equally dependent. "Antinomianism could not secure for women . . . practical earthly items . . . but it provided compensation by reducing the significance of these powers for men" (1980:221). Antinomian women used their feeling of an in-dwelling Holy Spirit to castigate male authorities, including their husbands (1980:219). Both rich and poor women joined the heresy, following the example of the assertive, highly intellectual, brave, witty, and outspoken Anne Hutchinson.

> Other Massachusetts women who wished to reach beyond the conventional, stereotypic behavior of "worthy and godly weomen" attached themselves to the emphatic example of Anne, and to God's ultimate power, in order to resist the constraints which they felt as Puritan women [Koehler, 1980:224].

Koehler claimed that some of these women, and certainly Hutchinson, were "primitive feminists . . . who consciously recognized that sexual inequalities existed in society, found these inequalities objectionable, and protested against them by design" (1980:228). Others, however, were not consciously rebelling against their sex roles, but were expressing felt frustrations that were indeed grounded in precisely those sex roles (ibid.) Hutchinson and a number of other "overly assertive women" in Boston and Salem were excommunicated and banished in 1637–38, and by the mid 1640s the Bay Colony had squashed the heresy completely.

For a brief period in the 1640s a small Anabaptist heresy appeared under the leadership of Lady Debora Moody, and it too attracted a disproportionate number of women. However, since nothing in its theology or practice was specifically relevant to Puritan women's need for increased freedom, prestige, or power, it lacked widespread appeal for rebellious women (Koehler 1980:240).

By the mid-seventeenth century a new heresy appeared in Puritan New England and "the female discontent which surfaced in the Antinomian years and festered in the Anabaptist years virtually exploded" (Koehler 1980:246). Between 1656 and 1664 large numbers of Quakers, especially female, traveled through Puritan New England seeking converts. In fact, the first Quakers to enter Massachusetts were two women. Every colony quickly enacted laws designed to "root out this new heresy" (1980:247). The Quakers were highly assertive and very courageous, and "men in particular felt it necessary to 'prove' their power over such women by beating them into submission" (1980:255). While Quaker men were also beaten, Koehler argued that, unlike the males, "female Quakers endured severe punishment partly because they had stepped outside their sexual bonds" (ibid.).

Why was Quakerism so appealing to women? Quaker theology was radically equalitarian, no less in terms of sex than social class. Ranks were irrelevant; salvation was available to anyone who opened her/his heart to God. George Fox, the founder, "accentuated the fact that Christ was as strong in the woman as the man." He and the woman he later married, Margaret Fell, are considered by Quakers as cofounders of the religion. Beginning in Britain, the religion spread quickly to the American colonies (Speizman and Kronick 1975:231). Fox argued for female ministers and permitted women to speak out in church. He even claimed that God sometimes (although not often) chose women to rule, so women could be mayors, justices, sheriffs, even monarchs, if God so directed them. All this was undergirded by equal education for girls and boys. Fox also stressed love and close companionship as the only legitimate basis for marriage. Quakerism did not treat the sexes totally equally, however. Women were still viewed as the weaker sex, still enjoined to be modest, still subject to the authority of their husbands in nonreligious matters, and in many places men and women conducted separate religious meetings (Koehler, 1980:257–58). Despite this, Quakerism

> provided them the opportunity to occupy one of the most prestigious positions in seventeenth-century society—that of preacher. It incited women to argue with men on an intellectual level . . . and to exercise dominion over their own religious lives. It removed women from the strict confines of the home, opening . . . an arena for very unfeminine missionary activity [Koehler, 1980:258].

Indeed, this appeal was not confined to the seventeenth century, nor to North America. Loukes (1965:126) provided data on Quakers in Britain in 1963: 57 percent of the members were female, and 57 percent of all elders and overseers were also female.

Clearly, seventeenth-century Puritan New England was a hotbed of female revolt, expressed primarily (but not exclusively) through a series of dissident religious movements, defined and persecuted as heretical by the established Calvinist authorities. Of this revolt Koehler said:

> Not always aware of the causes of their rebelliousness, they had no social formula for restructuring the world in which they lived. As women hungry for freedom but restricted by seventeenth-century awarenesses, they could do little more than adapt their religious beliefs into a vehicle for protest [1980:259].

The nineteenth century in America witnessed both strong revival movements and a plethora of new religious groups, many of which grew out of revivalism. Of revivalism generally,

> Women were especially important in this effort. They constituted a majority of those attending the revival meetings and they were among the most fervent in seeking the conversion of their family and friends. The more traditional churches had generally not allowed women to preach or to participate fully in worship, but revivalists . . . strongly encouraged innovations such as allowing women to pray in mixed public meetings. A few women even became itinerant evangelists . . . . They also provided new institutional means by which women could begin to participate more actively in the larger society. Moral reform groups, missionary organizations, Bible and tract societies and a variety of other groups all depended heavily on women, and indirectly encouraged them to become involved in the affairs of their society [Foster 1981:229; see also Epstein 1981].

A substantial literature exists concerning disssident religious groups such as the Shakers, Oneida Perfectionists, and Mormons. Some of this (e.g., Foster 1981; Kern 1981) went into extensive detail concerning their radical differences from established religions in their views about, and treatment of, women. However, nowhere have we been able to find any evidence that women were attracted to most of these groups in disproportionate numbers. Most authors have ignored this issue entirely. The scanty evidence that does exist suggests that the Oneida Perfectionists and Mormons attracted about equal numbers of males and females as converts (Anderson 1966:141; May 1983:61–63; Whitworth 1975:148). The Shakers, however, appear to have attracted substantially more women than men, at least in the later stages of their existence. Desroche (1971:131, computed from Chart 5) presented data for 1874 (100 years after Shakerism arrived in the United States) that shows that of a total of 2,415 members, 63 percent were female. Whitworth stated:

> It seems likely that the sexual dualism of the sect exerted a greater appeal to women than to men, but this cannot be demonstrated for the period of Shakers' expansion, although in the second half of the nineteenth century women converts were definitely in the majority [1975:39].

Bainbridge (1982:36) presented data that showed the following proportion to be female over time: 1840, 57.7 percent; 1860, 59.1 percent; 1880, 64.5 percent; 1900, 72.2 percent; and 1926, 86 percent. He argued that this probably reflected both greater male dropout rates and disproportionate female recruitment.

Shakerism, an offshoot of Quakerism, was founded in Britain by a woman named Ann Lee, who came to America in 1774. Shakers referred to her as the "female messiah," and perceived God as both male and female. Shakerism continued in existence well into the twentieth century, but in extremely small and ever-dwindling numbers. A central tenet in their faith was total celibacy for both men and women, which removed from women the burden of having and raising children, allowing them to concentrate on religious life. (It also meant that replacement of members was very difficult.) The sexes were equal at all levels of religious and organizational structure. But Shakers were highly traditional in their attire and in their strict division of work roles for men and women. They lived in rural, communal settings, in which women did all the domestic work, men the economic. This reflected, in part, the rural background of converts, as well as the formal theology of the Shakers. Each sex had complete authority within its own realm, and neither realm was considered superior to the other. In fact, the sexes were permitted little contact with one another at all (see Foster 1981, chap. 6; see also Kern 1981).

The feature of Shakerism on which scholars have focused most heavily has been the radical antipathy to all expression of sexuality, manifested both by Lee and by later converts. In the early part of the nineteenth century, female nature was defined by Shakers in a highly negative manner. By the 1870s, Shakers were embracing some issues associated with feminism such as suffrage, an end to the sexual exploitation of women, and especially of course, "sexual equality in religious life and ecclesiastical policy" (given that the women were redeemed by celibacy) (Foster 1981:229; Kern 1981:123–24). This change of emphasis may account for the increasing proportion of women Shakers over time, noted earlier. Their approach may be summed up with the often-suspect phrase "separate but equal." In this case, however, they really did believe in the equality of the sexes in their separate spheres, and this enabled them to attract "numerous capable women" (Foster 1981:229).

No discussion of women and religious movements can ignore the highly successful group, also founded by a woman, called Christian Science. It is likely that Christian Science, from its inception after the Civil War until today, has had a higher proportion of female members than any other major religious group. Citing another source, Wilson stated that of 23 principle denominations in the United States, Christian Science had the highest proportion of female members: 63 percent. The other denominations, especially the nonconformist ones, although having a majority female, "rarely had as many as fifty-eight percent" (1961:198).

The movement was founded by Mary Baker Eddy around 1866, whose book, *Science and Health*, remains today the central text for its adherents. She was described by Wilson (see also Fox 1978) as a highly charismatic leader whose followers viewed her as the prophesied Woman of the Apocalypse (Wilson 1961:138, 199). The first church was opened in Boston in 1879, with Eddy as its pastor (1961:137). The movement grew rapidly in the closing years of the nineteenth and early twentieth centuries under her leadership, spreading to Britain as well. By 1906 it counted 66,000 members in the United States, most of whom were drawn from the middle and upper classes. By 1926 every state in the nation had a Christian Science church (Wilson 1961:141).

The central focus of Eddy's theology is a denial of the material world; the only reality is spiritual. Humanity is perfect and, therefore, sin, death, illnesss, and suffering are mere manifestations of false belief. For her followers, then and now, the central component of Christian Science is nonmedical healing, which is correcting error with right thinking. The person who aids the sick in this is called a practitioner. Christian Science has no clergy; it has teachers and practitioners. Church "services" are really community gatherings around a teacher or leader whose knowledge is greater than that of other members. Teachers and practitioners are held in very high esteem and therefore often play a major role in the business life of the church. Both charge fees for their services, although practitioners rarely can earn a living from their fees.

Perhaps one major reason for the disproportionate appeal of Christian Science for women can be seen in Table 1.2. Practitioners throughout the world are disproportionately female: 88 percent worldwide (Wilson 1961:198). Teachers, who are also practitioners and in fact train practitioners, are 50 percent female, both in the United States and worldwide (1961:360). Also, women typically constitute at least half the church officers, readers, ushers, and board members of individual churches. (1961:199).

Table 1.2   Proportion of Female Christian Science Practitioners in Selected Countries, 1953

	Percent Female Practitioners	Total Number Practitioners
United States	88	8,111
Canada	86	207
South Africa	89	76
Australia	88	146
New Zealand	91	45
Ireland	100	10
France	93	29
West Germany	78	77
Great Britain	90	898
Holland	87	31
Norway	100	7
Sweden	88	16
Switzerland	88	69

Source: Computed from Wilson (1961:360, appendix E).

Not only is the church structure very hospitable to women; so too are Christian Science theology and Eddy's own views, as expressed in her writings. God is viewed as both male and female. "The perfect man . . . embraces both male and female qualities – gender being a quality only of mortal mind and not of God" (Wilson 1961:187; see also Fox 1978:411). A non-Puritanical faith, which proclaims that wealth, amusement, and pleasure are blessings to be enjoyed, "women are not inhibited by any exhortations against vanity and worldliness" (Wilson 1961:176–77, 183). Eddy herself considered chastity better than marriage and proclaimed that women did not have to become mothers. Contemporary followers, however, seem to regard sexuality and marriage as normal – not to be avoided on religious grounds (186–67). Despite the fact that she was not a feminist and did not want Christian Science to be a "woman's religion" (Fox 1978:410),

> on one . . . political issue Mrs. Eddy allowed herself to dwell in her writings, and this was the issue of women's rights: She . . . declared women to be "the highest species of man" and said "Civil law establishes very unfair differences between the rights of the two sexes." . . . She asserted that Christian Science equalized the sexes [Wilson 1961:179].

Fox explicitly defined Christian Science as "an unconscious protest movement" by women against their "social disabilities in the latter part of the 19th century" (1978:402). Both Eddy and her followers were seen by Fox as using Christian Science to enact "dominance roles," otherwise denied them, by becoming healers (practitioners) (1978:403). Eddy's earliest followers were female factory workers and shop girls, widows and unmarried women, who sought to make a living as healers (1978:410). It was also appealing to women members to have as healers other women, with whom the relationship was often that of close friend and spiritual advisor as well (1978:412). Fox concluded by defining Christian Science in the nineteenth century as building an "enclave in which female and male sex roles were less rigidly defined and more equalitarian than in the outside world," which it tended to ignore rather than attempt to change (1978:414).

One final example of women's involvement in dissident religious groups takes us to contemporary Mexico. Finkler (1981) has described a dissident religious movement called Spiritualism in this overwhelmingly Roman Catholic society. This heavily female group appeals primarily to the lower classes, in which, unlike the wealthier strata, women are normally denied any opportunity to gain public recognition or independence from their husbands. Spiritualist temples are structured to accord women equal, if not superior, access to positions of authority, "roles that women could not attain in the established church or in secular formal institutions" (1981:483). Finkler therefore concluded that movements like this "are a direct expression of opposition by women to the Catholic Church" (ibid.).

The movement was founded by a renegade priest in the 1860s. "His charter allocated 12 sacerdotal positions to men and 12 . . . to women . . . . the founder's earliest followers and functionaries were women" (Finkler 1981:485). The mother temple is located in Mexico City and has been and continues to be headed by a woman. In turn, this church supervises and controls the others. Twice a year, 5000 to 8000 people gather in Mexico City to hear a dialogue between Jesus, Mother Mary and Elias (the movement's founder) which is transmitted through mediums in a trance: a man and three women. In fact, the role of medium is of central importance in transmitting God's message and in curing the sick; they are predominantly women. At the top of the church hierarchy is the guide, who, when duty calls, "ceases her [domestic] activities, puts on her white habit, and is instantly converted from an ordinary housewife to a leader of men and women who issues orders" (1981:488).

In conclusion, women have often been strongly drawn to dissident religious movements, and often played important leadership roles in them as well. Such movements have varied widely in their definitions and treatment of the sexes, but at a minimum they gave women some sense of spiritual equality with men, if not opportunities to participate more equally in the religious structure. In so doing, they directly contradicted the theology and practice of established faiths. Where the established faith was sufficiently powerful, the movements were defined as heretical and persecuted. We have noted repeatedly that in their time and place, dissenting religious movements have often been the only mechanism available for women to voice their revolt. However, typically women gain some degree of equality in dissident religions only by sacrificing some major area of life in meeting the requirements of the religion, inasmuch as they have often been ascetic faiths or blatantly antisexual. Nonetheless, at least some of these movements can be appropriately viewed as incipient feminist movements, inasmuch as they called for a radical restructuring of relationships between the sexes in the secular as well as the sacred domains.

MORAL REFORM MOVEMENTS

Despite the pervasive, negative view and treatment of women characteristic of most Christian denominations, by the nineteenth century women had also come to be regarded by them as the bastions of morality. Especially during the Victorian Era in both the United States and Great Britain, femininity had come to be strongly associated with domesticity and moral purity, inasmuch as women were excluded from the corruption endemic to the political and business arenas of the time. Unlike men, women were basically dichotomized as evil and whorelike, or as highly virtuous and basically asexual, the later designation applying to those who remained in their "proper" domestic sphere. This same era witnessed the rise of a number of social movements which were concerned with reforming the moral tone of national life. The issues raised by these movements have, in some instances, persisted well into the twentieth century, albeit often in altered form, and new ones have been added during this century. Women have played a visible and active role in moral reform movements, often recruited through their religious involvements, especially Quakerism and Revivalism. Quakerism preached social equality and pacifism, as well as stressing the equal role of women in public life, thereby encouraging their activism in reform movements. Revivalism "simultaneously gave encouragement to two contradictory impulses: deference and obedience to superior authority and the need to take action on behalf of cherished values" (Epstein 1981:87).

In this section we will explore a few examples of moral reform movements in the United States. It should be noted at the outset that, as was the case of scholarly literature concerning religious movements, many of those studies which have dealt with moral reform movements have, at least until very recently, ignored the general role of women in their analyses.

In the early decades of the nineteenth century two reform movements emerged that were rooted in religion but went on to become intertwined with the Women's Rights Movement: abolitionism and temperance.

From the 1830s, the Abolitionist Movement was characterized by substantial female involvement (Donald 1970:18; Lutz 1968; preface). Donald commented that "for an age of chivalry and repression there was an extraordinary proportion of women in the abolitionist movement . . . who defied the convention that females' place was at the fireside, not in the forum" (1970:18–19). Likewise, Lutz noted that "women made an outstanding contribution to . . . abolition . . . at a time when the participation of women in public reform movements was frowned upon" (1968:preface). Given that many abolitionists were Quakers (Donald 1970:19; Dumond 1966:279–80; Lutz 1968:104), and given the sex composition of that sect discussed earlier, it is perhaps not surprising that women played such an active role in this movement.

Motivated in part by deeply felt religious commitments, women were present at the first meeting of the American Anti-Slavery Society, but they were not invited to sign its declaration. Instead, they were urged by the male leadership to form their own antislavery societies (Dumond 1966:275). In 1833 the first female antislavery society was found in Reading, Massachusetts, followed quickly by a host of others. By 1837, 300 such groups existed in ten states, including in their membership black as well as white women (Dumond 1966: 277–78; Lutz 1968:101). Friedman said of the female antislavery organization that it

> proved to be most exhilarating. It provided a means for women, on a daily basis, to cast out their periodic feelings of despair and uselessness—their sense of enslavement to a somewhat less than glorious hearthside and of deprivation from the full range of life's experiences. Simultaneously, it offered channels to replace that despair. Female antislavery organizations consciously opened doors to leadership and managment experience that had been closed to women in male-run institutions [1982:137].

In her analysis of female abolitionist leaders in New England, Hersh (1978; 197) noted that, while deeply religious, these women revolted against religious orthodoxy and its male clergy, who worked to keep women's activism in the movement confined to the private sphere of the family and centered on moral suasion only. They were also in revolt against the constricted opportunities available to urban, middle-class women. Many were seeking "to expand the boundaries of 'woman's sphere,'" and in part for this reason, they attached themselves to the Abolitionist Movement (1978:254).

In 1837 the first antislavery convention of women was held in New York City, led by the outspoken Grimké sisters, especially Angelina. She wrote "An Appeal to the Women of the Nominally Free States," which linked the struggles of blacks and women, and defined them both as part of a larger struggle for human rights. "The majority of women were completely in sympathy with these views" (Lutz 1968:104). This appeal was both sparked by, and in turn fueled, the great opposition which existed to women speaking publicly on this (or any other) issue. The press and clergy were especially outspoken in denouncing women's public involvement (Dumond 1966:275; Lutz 1968:105). Deeply committed to their convictions, the women defied the clergy and insisted on their right to step outside of "women's sphere" in pursuit of a moral goal (DuBois 1979:242–43). Such women as Lucretia Mott, Lydia Child, Elizabeth Cady Stanton, Susan B. Anthony, Lucy Stone, and the Grimkés were highly active in the movement in the ensuing years. However, the outspoken female abolitionists paid a high price in loss of social prestige and in being subject to insults and harassment (Hersh 1979:280).

The American Antislavery Society meeting held in 1840 with an attendance of 1000 delegates, in New York City, brought the issue of women's participation to a head. A woman was appointed to a commitee, prompting a walkout by several men, followed by the appointment of three more women to the executive committee (Lutz 1968:155–56). In the United States, women had won the right to participate publicly in the broader movement – not just their own groups. The "woman question" emerged again later in 1840, at the World Antislavery Convention in London, when female American delegates were excluded from participation. This is seen by most scholars as the primary impetus for the 1848 Seneca Falls Women's Rights Convention, which was called by Mott and Stanton, two of the women denied participation in London. In turn, this convention is usually defined as the starting point of the nineteenth-century Women's Rights Movement (about which more will be said later).

Besides public speaking, female antislavery activists held fairs to raise money and to gain new converts to the cause; "played an important role, sometimes a dominant one, in the work of the underground railroad"; began schools for blacks in the North; wrote books and pamphlets; and as teachers in public schools, introduced antislavery doctrine into the curriculum (Dumond 1966:278–81). During the Civil War, Stanton and Anthony founded the Women's National Loyal League to support the Union war effort and to push for a constitutional amendment outlawing all slavery. They collected 400,000 signatures on a petition to this effect. They disbanded in 1865 after passage of the Thirteenth Amendment (Allen with Allen 1974:139; Lutz 1968:284 ff.).

As the Women's Rights Movement developed, its meetings were held concurrently with antislavery conventions, as most female leaders were involved in both (Lutz 1968:293). In general, the males, even those sympathetic to the women's cause, wanted the issues kept separate and priority placed on abolitionism (Allen with Allen 1974:129). The split came during Reconstruction and during debate over the Fourteenth Amendment. Women were shocked to find that the amendment, which granted suffrage to former slaves, explicitly restricted it to males. Antislavery men supported the amendment as drafted (Allen with Allen 1974:139; Lutz 1968:294–95); women fought the amendment as phrased, but lost.

The Abolitionist Movement was relatively small compared to the major nineteenth-century reform movement, temperance (Epstein 1981:6). The Temperance Movement began in the 1820s as an offshoot of evangelical and revivalist Protestantism, from which it drew its members and its inspiration (Dannenbaum 1984:226; Epstein 1981:89; Gusfield 1963:72). From its inception women probably outnumbered men (Dannenbaum 1984:182), and until about 1850, women's roles were narrowly restricted to using moral suasion within the privacy of their homes to keep family members from consuming alcohol (Bordin 1981:xvi). They formed auxiliaries to men's organizations (1981:4). In the 1850s moral suasion gave way to attempts to legislate prohibition at the state level as the primary thrust of movement activity, and as this happened, women were left without a role to play (Dannenbaum 1984: chap. 6). This was the time that women began to demand a role in the more public, strictly male sphere of influence. Prior to and during the Civil War, women engaged in public action, destroying liquor and saloons and leading prayer sessions in saloons. Dannenbaum referred to their actions as "militant female vigilantism" (1984:205). During this time women tentatively began to link female suffrage to temperance, as they perceived the vote as the most practical tool in gaining their temperance goals (1984:184). The 1850s also witnessed the rise of new temperance organizations that did not discriminate against women in speaking or office holding.

With the men gone to war, women kept the movement going, only to have the men resume control after hostilities ceased (Dannenbaum 1984:201). The result was a phenomenon known as the "Woman's Crusade" of 1873–74, which marked the beginning of the almost total takeover of the movement by women. During that winter, Ohio church women began a "crusade" into saloons, "praying and pleading for their closing." This spread rapidly to other midwestern states (Gusfield 1963:90). Of the Crusade Dannenbaum wrote, it "focused the dissatisfaction women felt with the way men had run the temperance reform, and enabled them to take over the movement in large part" (1984:220).

The end of the Woman's Crusade saw the formation of the Women's Christian Temperance Union (WCTU) in 1874. A similar women's group formed in Canada that same year (Mitchinson 1981). From that time until about 1900, when the Anti-Saloon League took over, the WCTU led the movement (Bordin 1981:xviii). The WCTU was the largest women's organization of its time; indeed, it was the first mass female movement (men were excluded from voting membership) (1981:3,156). In 1892 it numbered 150,000 dues-paying members, by the turn-of-the-century 176,000. While smaller, the Canadian WCTU went from a membership of 969 in 1880 to 4060 five years later, and was the only truly national women's organization in that country (Mitchinson 1981:147,149). By the 1880s there was a chapter in every state and in thousands of communities in the United States (Bordin 1981:xvi). Although primarily composed of white, middle-class, evangelical Protestant housewives, the WCTU cut across racial and ethnic boundaries to include women "from nearly every sector of American life" (1981:156) in both large cities and small towns. "Among its members were seamstresses and the wives of artisans and clerks; women physicians, lawyers, clerks, and educators; . . . the wives of business and professional men" (ibid.). Blacks, Native Americans, and immigrants were all counted in the membership, and even became officers occasionally (1981:159–60). Indeed, so successful was the WCTU that it spread to Britain, New Zealand, and Australia in the 1880s, where before women had not been active in their nation's temperance movements (1981:159).

The WCTU began as a conservative organization narrowly focused on the issue of temperance, as in Canada (Mitchinson 1981:145). Temperance had long been defined by all as a "woman's issue" (Epstein 1981:100). Men drank; women suffered. Alcohol abuse was a real problem in nineteenth-century America, and the main victims were the wives and children of male abusers. First and foremost, alcohol was viewed as a threat to the home and family, which were, of course, women's domain. Drunkards beat their wives and children and drank up scarce resources, leaving their families destitute. Legally, women had no claim on their husband's wages, no control over their own (which he could consume in drink), and no claim to their children or family property. These legal liabilities left women "especially vulnerable to the abuses of an alcoholic husband" (Bordin 1981:7). Therefore, by common definition the Temperance Movement was perceived as a movement to defend the family and "home values" (Epstein 1981:1).

As Epstein (1981:101) noted, the husbands of these mostly middle-class women activists were not usually drunkards. Heavy drinking was most associated with poor and immigrant men. Gusfield's work is considered a classic concerning this movement (1963). He analyzed temperance as a class-based movement in which the older, Protestant middle class attempted to maintain its moral authority over newer, rising immigrant groups. More recent, feminist analyses see it in terms of sexual antagonism. Epstein, for instance, argued that "the crusaders were impelled . . . by a more amorphous set of fears about family life generally . . . . Alcohol . . . made it possible to talk about [their] . . . vulnerability [as women] without directly attacking men or challenging the structure of the family" (1981:103).

She recognized the class, as well as the sexual antagonism that motivated the movement by referring to temperance as the politicization of female cultural antagonism to male culture—especially working-class, immigrant male culture (Epstein 1981:90). Women were angry "over their subordinate status," (1981:4,89) and this led them both to revivalism and to temperance. Bordin saw temperance as "the medium through which nineteenth-century women expressed their deeper, sometimes unconscious, feminist concerns" (1981:162). Gusfield himself defined female concern for temperance as "an act of controlling the relations between the sexes" (1963:89). In addition, some scholars have noted that temperance provided an avenue to engage in the public sphere and in leadership roles when few other avenues existed. Bordin stated that "women found temperance the most congenial cause through which to increase their involvement in public life" (1981:xvi). Furthermore, "the WCTU offered them opportunities for creative service and self-fulfillment that they were unlikely to find elsewhere" (1981:12). Epstein claimed that temperance "gave women an opportunity to explore at least one part of the world that nineteenth-century men inhabited" (1981:107).

If the Temperance Movement and the WCTU began as conservative phenomena, for women that changed substantially after 1879, when the dynamic Frances Willard became president of the WCTU; a similar phenomenon occurred also in Canada (Mitchinson 1981:151). It was to her charismatic leadership that the phenomenal success of the organization is attributed by most (Bordin 1981:xvi–xvii). For the rest of the century, the WCTU became a broadbased reform organization, supporting such diverse issues as (1) women's suffrage, (2) safer working conditions, (3) unemployment protection, (4) prison reform, (5) creation of kindergartens, (6) change in women's clothing styles, (7) punishment of prostitutes' clients, and (8) practical education for poor women. Willard herself subscribed to Christian socialism, although most of her followers did not. The underlying logic remained the defense of home and family. Earlier, the Temperance Movement had seen alcohol abuse as the cause of poverty and other social ills. Conversely, under Willard, the WCTU defined social and economic problems as the cause of alcoholism, hence within its realm of concern. Epstein (1981:4), among others, felt that the WCTU converged with feminism during the last quarter of the nineteenth century, while Gusfield (1963:88) noted that most leaders of the Women's Rights Movement had, at some time, been active in the Temperance Movement. In a study of 51 female abolitionist leaders, who were among the early women's rights advocates, Hersh (1978) found that at least 20 were involved in the Temperance Movement as well.

Despite the broad array of issues, including suffrage, taken up by the WCTU under Willard's leadership, the ideological underpinning of the organization remained, in Willard's own terms, "Home Protection." Suffrage was seen as a necessary means to accomplish that end by getting prohibition legislation passed, not as an end in itself or as a manifestation of women's natural rights. Predicated on the very traditional notion that the chief priority of women was the sanctity of the home and family, the "WCTU assumed rather that criticized male dominance. . . . " (Epstein 1981:133). Women could, in fact should be publicly active, but in the service of the sanctity of the family and other related moral values. Ultimately, women's equality and conventional morality were inimicable, inasmuch as "conventional morality was in fact defense of the male-dominated family" (1981:132). In this sense, as Bordin (1981:9) noted, "the WCTU was a 'safe' women's movement." It did not challenge traditional sex roles. In fact, even Willard never called herself a feminist (Epstein 1981:147). But Bordin also argued that the WCTU made the Nineteenth Amendment possible because it was "one of the most powerful instruments of women's consciousness-raising of all times" (1981:157). The early Suffrage Movement was too radical for most women, so it remained small. The WCTU helped more conservative women to see the need for broader changes, including suffrage, in the direction of greater sexual equality (Bordin 1981:158; see also Epstein 1981:146–47). Willard died in 1898 and after that the WCTU returned to a more narrow focus on temperance and lost the lead even in that movement.

The Abolitionist and Temperance movements were, in some important ways, very similar to one another. In both movements, women were originally primarily motivated by the same forces which motivated male activists: moral indignation rooted in part in deeply felt religious commitments. Women were in revolt against perceived social wrongs, along with their male class, ethnic, and religious counterparts. In the process of pursuing reform, however, women in both movements came to see that the extensive social and legal handicaps from which they suffered impeded their ability to pursue their religious-moral commitments effectively. First the right even to speak publicly was sought and ultimately gained. Soon the right to play leadership roles within movement organizations was sought and eventually gained. Finally, the realization that without suffrage women's voice was still ineffectual led women in both movements toward feminism, the ultimate female revolt. Hersh noted that the rhetoric of abolitionism, temperance, and feminism "shared a common theme, the emancipation of women from man's brutality and oppression" (1978:48), despite the fact that many female abolitionists and temperance women were not feminists and never rejected the main components of the traditional role of women: the emphasis on domesticity and family, as well as the moral superiority of women.

Another type of moral reform movement in which women have often been very active, especially during this century, has been the Peace Movement. Like temperance, women do not tend to participate directly in the "evil"—in this case war—so much as they suffer the consequences, as widows and mothers of dead and maimed soldiers, and as victims of rape and abuse when their nation is defeated (Roodkowsky 1979). The traditional emphasis on women's nurturant role may make the issue of peace especially pressing to them. Numerous public opinion polls have shown that, compared to men, women tend to be less favorable toward wars in which we have been involved, and more supportive of arms reductions and negotiations (Chafetz 1978:163). In addition, the traditional masculine role is identified in the United States (and elsewhere) with a willingness to fight, which may make pacifism appear to many men as "unmanly."

Steinson (1982) wrote a detailed history of women's involvement in World War I. Before 1914, women were little involved in the Peace Movement, which itself was declining (1982:397). By January 1915, the Women's Peace Party (WPP) had been organized, and subsequently women "supplied much of the leadership, enthusiasm, and determination, and performed much of the difficult, but unrecognized, behind-the-scenes organizational work" of the movement (1982:1). Basically an urban, middle-class movement, the WPP had large active branches in San Francisco, Philadelphia, Chicago, St. Louis, Washington, New York, and Boston. Communications problems made it vitually impossible to organize smaller towns and rural areas, but many women in such places contacted the party and were supporters (1982:120,47).

The women's peace efforts were intertwined with the Suffrage and other reform movements of that time. Like those movements, it was also based on "traditional views of women as the nurturing and protective sex" (Steinson 1982:2). Women were said to have a "special right to protest against war" in their role as mothers of soldiers (1982:9). Indeed, women took to arguing for suffrage on the basis that since they were more "gentle, pacific, and humane" than men, the United States could be kept out of war by them (1982:6).

When war broke out in Europe in August 1914, a group of women decided to stage a Women's Peace Parade, which was held that same month in New York

City. About fifteen hundred women attended. Led by Quaker suffragist Jane Addams, the WPP organized five months later and included "some of the nation's most influential and prestigious women." For the next two years the WPP "played pivotal roles in the World War I mediation movement, often taking the initiative and acting independently of men" (Steinson 1982:48). They, along with counterparts throughout Europe, organized an International Congress of Women, which met at the Hague in April 1915, and which demanded an end to bloodshed and the start of peace negotiations, as well as general disarmament and the formation of a permanent world organization (1982:49–60). This was the only international peace organization that met after the war began (1982:397). It established the International Committee of Women for Permanent Peace.

Steinson (1982:62 ff.) described the very active role of Jane Addams and other women in trying to get President Wilson to mediate the European war, and she attributed both the 1916 Conference of Neutrals called by Wilson and much of Wilson's own peace program to the influence of these women.

> Although the mediation movement attracted several men . . . what is remarkable about the effort is the extent to which it was a female enterprise. Women dominated the movement in formulating policies and proposals, in undertaking concrete actions to secure international discussion of peace proposals, in publicizing mediation schemes, and in establishing linking mediation organizations [Steinson 1982:112].

In the years before the United States became involved in the war, in addition to the strictly female peace groups, women were also "leaders of American Union Against Militarism" and the " 'moving spirits' behind the American Neutral Conference Committee, the Emergency Peace Federation, and the People's Council" (Steinson 1982:1).

Although the WPP continued to exist after the United States entered the war, most of its antiwar activity ceased. Immediately after the armistice in 1918 it became active again and was instrumental in convening a Women's International Congress in Zurich in 1919. It was one of the first international peace meetings of any kind after the war (Steinson 1982:397). After that, the WPP became the U.S. branch of the Women's International League for Peace and Freedom (WILFP), which was still active at the time of our involvement in Vietnam.

In summarizing women's role in the World War I Peace Movement, Steinson noted that the women believed that they "had a special relationship to war that would not be recognized in organizations directed by men" (1982:381). Also, many of the female activists "believed that for the first time in their lives they were doing something important" (1982:385). Finally, "for many women, the WPP was the one group in which they could express their thoughts without fear of censure" (1982:399).

The WILFP continued women's involvement in the Peace Movement, but after 1920 it no longer justified its existence in terms of an ideology of motherhood (Jensen 1983:202). Initially, in 1919 it numbered but 52 members and, while not growing very rapidly, by 1923 it had 5000 members (1983:206) and by 1924 was large enough to set up an office in Washington with seven paid employees. Jensen noted the heavy Quaker influence in this organization, which we have seen in other contexts. Its leadership included two Nobel Prize winners (Jane Addams and Emily Greene Balch). In 1920 a new female peace organization also began, Women for World Disarmament. The 1920s witnessed coalition formation among a large variety of women's groups—including even the Daughters of the American Revolution—seeking a reduction in defense budgets and the size of the army, and related issues. In turn, women's peace efforts, and especially the WILFP, were attacked as treasonous and Bolshevic by both the Defense Department and various patriotic groups (red-baiting was almost as common in the aftermath of World War I as it was after World War II). The 1930s witnessed a WILFP attack on the munitions industry, which prompted a Senate investigation of that industry. And as World War II approached, its membership swelled to 13,000, with 120 branches in the United States and eleven paid staff members (1983).

After World War II, the WILFP declined in membership and influence, and during the McCarthy years Peace Movement activists were under virulent attack. Women's involvement in peace efforts resurfaced abruptly in November 1961, when a group of five women, active in SANE (Society Against Nuclear Energy) became frustrated with its male leadership's reluctance "to deal with 'mother's issues' such as contamination of milk by radioactive fallout from nuclear tests" (Swerdlow 1982:509). Using contacts with a variety of women's groups, along with personal contacts, they called for a Women's Strike for Peace (subsequently the name of their organization) to protest nuclear testing and nuclear war (Swerdlow 1982:493 ff.; Toch 1965:186). An estimated 50,000 women heeded the call to strike, in the largest female peace action in U.S. history (Swerdlow 1982:493). Within a year, the organization had branches in 60 communities and offices in 10 cities, although it was very loosely structured, had no headquarters, leaders, or membership lists, this to protect itself from the House Un-American Activities Committee (HUAC) (1982:495).

The ideological basis of Women Strike for Peace was the traditional one we saw in our discussion of the Women's Peace Party: women's right to influence on the basis of their motherhood. They were defined by the press as "unsophisticated wives and mothers" (Swerdlow 1982:497) and indeed, often brought their children in strollers to their marches and rallies (1982:494). Many of these women were called in for examination by HUAC, which was convinced that the movement was Communist inspired, or at least infiltrated (the FBI collected 43 volumes of material on them) (1982:497). The women responded by defining patriotism as "the extent of one's dedication to saving America's children from nuclear extinction" (1982:500). The first HUAC witness, a retired schoolteacher, stated:

> This movement was inspired and motivated by mother's love for children. . . .
> When they were putting their breakfast on the table, they saw not only the

> Wheaties and milk, but they also saw strontium 90 and iodine 131 – They feared for the health and life of their children [Swerdlow 1982:502].

The women perceived their confrontation with HUAC as a "contest between the sexes," female "common sense, openness, humor, hope and naiveté versus male rigidity, solemnity, suspicion, and dark theories of conspiracy and subversion" (Swerdlow 1982:504). Evidently, the women made HUAC appear rather silly and the press ended by ridiculing the committee's attack on the women (see Swerdlow 1982; Toch 1965).

The members of Women Strike for Peace were mostly white, middle class, politically moderate, well educated, and in their late 30s and 40s. They were active in local religious, school, and civic groups, but few worked outside the home. They took their motherhood very seriously (Swerdlow 1982:513–14). In short, they were bastions of the postwar feminine mystique, who differed from other mothers only in that they felt compelled to act politically, not just privately, in defense of children (1982:515). They used the feminine mystique to

> legitimize women's right to radical dissent from foreign and military policies. . . . But by emphasizing the fact that men in power could no longer be counted on for protection in the nuclear age, WSP implied that the traditional sex-gender contract no longer worked [Swerdlow 1982:515].

A few years later the Peace Movement gathered new impetus with America's growing involvement in Vietnam. Swerdlow (1982:516) argued that women's participation then was no longer as mothers but as autonomous persons. this was undoubtedly true for many, perhaps for most of the female activists. In a comprehensive listing of groups involved in the Peace Movement during the Vietnam era, Heath (1976:xxxi–xxxix) listed a large number of women's liberation groups, a number of women's organizations whose primary focus was something else, and about ten specifically female peace groups, such as Women Against the War, Women for Peace, the WILFP, Women's Peace and Unity Club.

One organization, at least, carried on the tradition of linking women's role as mothers to pacifism: Another Mother for Peace. This was a California-based organization, formed in 1967 to protest U.S. involvement in the war in Vietnam, which quickly spread nationwide. Although membership was not restricted to women, most of its organizers and a majority of its members were middle-class, college-educated women. At its peak in 1973, it numbered 165,000 members, although by 1984 it had less than 20,000 (Encyclopedia of Associations 1984). Its motto, War is not healthy for children and other living things, as well as its title, reflected maternal values. The central strategies of the organization were consumer boycotts and letter-writing campaigns to the president and to other elected officials. Members were urged not to buy consumer goods manufactured by companies that participated in the war effort. In its later years, as U.S. involvement in Vietnam ended, the organization turned to other issues such as nuclear disarmament and amnesty for draft evaders living abroad.

After Vietnam, women continued to protest militarism at least in part on the basis of their role as mothers. In November 1981, 2,000 women demonstrated at the Pentagon to end "that [military] dominance which is so dangerous to women and children at home" (Gelder 1981:66). And we might also note in concluding our discussion of peace movements, the visible and active leadership roles played by both Protestant and Catholic women in attempting to bring peace to Northern Ireland. the Irish People's Peace Movement is led by women (Roodkowsky 1979:256). Irish women, too, often justify their involvement by referring to their motherhood and to children.

Moral reform movements have been comprised of both males and females. Participants have been motivated by deeply held commitments, often, if not usually grounded in religious beliefs. For women, in addition such movements have often served as an outlet for energies that, at least until the end of the nineteenth century, had few other avenues of expression. Women have revolted against what they perceived as the moral iniquities of their time—as have men. But for women, who usually have been committed on the basis of highly traditional ideas concerning their own roles, their experiences in reform movements have often been radicalizing. In these movements they discovered their inability to pursue moral reform effectively because of traditional role expectations and legal handicaps. This, in turn, has often had the ironic consequence of spurring revolt against aspects of the sex stratification and gender role systems of the society.

FOOD RIOTS

Riots, or hostile crowd outbreaks, have occurred throughout recorded history, triggered by any number of strains experienced by the common people. One type which has appeared in many times and places is the food riot, which is typically triggered by food shortages and/or abrupt increases in food prices, and is primarily an urban phenomenon. Unlike many other forms of riots, food riots have often involved large numbers of women. Indeed, it is not unusual to find that women have instigated and led such riots. It is our contention, as well as that of numerous historians (Hufton 1976:161–62; Sharp 1980:36; Stevenson 1979:101; Thomis and Grimmett 1982:30), that when food becomes scarce or very expensive relative to average income, men and children suffer along with women; however, since food acquisition and preparation is overwhelmingly a female task (Boulding 1976), women may be more cognizant of, and quick to react to, sudden scarcity or abrupt price rises.

Food riots have been especially well documented in England, Scotland, and France where they were a frequent occurrence from about the seventeenth century until the early decades of the nineteenth century (Tilly 1978:156). Sharp (1980) analyzed the seventeenth-century riots in England and found that women were most heavily involved in those which took place in port towns and food distribution centers (1980:36). For instance, in 1595 women seized the corn in the market at Wye; in 1608 a group of Northamptonshire women boarded a ship and forcibly unloaded its corn. Sharp argued that " . . . women . . . had their own discontents, stemming from their immediate and direct experience, as purchasers, of high prices and the sharp practices of middlemen in the market place" (1980:36).

In discussing the eighteenth- and early nineteenth-century English food riots, Stevenson also remarked upon the prominent role played by women:

> It was women who had to go to market and were faced with the stark imperative of feeding their family and satisfying all the complex demands of preference and status that went into the family budget. It is hardly surprising then that market riots were so often the province of women; it was they who felt most acutely the frustrations and anxieties of fluctuations in price [1979:101].

He went on to explain that mobs comprised of both men and women were also common, the result of women complaining about prices to their husbands, who subsequently were urged to join the violence (Stevenson 1979:102). He cited riots by women in Dover (1740), Taunton (1753), Blandford Forum (1800), and in Aylesbury (1795), where women seized the wheat in the market and sold it at their own prices. Likewise, in mid-nineteenth-century Scotland a series of food riots erupted, about which Richards (1982:21) said, "In the recurrent pattern of events women took the initiative and then roused the involvement of men."

Across the Channel French women in the eighteenth and early nineteenth centuries were equally instrumental in food riots. Like their English counterparts, in France "the woman had both to procure food and to cook it; all her husband had to do was eat what she prepared and judge whether he was hungry or not. What she got was often the result of hours of waiting" (Hufton 1976:161–62).

Rudé (1959) has written a detailed account of riot behavior during the French Revolution. He argued that after September 1789, for women "the bread crisis was peculiarly their own and, from this time on, it was they rather than the men that played the leading role in the movement" (1959:69). Indeed, Rudé (1970:113) argued that the common people participated in the French Revolution primarily because they were concerned about food shortages, not politics.

On September 17, 1790, angry women beseiged the Hôtel de Ville, complaining abut the prices charged by bakers. In October they led a series of market riots in which "it appears that . . . women of every social class took part" (Rudé 1959:73). They forced the bell-ringers to toll the bells to call citizens to arms. They again attacked the Hôtel de Ville in search of bread as well as arms and ammunition for the men. They disarmed the guards, and gave the weapons to the men who "followed behind the women and urged them on" (1959:74). The women themselves were armed with sticks, pikes, axes, crowbars, bludgeons, and muskets. Next they set out for Versailles to petition the king and the Assembly for bread, compelling women of all classes whom they met along the way, to join them, until their numbers swelled to between six and seven thousand. As they marched they chanted, "Let us fetch the baker, the baker's wife and the little baker's boy" (1970:113). They included market "stall-holders, fish-wives and working women of the market, well-dressed bourgeoises, . . . and other women of various social classes" (1959:181). It was this women's mob that brought the royal family back to Paris, where they hoped the king's presence would ensure a plentiful supply of bread. When that failed to happen, the women continued to riot until finally the Assembly cracked down on rioting and took steps to ensure an adequate supply of flour (1959:74–78). More food riots, again led by women, broke out with renewed food shortages in 1792 and 1795.

In their review of food riots of the first half of the nineteenth century, Thomis and Grimmett argued that they were probably less of a strictly female phenomenon than most observers think. However, "one thing that does seem certain is that whatever weight women threw into food riots, either as leaders or as supporters, they were widely recognized as *agents provocateurs* who incited men to greater action" (Thomis and Grimmett 1982:32). They went on to point out that women usually had "very precise targets" of attack, primarily the shops of bakers and mealmen, as well as market stall owners, warehouses, storehouses and mills, and sometimes specific individuals such as the millers" (1982:35–36). "The other common . . . target consisted of boats, barges, and carts on which food was moved" (1982:36). The attacks varied in degree of violence, but "there is plently of evidence to suggest that they acted on occasion with a more passionate commitment . . . than comparable crowds of men" (1982:38). They used verbal taunts and stone-throwing, overturned carts, stopped wagons and carried away sacks of flour, and even confronted soldiers directly. And they announced their defiance by having the local bell-man circulate news of their achievements (1982:39). Finally, although women undoubtedly constituted at least half of the rioters, far fewer were arrested. Thomis and Grimmet cited figures for the Scottish riots between 1780 and 1815 showing that only 28 percent of those arrested and charged were female. They argued that the authorities were lenient with women because they were often sympathetic to their plight: "The 'right' of women to raise a food riot in particular circumstances is something that cannot be entirely discounted" (1982:41). Hufton (1971:94) made the same point less equivocally in speaking of the French food riots.

Although food riots are best documented in France and Great Britain, there is evidence that women have played a major role in such riots elsewhere. Tilly, Tilly, and Tilly (1975) talked of female participation in Italian food riots: in Naples, Terra Di Lavora, Compania, and Apulia in 1860 (1975:136); in Ancona in 1898 (1975:151–52); and a specifically female-initiated bread riot in 1917 (1975:167). Hoerder (1977:360–61) discussed a 1777 riot over coffee led by 100 women in Boston, which was followed by a series of other such incidences. In speaking of his personal experiences in Russia on the eve of revolution (1916–17), Sorokin noted that poor women and children rioted over "bread and herring," turning over tram cars, breaking into shops, and attacking police. Joined by men, the strikes and riots spread. He then stated that "the Russian Revolution was begun by hungry women and children demanding bread and herrings"

(1963:99). In India, 1973 witnessed soaring grain and oil prices and scarcities. Riots broke out in the state of Gujarat, which were apparently heavily comprised of women and children, inasmuch as Jones and Jones (1976:1026) noted that local police became "unwilling any longer to attack women and children." Omvedt (1980:77) discussed a series of food strikes and demonstrations, primarily by housewives, in several parts of India during the famine of 1970–73.

Several of those who have written about riots have noted explicitly that the unusual feature of food riots has been precisely the active and visible role of women compared to other types of riots. Thomis and Grimett (1982:33) debated the assertion that food riots were essentially female in composition, yet argued that in relative terms, given their absence in other forms of riots, this should certainly be considered a female activity. In speaking of other early nineteenth century riots in England, which were mostly labor riots, Stevenson (1979:242) explicitly stated that women were underrepresented. Rudé argued that women were particularly active in episodes where " . . . food prices and other bread and butter questions were well to the fore; we find women playing a less conspicuous part in . . . essentially political movements" (1959:184). Finally, Tilly noted that during the nineteenth century, there was a

> notable shift of collective action away from routine assemblies such as markets . . . toward deliberately called gatherings as in demonstrations and strikes. . . . In that process, the participation of European women in collective action declined noticeably. The segregated worlds of politics and labor organization became male preserves [1978:16].

In conclusion, one major expression of collective female revolt historically has been the food riot, often led by, and even more often heavily comprised of, women from a variety of backgrounds. Their participation has been grounded in the traditional female role of food purchaser and preparer. The strains of shortage or unaffordability have been most evident to them, although by no means exclusive to them. Sometimes such riots have been part of broader sociopolitical upheavals, but women seem to have been most directly involved when food was explicitly at issue. Food riots, therefore, really manifest a collective response to strains that impede the fulfillment of traditional role obligations, rather than a form of revolt against the gender role and sex stratification systems.

MOVEMENTS FOR HUMAN EQUALITY AND/OR LIBERATION

The past century and a half has witnessed an enormous array of movements on a worldwide scale, whose purpose has been to advance the well-being of a deprived category of people (theoretically inclusive of both sexes) within a society, and/or to liberate an entire society from colonial or foreign domination. The latter are called national liberation movements. The former have taken many forms, including labor, socialist, communist, and civil rights movements. Women have participated substantially in many of these movements, especially during the past century, reflecting the fact that besides their sex, women also have statuses based on their class, race, ethnicity, religion, and nationality. Where the moral reform movements were primarily phenomena of the more privileged classes, these movements have involved women in the lower reaches of the socioeconomic hierarchy. One central point will be emphasized, already noted in our description of the Abolitionist Movement, and cogently stated by Lipman-Blumen:

> when women in the forefront of major social movements did try to address women's equality, they were forcefully reminded that the "women's issue" must wait until the "larger" social question was resolved. Abolitionists, socialists, Zionists, nationalists, civil rights workers all admonished women that they were selfish, elitist, or politically inept to press the women's question as an explicit component of social justice and power relationships [1984:40, 181–82].

In discussing food riots, we noted that they all but disappeared in the early nineteenth century in the West. During that century, all kinds of spontaneous collective behavior in response to deprivation gave way to more organized, sustained movements oriented to basic structural change (see Tilly 1978). Initially, women were absent from these new movements. Given the nineteenth-century definition of "women's place" that we saw in our discussions of dissident religious, abolitionist, and temperance movements, it is scarcely surprising that the newly emerging labor and socialist movements were devoid of women. These new movements were squarely in the male domain, concerning themselves with issues of political and economic structure and practice. By the closing decades of that century, as we have seen, women's public roles in religious and moral reform movements were broadening. Moreover, women were, albeit in relatively small proportion, increasing their formal labor force participation—both in the industrial work force and in the professions and semiprofessions. Activism in moral reform movements often alerted women to the plight of the poor as well, as we found in the WCTU under Willard's leadership. These factors contributed to the fact that by the end of the nineteenth century, women had become active in many movements for human equality and/or liberation.

Organized protest on behalf of the poor appeared earliest in the society that was first to undergo the Industrial Revolution: Britain. By the early decades of the nineteenth century, Britain was already heavily industrialized, a process which not only radically restructured society, but initially further impoverished a large proportion of the common people. In about 1812, a movement arose among working-class men to reform the British Parliament, known as the Reform Movement. Its goals were universal *manhood* suffrage, vote by ballot, a free press, and annual Parliaments, all seen as political changes which would result in a reduction of the misery that was the lot of the common worker (Thomis and Grimmett 1982: chap. 5). By 1819 this movement involved working-class women, although only in relatively small numbers, and only after several years of debate as to whether they should be involved in politics. Both men and women perceived the reason for female involvement in traditional terms:

> Their duty arose from their very role within the home and the family, the suffering they had witnessed and undergone, and their own obligation to attend to the food, the clothing, and the domestic well-being of their families, undermined by the economic conditions which they were experiencing [Thomis and Grimmett 1982:98].

No separate programs for women were developed, although they were organized separately into their own reform societies. Only a few women eventually were to argue that universal suffrage should include women (Thomis and Grimmett 1982:109). Most simply felt that their role was to be supportive of the men's purpose (Rowbothem 1976:33–34). Women engaged in protests and demonstrations along with the men, as well as sharing governmental repression. In the 1819 Peterloo Massacre, 600 persons, including 113 women, were wounded when soldiers fired on the demonstrators. The wives of working-class men organized the Friends of the Oppressed in 1832, to aid "the wives and families of those who suffer in the peoples' cause" (Thomis and Grimmett, 1982:106). It worked closely with the male National Union of Working Classes. These women were "not strident" and subscribed to the prevailing notions of the feminine stereotype. They presented themselves "with reluctance and apology and almost always on behalf of their men" (1982:108–9).

The first truly national working-class movement in Britain, and the first to involve tens of thousands of women in Scotland, Wales, as well as England, was the Chartist Movement, which began in 1835. This movement was oriented to the entire socioeconomic structure and its relationships to politics (Thomis and Grimmett 1982:111), including in addition to the changes sought by the Reform Movement, repeal of the Poor Laws and reduction of work hours (Rowbotham, 1976:31). Again, women became active (beginning in 1838–39) primarily because deteriorating economic conditions meant that they could no longer discharge their traditional family obligations. Between 1837 and 1844 there were an estimated 80 female Chartist organizations (Thomis and Grimett 1982:124). Chartist women proclaimed, "Even woman, domesticated woman, leaving her homestead, will battle for the rights of those that are dear to her. . . . Women would not have been interested in politics if they had not suffered by politics" (1982:112). Both sexes defined the role of women in the movement as that of "helpmate" and, organized separately into their own Chartist groups, women even came to see their involvement in religious terms (1982: 114–15). The men generally welcomed women into the movement but only in subordinate roles, and "there was a fairly general tendency for male Chartists to exploit their female supporters." (1982:119–120). Women's leadership roles were confined to their own organizations, and when, in 1840, a Committee of the National Charter Association formed, women were not even permitted to address its mixed audience

(1982:125). Women raised funds for the movement, marched and demonstrated, and engaged in boycotts of merchants unsympathetic to the movement. Two charters were presented to Parliament. Of the signatures to the 1838 Charter, 17 percent were female, that of 1848 only 8 percent (1982:125). Some women did see the connection between women's suffrage and the Chartist Movement, and became interested in the general issue of women's rights. The few males who were sympathetic to this, however, feared "that advocacy of the women's cause was likely to delay the achievement of their own." The Chartist Movement failed, and after about 1850 men turned to union activity to pursue their goals.

Women's activism in the British Reform and Chartist Movements differed little from their roles in moral reform movements or in food riots. As wives and mothers faced with problems that interfered with the discharge of their traditional obligations, they joined their menfolk in revolt, but were confined to a segregated and subordinated existence within the movements. A few began to notice their own deprivations as women, but the male response was either hostile or else they vowed that they would grant this issue future priority, after their own aims had been achieved.

The nineteenth- and early twentieth-century union movement in both Britain and the United States received relatively scant female support. Women were hired primarily because they constituted cheap labor. As such, men saw them as competitors for scarce jobs, who suppressed the wage scale, and as strike-breakers on occasion. Male unions were thus "overtly hostile" to women workers (Thomis and Grimmett 1982:70). Women did sometimes unionize, usually in their own unions, and both struck and supported male strikers. But women's unions tended to be weak and short-lived (Foreman 1977:133–34). Union men's prevalent attitude was to gain a wage for themselves that would permit their wives to return home (Kessler-Harris 1975; Thomis and Grimmett 1982:80).

By the late nineteenth century, in Britain males had become more sympathetic to female workers and had begun to see the need to cooperate with them (Rowbotham 1976:60). However, male-dominated unions defined issues in totally industrial terms, ignoring those of central interest to female workers, such as child-care (Foreman 1977:134–35). The Trade Union Congress became committed to women's suffrage after 1884, "but in a pious rather than an active manner" (Rowbotham 1976:63). And, as late as 1877, a major leader of the British Labor Movement argued that "the trade union movement should direct its 'utmost efforts' at securing women within the home" (Foreman 1977:133).

Kessler-Harris (1975) noted the same phenomena in the U.S. union movement in the late nineteenth and early twentieth centuries: (1) a low proportion of female members (never more than 1 in 15, compared to 1 in 5 men who were industrial workers); (2) after the early 1900s a verbal commitment to organize women accompanied by active efforts to return women to the home; (3) an unwillingness to consider issues of interest to women that were not strictly "industrial" ones; (4) unequal pay for female union organizers; and (5) a dearth of females in leadership positions. In the United States, by 1903 middle-class feminists and working-class women organized the Women's Trade Union League as a combination feminist and trade union organization. It peaked in the 1920s, and lasted until about 1950, but after about 1912 it changed its priority from unionizing women to seeking protective legislation for them (Jacoby 1975). As late as the 1930s and 1940s, the International Ladies Garment Workers Union was 70 percent female, but women had no leadership roles above the local level, it paid its female organizers less than its male, and it signed contracts calling for lower pay rates for women (Hield 1979). Of this period in American union history Scharf and Jensen wrote:

> The common concerns of industrial labor – male and female – stopped where the special problems of women or the integration of women into positions of leadership were involved. . . . As unions modified economic inequities, they ignored the basic inequities of race and sex [1983:12.]

Similarly, in terms of the National Unemployed Workers Movement in depression Britain of the 1930s, Rowbotham wrote:

> If they were separate from the men they could build up confidence but their capacity for effective action was reduced. If they united with the men their specific problems could often be shelved as not of "general" importance. The men felt their interest was the general interest and the women's concerns a diversion [1976:134–35].

Although working-class women were generally unable to express their revolt through union channels, they found a more hospitable reception in the growing Socialist movements in late nineteenth- and early twentieth-century Europe. Here, they were often joined by radical middle-class women, and the Feminist and Socialist movements became deeply intertwined. However, as we shall see, the Socialist Movement was not free of problems for women either.

In Britain, the union movement and socialism found political expression in the International Labour Party, which began its rise to power just after the turn of the century. Closely allied with the Labour Party was the Women's Social and Political Union (WSPU), a Socialist, suffragette organization. However, in 1904 the Labour Party refused to commit itself to women's suffrage, seeing the issue and the WSPU "as a diversion from the main concerns of the day" (Foreman 1977:136; Rowbotham 1976:77). Many of the socialist women, such as Emmeline Pankhurst, and especially those of the middle class, withdrew from the party and from socialism after about 1912. At that time, only propertied males could vote. The Labour Party was concerned that women's suffrage would extend the vote to propertied women, thus further undercutting working-class strength (1976:82). Thus, although committed to women's suffrage "in principle," the Labour Party (as well as the Liberal party) were "lukewarm" in practice and divided in tactics, insuring the continued defeat of female suffrage efforts until after World War I (1976:83). Labour Party women, and especially those of the working class, had other problems within the party. They had a hard time convincing the primarily male leadership that "details of domestic life" were political issues, or even that women had "distinct interests" (1976:92). In her discussion of British socialism, Rowbotham came to a conclusion which will be echoed in our discussion of Socialist movements in other nations:

> Socialist women were . . . afraid of antagonism between the sexes because they felt it would have a destructive effect on the movement. However, women became aware of their own subservience and passivity. They hoped that in comradeship they would find . . . sexual equality. But the hope and aspirations of women were still at variance with their actual predicament [1976:105].

In response to feminist activism the Labour Party did establish a Women's Labour League in 1906, but it was not to be "concerned with . . . developing a socialist feminism" (Rowbotham 1976:94), but rather with some concrete issues relevant to working-class mothers. When the Labour Party gained power after World War II, it instituted a set of maternity and child allowance policies, as part of the welfare state, that fully supported a definition of women's place as the home (Foreman 1977:141).

The role of women in continental socialist movements, especially the German and Russian, has received extensive attention by feminist scholars in recent years (e.g., Boxer and Quataert 1978; Engel 1977; Jancar 1978; Heitlinger 1979; Honeycutt 1979). Socialist movements typically have distinguished between "socialist feminism" (which is acceptable) and "bourgeois feminism" (which is not). Based especially on the writings of Marx's collaborator Engels, and Bebel, the famous leader of the German Social Democratic Party (SPD), socialist feminism, indeed socialism generally, has assumed that the root of women's problems lies in the capitalistic system, which distorts family life and relations between the sexes. The solution to women's problems is therefore to be found in socialist revolution. Thus, first priority must always go to the worker's movement toward revolution. As Jancar wrote:

> A woman was labeled proletarian only if she adhered to the socialist movement. Thus, the male socialists subordinated women to the Revolution and relegated the "women question" to second place after the Revolution had been accomplished [1978:74].

Indeed, for many socialists, there was no separate "women's problem"—the new society which will appear after the Revolution will automatically be one of equality between the sexes. From this perspective, women's oppression has been reduced to class oppression, to be solved, *by definition*, with the solution of the class issue. Those who have seen women's issues as a first priority, or as requiring solutions other than, or beyond socialist revolution, have been perceived as "bourgeois feminists."

With this the view of virtually all male socialists, and many females as well, it is little wonder that "socialist women . . . at times failed to advance their feminist goals [even suffrage] for fear of disrupting proletarian unity" (Boxer and Quataert 1978:15). Nor is it any wonder that socialists basically have ignored issues and policies concerned with women's role in the family (1978:16). Honeycutt (1979:37) noted that the Italian, Russian, and French movements made conscious decisions to disregard totally the "woman question," while in Germany, it explicitly sought only political emancipation for women. In 1896 Austrian socialist males opposed working for female suffrage for fear that it might "prejudice" their struggle for universal manhood suffrage; they wished to postpone the issue of female suffrage until after all men were enfranchised (Heitlinger 1979:49–50). Heitlinger expressed a cynical view of the movement's concern for women. Noting that unorganized working women constituted a "threat" to the movement, "the origin of the Socialist women's movement, both within social democracy and within communism, is best understood as a short-term political need to win the support of women workers, a specific social group of potential followers" (1979:52).

It should be noted, however, that by and large socialist feminist women concurred with these practices, priorities, and party ideology. Especially "when crucial international controversies arose [such as the rise of Fascism], all of these women, with rare exception, put their feminist concerns aside," leading to a "greatly diluted" feminism by the 1920s and 1930s. In this context, "many women felt emphasis on the issues of their own sex would be selfish" (Slaughter 1978:61–62).

Let us examine more closely the largest and strongest turn-of-the-century socialist movement, the SPD in Germany, and the first to achieve a revolution, the Russian. In its earliest years in the 1860s, the SPD believed that women's place was in the home, and indeed, there were few female members (Heitlinger 1979:36). Under Bebel's influence, the last three decades of the nineteenth century witnessed the development of the ideology just as discussed: that women ought to be emancipated but that they could be only by a socialist revolution, so top priority must be given the proletarian struggle (1979:36–37). The only women who mattered were working women, not the wives of workers (1979:38), yet most of the female members of the SPD were housewives married to male socialists (Honeycutt 1979:31). Unlike the rest of Europe, the class antagonism in Germany was so strong that virtually no middle-class women were involved in the SPD. On the eve of World War I, women members of the SPD numbered 175,000 and constituted 16.1 percent of the membership (Boxer and Quataert 1978:2).

The SPD was a male-dominated organization that treated women as an auxilliary (Honeycutt 1979:30). The men did not want the women to organize separately, and nineteenth-century law in most German states prohibited women from assembling for political purposes. Therefore, under the guise of apolitical associations, the women did organize separately as their only means of participation (1979:31). The women actually preferred such segregation as a means of pro-

Table 1.3   Percentage of Female SPD Members and Party Congress Delegates in Pre-World War I Years

Year	Percent Female Members	Percent Female Delegates to Party Congress
1909	9.8	5.8
1910	11.5	6.4
1911	12.9	10.6
1912	13.4	8.6
1913	14.4	7.5

Source: Honeycutt (1979:36, footnote 7).

tecting themselves from male discrimination, learning to make their own decisions, and "securing representation for women's special interests" (1979:32).

After 1890, the official program of the SPD called for women's suffrage and an end to all legislation discriminatory against women. Women were placed on party commissions, as well (Honeycutt 1979:33). In 1908 the government abolished its restrictions on female political organization and the SPD immediately abolished the separate women's organizations, and with these the autonomy of female socialists. Ostensibly integrated into the party structure, women were henceforth controlled by the party Executive Committee, on which sat but one female, a relatively "moderate, accommodating figure," not one of the radicals. She was "quickly co-opted by the Executive Committee and came to view her office as representing the interests of that committee to socialist women rather than vice versa" (1979:35). Many of the women were dissatisfied with these changes, and "some evidence of hostility and indifference to the new female members and their interests" existed among the men (1979:35). Nevertheless, because it was now legal to join, women's involvement increased rapidly, from 30,000 in 1908 to 175,000 in 1914 (1979:36). Despite this, "women were discouraged from participation" in party politics and were pushed into the areas of social welfare and communal affairs, "for which they were allegedly better suited." There was in fact more sex segregation than when women were legally separate (1979:36). As Table 1.3 indicates, women were consistently, and in most years substantially, underrepresented in policy-making and leadership roles, as manifested by their participation as delegates to the party Congress.

The majority of female members held "traditional values regarding the family and women's role within it." Women were enjoined to transmit socialist values to their children as their major contribution. Women's rights were viewed as a means to be used to combat capitalism, not as an end in itself (Honeycutt 1979:37). It appears that both sexes accepted the notion that women's role was within the home, as housekeeper and as mother:

> Instead of seeking to institute sexual equality within their movement, they [women] glorified women's traditional female roles of mother and helpmate,

since they knew that in these roles women could be of significant service in the struggle for working-class emancipation [Honeycutt 1979:41].

Turning to prerevolutionary Russia, before the 1860s women were absent from radical movements. During that decade, some daughters of the nobility and other privileged classes became members, but played a peripheral part and were not permitted to assume any leadership roles by the men (Engel 1977:92–100). The 1870s witnessed a peak of female activism in radical and terrorist groups— again primarily idealistic young women of the upper classes. About 15 percent of those arrested in 1873–77 were female (1977:96), and Boxer and Quataert (1978:2) estimated that about half of the terrorists in the 1870s and 1880s were female. One third of the committee membership of the terrorist group, the People's Will, were female, and women were involved in their actual terrorist attacks. Despite their ideological commitment to sexual equality, however, "in the first printing press of the People's Will . . . only the women did housework, cooking, and cleaning, while the men set type. . . . the women did not like doing it much . . . and preferred to work at the press" (Engel 1977:99).

On the eve of World War I and the Russian Revolution, 15 percent of the socialists were female (Boxer and Quataert 1978:2). Both the Bolshevik and the Menschevik factions "opposed acknowledgment of the distinct problems of women within the working class" (Slaughter 1978:58; see also Jancar 1978:74). The revolution of the proletariat was the first priority, and men and women workers were to work side by side toward this goal. Even the female leaders defined women's roles in these terms, along with bearing and raising revolutionary children. The famous Russian female socialist, Rosa Luxemburg, "went so far as to deny that there really was a woman's problem" (Jancar 1978:74). Those few women who insisted on priority for a women's movement, left the party (ibid.). In prerevolutionary Russia, the Bolsheviks did not permit separate female organizations, for fear that they "might create a feminist deviation, splitting the revolutionary movement" (1978:105). Immediately after the revolution, however, they realized that they had to appeal to women, so in March of 1917, they began setting up local women's bureaus. Nonetheless, these remained firmly under the control of the male-dominated central committees, and women were forbidden (as were all other groups) to organize themselves (ibid.).

Nearly 70 years after the first successful socialist revolution, the promise of sex equality that would follow automatically in the wake of the proleterian revolution has yet to materialize beyond the legal sphere in Russia or in any other nation with a socialist/communist government. Indeed, in World War II Yugoslavia,

> two million women participated in the Communist-directed National Liberation Movement, and . . . 620,000 gave their lives for the cause. No women, however, were appointed to the Provisional Government in 1943, and only two women . . . were appointed to the 64-member presidium of the provisional legislature [Jancar 1978:113].

Before turning to nationalistic movements, many of which (like Yugoslavia) also have been partially or completely socialistic in inspiration, we will briefly examine the role of women in a late nineteenth-century U.S. movement on behalf of a deprived population: the Southern Farmer's Alliance. Jeffrey has analyzed this phenomenon of the 1880s and 1890s which, at its height, had millions of members. It was "a rural protest against the inferior social, economic, and political position" (1975:72) of farmers, which included farmers of all social strata, and originated in the depressed state of rural southern agriculture. Included in its agenda was a call for better education, job opportunities, and financial self-sufficiency for women. Women were not only welcomed into, indeed specifically sought out as voting members of the organization; they were encouraged to speak out and to assume leadership roles within it. Yet neither sex supported societal political rights for women: "The meaning of equality for women was constricted by the organization's main goal of reviving southern agriculture" (1975:74). Some male opposition to women's participation did exist, and even some of the women questioned the propriety of such an active role for their sex (1975:76). Nonetheless, women constituted as much as a third to a half of the membership in many local organizations (1975:77), and were at least occasionally elected to local office—although not that of president (1975:78).

Women's activism in this cause, as in so many others we have reviewed, was predicated both on their supposedly greater morality, and on their role as supporters and encouragers of men; as "helpmates" (Jeffrey 1975:79). The improvement of women's lot was part-and-parcel of the improvement of agriculture, inasmuch as farming was a family concern in which women were deeply involved. Jeffrey concluded:

> The part that the Alliance encouraged women to play . . . was more expansive than the traditional role of the southern lady at the same time that it had definite limits. Women need no longer cultivate . . . genteel passivity; they required education as the preparation for a useful life. But the Alliance defined utility in terms of the organization's overall objectives, the profitability of agriculture and the prosperity of the state. Thus, it was vital that women learn to be skilled managers or teachers. Whether spinsters or widows women must never be parasites on their families or on their state. Beneath the rhetoric, the lifestyle the Alliance support [sic] for women was one of constant hard work and low wages, if women were to be paid for their labor at all [1975:84].

Turning now to nationalist movements, a major part of the Zionist movement of the early twentieth century was both socialistic and nationalistic. Its goal was to establish a Jewish homeland in Palestine, but one structured along socialist lines. The role of women in this movement has been analyzed by Izraeli (1981). In the late nineteenth century a series of violent pograms occurred in Russia, bringing death and destruction to Jewish communities. Beginning in the first decade of the twentieth century, idealistic young Jewish men and women began leaving Eastern Europe, especially Russia, for Palestine. In Russia they had espoused an ideology of equality – sexual as well as social. The women had not been organized separately, but they had tended to be "assigned specialized roles" (1981:88–89) which emphasized the cultural rather than the political activities of the group. And, as we have repeatedly seen in discussing socialism, despite a general ideological commitment to sexual equality, no concern was shown for "issues of women's emancipation"; the elimination of exploitative class relationships was to automatically solve women's problems, when the new society was formed in Palestine (1981:89). In addition to the problem women faced based on socialist doctrine, "the Zionist movement defined the problem of Jewish existence as the fundamental and overriding social issue to which all efforts had to be directed. Jewish women were told that their first commitment was as a Jew" (1981:89). On two counts, then, women in this movement were to postpone their claims.

Women comprised about 30 percent of the early immigrants to Palestine (Izraeli 1981:90). The new migrants began the work of establishing communes (*Kvutza*, later called *Kibbutzim*). The work was hard – converting malaria-infested swamplands into farms – and dangerous – fighting off Arab "marauders." The "women were automatically assigned to the kitchen and laundry," as both they and the men felt that "plowing and loading crops were . . . too strenuous and even harmful for women" (1981:91–92). However, the highest value was placed on "productive" work in the fields, and domestic work was of low status. In light of this division of labor, communes accepted 10–30 men, but only 2–3 women, because "women were economically less productive." In June 1909, of 165 Jewish workers on *Kvutzot*, only 11 were female, while by 1912, only 30 of 522 were (1981:92). So, in the face of the realities of pioneer existence, the ideology of sexual equality was an early casualty among socialist Zionists.

Nor did their Arab sisters fare better. Beginning in 1929, Palestinian Arab women organized to support Arab nationalism, to get the sentences of political prisoners mitigated and to stop the flow of arms to Jews. Rowbotham pointed out that not only did the Arabs fail in these endeavors, but "Palestinian women were not able to establish any social basis for the liberation of Arab women" (1972:204).

In Algeria, out of "urgency and necessity" women became active in the revolt against the French after 1955. Women from diverse socioeconomic strata, married, widowed, divorced, and even single, became involved, often against the wishes of their families (Horne 1977:402). They acted as messengers, carried weapons, were imprisoned, tortured, raped, and killed. In many families "it was the women who provided a hard nucleus of anticolonial militancy" (1977:401). But the men remained "profoundly hostile to the liberation of women" and the women "operated in an atmosphere which was completely defined and controlled by men" (Rowbotham 1972:240). "Although the party piously promised women posts, when each instance arose the men automatically decided that women were still too backward, too inexperienced, not sufficiently educated" (Rowbotham 1972:241). Whatever freedoms Algerian women achieved while working in the movement, they were quickly rescinded after independence.

As the movement for independence from the British spread in India during the 1920s and 1930s, women became very active. "They demonstrated, picketed shops, were imprisoned and faced police charges with great courage" (Rowbotham 1972:205). Most explicitly rejected feminism because they believed that it would be unpatriotic to "put women's rights before those of the nation" (Forbes 1982:529). Nonetheless, reform of women's legal status was a major issue for these women, and ultimately a split occurred between those who put national independence first, and those whose first priority was women's rights (1982:531). Ghandi, Nehru, and other leaders were sympathetic to issues of women's rights, but were convinced that they would result only from national liberation, which therefore had first priority (1982:532). After independence the laws indeed changed to grant women equality, but the laws are widely disregarded and the sexes still highly unequal.

We shall end this section with a brief discussion of the role of American women in the black and Chicano civil rights movements of the 1960s. Despite a plethora of research, there is actually a limited amount of data on the magnitude of female participation in these movements. Perhaps because the black civil rights movement predates the interest in women's issues, investigators did not count by sex, only by race and class. Even national surveys of minority attitudes toward the movements tended to ignore sex as a variable, despite the fact that the survey instruments enumerated the sex of respondents (see e.g., Brink and Harris 1963, 1966). However, in a survey of "conventional militancy" among black Americans (willingness to endorse civil rights activism as well as riots), G. Marx (1967:53–54) did report that men were more militant than women (32 percent compared with 22 percent). Likewise, the National Advisory Commission on Civil Disorders (the Kerner Commission) reported in 1968 that among arrestees during the Detroit riot of 1967, 89.3 percent were males. Of course, the likelihood of arrest was a function of the seriousness of the act and differential enforcement behavior by the police, both of which might reduce the percentages of women counted. Fogelson and Hill (1970:379–80) estimated that between 40 and 50 percent of the urban rioters in 1967 were female. Survey data reported by the Kerner Commission support the lower figure, as it noted that 61.4 percent of the self-reported riot participants were male (1968:172–73). Nevertheless, Caplan (1970) depicted the black militant of the times as "the new ghetto *man*." It is no accident then that the names that are recalled today as constituting the leadership, first of the nonviolent civil rights phase and later of the more violent black power phase of the movement, include virtually no females: Martin Luther King, Andrew Young, Jessie Jackson, Huey Newton, Eldridge Cleaver, Stokely Carmichael, Malcolm X, Immamu Baraka (Leroi Jones), and so forth. In a study of post-World War II black social activism in New Orleans, Thompson found that women were often active, but rarely played any kind of leadership role (1963:26).

Many writers, black and white, male and female, have noted that at least by the mid 1960s, as feminism was beginning to reemerge within the white community, black leaders and scholars were explicitly defining women's role as subordinate and domestic. Moreover, they totally rejected the Women's Liberation Movement as a white women's issue, irrelevant to black women and divisive of the black movement (Deckard 1983:344; Hare and Hare 1970; La Rue 1970; Staples 1973:175–79). A common quip in the black power movement, attributed to Stokely Carmichael, was that "the position in the black movement for black women is prone." The "home and babies" emphasis was particularly evident among Black Muslims (La Rue 1970:61), but opposition to birth control and abortion was widespread among black leaders, who defined these as whites' efforts toward black genocide (Deckard 1983:344; La Rue 1970:64). Women were to produce babies for the revolution as their major contribution. In addition, black scholars and leaders accepted the notions of a black matriarchy and black male (symbolic) castration by black women, propounded first by the white male sociologist Daniel Patrick Moynihan. This myth led black men to focus blame on black women as a source of their problems (Deckard 1983:344; La Rue 1970:63): "Black men were telling their women to take a subordinate position so as to build up the damaged black male ego. In effect, women were being told that the black liberation movement could succeed only at their expense" (Deckard 1983:344; see also Hare and Hare 1970:66).

Most black women accepted this logic, if for no other reason than fear of creating dissensus within the black movement (La Rue 1970:64; Hare and Hare 1970:68). Many also felt that black male freedom ought to come first, after which attention could be focused on their plight (see La Rue 1970:62), or that racism was more oppressive than sexism (Hare and Hare 1970:90). Therefore, they took "pains to avoid the appearance of posing a threat to black men as leaders" (1970:66).

Some black women clearly did perceive their unique problems as women, both within the general society and within the black movement. The first feminist protest came as early as 1964, when a radical black woman presented a paper protesting the treatment of women by the male leadership of the Student Non-Violent Coordinating Committee: "The men's violent reaction . . . made it clear that women would have to choose between feminism . . . and black liberation. . . . the men were not willing to incorporate feminist demands into their basic program" (Deckard 1983:344).

As we have suggested, most black women chose to work within the black movement. As the 1960s wound to a close, however, black women began to form their own feminist organizations, separate both from the white women's movement and the male-dominated black movement. Gradually, black males became more receptive to the concerns of these women, but by then the black movement was past its apex (see Deckard 1983:345–46).

Chicanas (Mexican-American women) have faced almost the identical situation as black women, and responded in like fashion. The Chicano movement, which emerged in the late 1960s, has been primarily male-dominated, with women "largely underrepresented in policymaking positions." Some token female representation has occurred, largely since the mid-1970s (Gonzales 1978:68). Male leaders declare that "when discrimination has been defeated, then [we] will see to the Chicanas" (1978:68). Like black males, Chicanos have viewed women's liberation as a white ("Anglo") issue, which can serve only to divide the Chicano movement; and the women have been accused of divisiveness if they attempt to raise feminist issues (1978:72). Most Chicanas have chosen to remain within the Chicano movement (Deckard 1983:344) and accept their subordinate position. Ideologically, the Chicano movement has been very similar to the black movement: "When Chicano men talk about maintaining 'la familia' and the cultural heritage of La Raza, they are in fact talking about maintaining the age-old concept of keeping the women barefoot, pregnant and in the kitchen" (1978:73).

Recent analyses by Cortera (1980) and Melville (1980) chronicle the substantial participation of women in the Chicano movement. These authors cited numerous women activists who served as leaders in portions of the movement and enumerated no less than three dozen conferences, seminars, and workshops organized by Mexican-American women between 1970 and 1975. It is significant to recognize that these conferences addressed and endorsed both feminist and Chicano Liberation goals, and each occurred after the emergence of the Women's Liberation Movement. The minority of Chicanas who have become unwilling to sacrifice feminist issues have, thus, sometimes formed their own organizations, but also have sometimes worked (with varying degrees of success) within primarily Anglo feminist organizations.

In conclusion, it is clear that movements for *human* equality and/or liberation have typically been de facto movements for *male* liberation and equality. Some have explicitly argued for a traditional and subordinate role for women; others have been ideologically committed to sexual equality. But even in the latter cases, women have been told repeatedly to "wait" until after the "more important" issue was resolved. Women's problems have been literally defined out of existence by many groups ostensibly devoted to human equality. Women who have argued for the unique nature of their problems—and therefore the need for unique solutions—have been defined as divisive and uncommitted to the "true cause." Yet women in large numbers have marched and demonstrated, raised funds, borne arms, gone to jail, and suffered torture and death in these causes, side by side with their male comrades. Finally, in those instances where "the cause" has triumphed, women have often been little better off years later than they were before the revolution.

WOMEN'S MOVEMENTS

It should be clear from the preceding descriptions of the myriad ways in which women have protested, individually and collectively, against a rather full range of injustices that they have not simply been passsive spectators to history, nor have they been passive victims of their own social and cultural oppression. Millions of women have participated in revolt, but rarely has it been specifically and explicitly on behalf of their own sex, and more rarely has it called into serious question the basic structures of the sex stratification and gender role systems. Until at least the nineteenth century, social and political conditions probably made a more complete revolt impossible. In short, women used the avenues open to them to express their sex-based frustrations, but these avenues were very limited.

All the forms of revolt discussed in this chapter share one or both of two characteristics that distinguish them from women's movements. First, in several instances revolt has been based upon membership in, or concern for, a deprived category comprised of members of both sexes, but women's status qua women has been either ignored or relegated to low priority within the larger movement. When female abolitionists began to note the similarity of their status to that of black slaves, even male abolitionists sympathetic to their plight asked that they wait until the slavery issue was settled. In our discussion of movements for human equality and/or national liberation we noted repeatedly that the issue of women's emancipation was not raised at all (Reform and Chartist Movements), defined out of existence (socialist movements), and/or women were told to wait until a more "important, general" goal was achieved. In many of these cases, at least some women departed the movement in question to devote their energies to women's own cause. Second, in several cases women indeed have revolted directly against their inferior status and role constraints as women, but not *explicitly* on behalf of their sex, and their revolt often has been unconscious as well. Witchcraft was seen as just such a form of revolt, wherein self-proclaimed female witches have achieved through magic a degree of power normally denied members of their sex. Yet no direct challenge to the sex stratification or gender role systems, other than through the example of their own behavior, has usually been voiced by witches. Likewise, religious heresies and dissident religious movements have rarely challenged the secular sex stratification or gender role systems, although often explicitly questioning religious distinctions made on the basis of sex. In fact, their theologies have addressed both sexes and called for religious changes designed to make people (not just women) more righteous.

In short, in all the phenomena discussed to this point, women have been engaged in revolt. In many cases they have revolted over what may be described as "women's issues." What was lacking in such instances, however, was conscious and collective revolt on behalf of women, defined as a general category with a set of problems and needs specific to themselves, which in turn are created by a sociocultural system that categorically disadvantages them relative to males. When led by their involvements in various forms of revolt to the conscious realization that they have been unfairly handicapped by existing custom and law, some women have developed their own movement to fight for secular changes on their own behalf. At that point, they have developed or participated in a women's movement, as we saw in case of some of the abolitionists, socialists, and temperance activists.

Four characteristics distinguish women's movements from the types of revolts already discussed. First, they focus attention on problems specific to women as women. Their first and major priority is to change the sex stratification and/or gender role definition systems as an end in itself. In this connection, and regardless of who actually participates in the movement, women's movements purportedly work on behalf of all women, irrespective of other distinctions such as social class, race, ethnicity, and religion.

Second, several specific problems are explicitly seen as interrelated to one another and, in turn, collectively a function of a system of female disadvantage. In short, women's movements are ideologically (if not tactically) oriented to a relatively broad range of specific issues, problems, and proposed changes relevant to women. This constitutes a variable dimension, and the more fully feminist the movement, the larger the number of specific issues that are linked together.

Third, a movement is not simply a sporadic outbreak, such as a riot. Rather, it is more highly organized and conducts sustained activities, utilizing a variety of tactics and strategies, over a period of years. This is not to say, however, that some movement activities may not be riots or other forms of sporadic outbreak.

Fourth, movements are broader than one organization, such as a particular religious group or party. Movements consist of a number of organizations, along with "fellow travelers," who agree with some, many, or virtually all the positions taken by specific movement organizations and spokespersons, but who may not join any specific organization, or even apply the movement label to themselves.

These four characteristics really reflect two fundamental traits. The first is the degree to which the *ideological focus* of a women's movement analyzes a variety of specifically female problems said to result from structured systems of sex inequality and/or gender role differentiation, and this ranges from ameliorative to feminist. Second, movements must be sufficiently *organized* to sustain a variety of activities over a span of years, through which they attract a relatively large number of supporters for the issues raised.

Clearly, there is vagueness in such terms as *span of years, relatively large number of supporters,* and *network of organizations.* At no precise point can one establish that a handful of activists have attracted enough adherents to constitute a movement. The distinction is important, however, because small numbers of vocal feminists probably exist in most socities today and in many societies in the past, while only some societies can be said to have developed women's movements, and those only during the past century.

2 Existing Explanations: Causes in Search of a Theory

In the last decade and a half a plethora of books and essays have been written concerning the current feminist movement in the United States and elsewhere, and turn-of-the-century movements as well. In general, the issue of why, given the centuries of female oppression, women's movements emerge only in certain times and places, has been ignored or glossed over by most scholars. When the issue had been addressed, a rather vast array of historically specific processes and events has been adduced to account for the emergence—or reemergence—of such movements. Many tend to read like a catalog of socioeconomic and political trends and events that might influence substantial numbers of women to revolt (e.g., see Banks 1981: introduction; Burke 1980: chap. 1). Considerable attention has also been paid to the individual characteristics of movement participants and/or leaders, including in some instances detailed accounts of their "conversion" to feminism (see, e.g., Carden 1974). These tend to lack a framework which identifies the relationship between social-structural and individual-level variables. Absent from almost all of the literature (for a notable exception see Freeman 1975: chaps. 1, 2) is any theory that could allow a reader to decide which sociohistorical factors are most important and why; and what specific processes link broad socioeconomic, political, and demographic changes to the emergence of women's movements in given times and places (see chap. 3). In this chapter we will review the more frequently mentioned factors adduced in the literature to account for the rise of such movements, especially in the United States. These factors will be subsumed within five categories: demographic changes, educational and intellectual factors, political and organizational phenomena, economic trends, and "contagion" from other movements.

DEMOGRAPHIC CHANGES

The post–World War II era has been a time of substantial demographic change in both the United States and most of the other industrial societies, although some of the changes had begun before the turn of the century. Those which have been cited as salient to the emergence of the contemporary feminist movement include increasing longevity and divorce rates, substantially reduced family size (especially since 1964 and the end of the "baby boom"), increasing age of marriage and childbearing (again, especially since the early 1960s), and a low societal sex ratio (a surplus of females). In discussing several of these changes, scholars have linked them to one or both of at least two other phenomena, which we will discuss later in this chapter. First, these demographic changes have typically been viewed as highly influential in their effects on increasing women's labor force participation, which, in turn, has been seen as a major impetus for the recent reemergence of feminist activity (Chafe 1977:121; Huber 1976). Second, and less important, some of these demographic changes (and some related ones in the nineteenth century) have occasionally been viewed as instrumental in freeing women's time and energy for participation in movement activities.

Longevity has been gradually increasing in the Western world for several hundred years, and in recent decades has reached the point where most females may reasonably expect to be alive and healthy for at least three decades after the responsibilities of childbearing, and especially rearing, are all but completed. While it has long been normative for unmarried women to participate in the labor force, among nonpoverty families it was primarily the mothers of the "baby boomers" who, in the 1950s, began the extensive trend of returning to the labor force as their children entered adolescence. These middle-class, married women were primarily seeking money to help maintain and increase their family's middle-class life-style, and to save for the anticipated financial burden of college expenses. They may also have been seeking something to do with the long stretch of years before them. Regardless, they reentered the labor force with about 25 years of work before retirement—a function of relatively small families (averaging around 3 children), relatively early childbirth (families completed during the women's 20s) and increased longevity.

Industrialized nations worldwide have witnessed rising divorce rates in recent decades, but the United States has the highest rate. Due to this phenomenon, women are further impelled toward labor force participation (see Huber 1976:382)—both as divorced persons who must support themselves and often their children, and as married women fearful that they had better be prepared for independence because of the possibility of divorce. However, relatively high divorce rates (and their functional equivalent, early widowhood) have existed in other times and places, including many tribal societies, and have been accompanied by women returning to their parents or other family members for protection and support. In other words, high divorce rates do not necessarily impel increased labor force participation and are therefore probably not linked in any necessary fashion to the emergence of women's movements.

Since about 1964 the birth rate has declined sharply, reaching the lowest point in our history by the late 1970s (at an averge of less than two children per family) and remaining low ever since. Again, low birth rates characterize the entire industrialized world. However, unlike the situation in the United States and in a small handful of other societies (Canada, Australia, and New Zealand), the rest of the industrialized nations never experienced the postwar baby boom. Except for the period 1947–63, the United States, like the entire industrialized world, has been experiencing a gradual trend toward smaller families for at least a century. Ample evidence from around the world links small family size to increased female labor force participation (see Chafetz 1984:67–71).

Also since the 1960s the average age of first marriage for both sexes has increased—by more than one year—accompanied by a substantial increase in the average age of women at the time of first births. Since for several decades American females have typically entered the labor force after completion of schooling and before marriage and childbearing, these changes mean that females tend to spend a longer time in the labor force at a younger age. This has been said to increase women's attachment to the labor force by increasing their "human capital" (i.e., experience and skills), hence the status and pay they receive from work. The result is said to lead to a greater reluctance to leave the labor force at all, or for very long, for childrearing; and a greater probability of recognizing continuing sex discrimination in the labor force and hence attraction to the women's movement.

The demographic changes we have enumerated to this point function together to increase women's labor force participation in terms of both the proportion of women working outside the home and the number of years women do so. In turn, this ostensibly increases their feelings of commitment to nondomestic work (Chafe 1977:119–23; Freeman 1975:28–29; Huber 1976). However, these demographic changes have occurred within a context of a relative lack of change in two related phenomena: the amount of domestic work performed by men, and the degree of occupational sex segregation and resultant pay inequities for females. The latter issue will be explored in greater depth later in this chapter. The former is said to also spur feminist consciousness by increasing substantially the number of women (but not men) who suffer from work overload. Married women employed outside of the home also average about 30 hours of household labor per week, compared to about 5 for their husbands (Barrett 1976; Kahne 1976). In turn, women are said to better perceive the inequities of the sex stratification and gender role systems because of this double burden (Carden 1974:154; Huber 1976). It should be noted, however, that in some agrarian, many horticultural, and most socialist/communist societies women also routinely work longer hours than men, shouldering the double burden of domestic, childrearing work, and economically productive labor, yet they have not revolted or developed a feminist consciousness. Work overload does not automatically translate into consciousness and activism, any more than does extensive disadvantage per se. A "transmission mechanism" that can account for how and why overload comes to be perceived and defined as unfair must be specified—and generally it hasn't been in the literature.

Recently, Guttentag and Secord (1983) have focused attention on the effects of differing sex ratios on social life. They argued (in a somewhat overstated fashion) that low sex ratios (a surplus of females) constitute a "strong impetus" to the development of women's movements (see also Caine 1982:539–40; Edmondson

1984:7). Given a situtation where there are "too many women" and women have markedly less "structural power" than men (i.e., women are a disadvantaged category), men have weaker commitments to individual women, since there are so many available from which to choose. The result, argued Guttentag and Secord, is heightened misogyny, increased sexual promiscuity, a large number of women who have experienced hurt and rejection by males, and therefore a large number of women who seek independence from men. At the very least, a low sex ratio implies that many women will need gainful employment in the absence of husbands who can provide for them. In turn, these pressures presumably inspire women's movements. Defining the Beguine Movement (which we discussed in chap. 1) as a feminist movement, Guttentag and Secord (1983: chap. 3) documented the low sex ratio characteristic of Western Europe at that time. Likewise, they demonstrated that the sex ratio among marriageable Americans in the late 1960s, early 1970s was quite low (1983: chaps. 7, 8). However, the data they presented concerning black Americans (1983: chap. 8) showed them to have a markedly longer-lasting and lower sex ratio than that characteristic of whites (1983: chap. 7). By their own logic, blacks should be more committed to feminism than whites, yet as we suggested in chapter 1, this is not the case (see also Freeman 1975:38). We suggest that Guttentag and Secord's argument concerning the effects of low sex ratios may have utility in terms of developing an understanding of the emergence of collective female revolt, but not the form of that revolt. In other words, low sex ratios in the context of substantial female disadvantage may well prompt substantial numbers of women to seek new roles for themselves, to question the status quo in some fashion, but not necessaily to advocate *feminism* — at least as we are using that term.

EDUCATIONAL AND INTELLECTUAL FACTORS

A number of scholars have cited the publication of several books in the late 1950s and early 1960s as highly influential in precipitating the Women's Liberation Movement. Kontopoulos (1972:356) provided a fairly comprehensive list, going back as early as a 1949 book by Margaret Mead, and including scholarly works by Flexner (*Century of Struggle* 1959) and by Sinclair (*The Emancipation of American Women* 1965), de Beauvoir's esoteric *The Second Sex*, and Friedan's 1963 best-seller, *The Feminine Mystique*. Yates (1975) likewise cited several influential books, including Flexner and Friedan again, Newcomer's 1959 *A Century of Higher Education for Women*, Smut's *Women and Work in America* (also 1959), and a special issue of the journal *Daedalus*, published in 1964, devoted entirely to women. Carden (1974:154) presented yet another list, with some overlap of names like Friedan and de Beauvoir, and the *Daedalus* issue. With the exception of Friedan's book, it is unlikely that any of the rest of the works cited in these analyses were read by more than a small number of academics. In fact, it is likely that these books were more widely read after the movement began than when they were first published. Friedan's book was widely read at the time of its publication, and we are inclined to agree with the authors who argued for its influence in developing the movement (see also Deckard 1983:321; Flexner 1975:ix; Freeman 1975:52). Altbach (1984:456) and Everett (1983:20) both spoke of the influence of foreign feminist books on the development of women's movements in Germany and India, respectively.

Of greater significance than a few books was probably the dramatic increase in the educational attainments of women in the postwar era. The baby boom generation, even more than those born a few years earlier, went to college in massive and unprecedented numbers. Both sexes increased in their proportion of college-educated, but women more so than men. Explanations of the Women's Liberation Movement have typically included mention of this phenomenon. It is said to have influenced the emergence of the movement in two ways: through its direct impact on women, and indirectly through its impact on women's labor force participation. Indeed, in discussing the nineteenth-century women's movement, O'Neill (1969a:19; see also Howard 1974:141–42) claimed that increasing educational opportunities for middle-class women, which emerged after Oberlin College opened its doors to women in 1841, was an important factor in the origins of that wave of activism, while Rosenthal (1977:374) made a similar observation concerning nineteenth-century Russia, and Everett (1983:19) concerning contemporary India.

Lipman-Blumen viewed higher education, in and of itself, as "a radicalizing force" (1984:205; see also Everett 1983:19). Guttentag and Secord argued that higher education serves as an impetus to feminism because of several direct consequences:

> First, it creates a pool of women who are more apt to respond to media communications concerning women's rights and women's roles, and who are more apt to be in a position to participate in or respond sympathetically to organizational efforts concerning women. Second, educated women are apt to be more aware of the alternatives that are available to them with respect to careers and lifestyles, and thus to be more ready to accept feminism. Finally, they constitute a large pool of women who can serve as leaders of the feminist movement [1983:32].

Yates (1975:3) claimed that higher education produces disenchantment with domestic life, which in turn contributes to the development of feminism. Also, in college women and men are presumably given the same education and women also gain a degree of independence from males (husbands or fathers) (Freeman 1975:35). We agree that there is a relationship between expanded education and the rise of a women's movement, but its precise nature needs to be clearly spelled out theoretically, and this has not been done.

Huber and Spitze (1983:43) pointed out what is probably the more important linkage between higher education and feminism: labor force participation, a linkage echoed by Howard in his discussion of the nineteenth century (1974:142). The proportion of a woman's life spent in the labor force is in part a function of how much education she has: college-educated women are more likely to be employed. Freeman (1975: chap. 1), in the most theoretically sophisticated analysis of why the Women's Liberation Movement arose, argued that college-educated women were (and presumably still are) the most likely to feel relatively deprived (see also Carden 1974:154). In turn, revolt, including feminist revolt, springs from a sense of relative (not absolute) deprivation. Our own theory, to be explained in chapter 3, will develop this issue. Noting continued segregation and inequality in the work force, Freeman stated about college-educated women: "This group of women is more likely to compare themselves to people of similar educational attainment than to those of the same sex status. In particular, their comparative reference group is more likely to be their husbands and their former classmates" (1975:31). She continued by arguing that there is relatively little discrepancy between what lower-class, less educated women receive and what they feel entitled to. But for the college-educated professional, "married to or simply associating with professional men," what she receives is far less than what, on the basis of her educational credentials, she has come to define as desirable, feasible, and legitimate to obtain (Freeman 1975:32–33). Feminism arises, therefore, because "In general, college-educated women have greater expectations and lesser opportunity for realizing them" than either men or other women (1975:35).

POLITICAL AND ORGANIZATIONAL PHENOMENA

Several specific political and organizational events of the early 1960s have been enumerated by many writers in discussing the emergence of the Women's Liberation Movement. The first of these was John F. Kennedy's creation of a Presidential Commission on the Status of Women in 1961. He did this in response to pressure from a group of political and professionally employed women (Yates 1975:4). It was "the first official body to make a thorough study of the status of women in the United States" (Deckard 1983:321), and resulted in a lengthly published report (see also Carden 1974:154; Freeman 1975:52). Everett (1983:20) reported an analogous phenomenon in India in the early 1970s as part of her analysis of the emergence of an Indian women's movement. In turn, Kennedy's commission spurred the establishment of a large number of state commissions on the status of women during the ensuing few years (Freeman 1975:52). In 1963 the Equal Pay Act was passed by Congress (Carden 1974:154; Deckard 1983:321), followed by the 1964 Civil Rights Act. Almost by accident, this piece of legislation, which was basically designed to protect blacks, included sex as a category that could no longer form a basis for differential treatment by employers. It became immediately apparent, however, that the EEOC (Equal Employment

Opportunity Commission) charged with enforcement was ignoring the sex provision—that is, ignoring discrimination against women. The last major specific event usually cited to explain the emergence of women's activism is therefore the 1966 organization of NOW (National Organization for Women), the initial impetus for which was concern over enforcement of the sex provision of the Civil Rights Act (Deckard 1993:322; Freeman 1975:54).

Nearly all scholars who have concerned themselves with the origins and/or early history of the Women's Liberation Movement in the United States have spoken of two separate paths to the movement, which emerged more or less simultaneously, and which began to converge after about 1970 (see, e.g., Carden 1974; Chafe 1977: chap. 5; Deckard 1983: chap. 12; Freeman 1975; Huber 1976; Yates 1975). The first was comprised primarily of somewhat older, professionally employed women, whose interest was focused primarily on legal and economic problems, and whose tactics were primarily political (Freeman 1975:49). These were the women who organized NOW, and in very short order other national groups such as WEAL (Women's Equity Action League) and the Women's Political Caucus, and allied themselves with national organizations of like-minded women already in existence (e.g., the YWCA, the League of Women Voters, and various professional and business women's groups). The second stream emerged from the the New Left Movement, including women who had been active in the Civil Rights, Student, and Antiwar protest movements of the 1960s. They tended to be younger and more oriented to personal, educational, and service work issues (Freeman 1975:49). Based on their experiences in these male-dominated movements, some of which were discussed in chapter 1, and all of which mirrored the experiences of women in movements for human equality and liberation, radical women began organizing themselves locally. Many accounts of this phenomenon catalog a lengthy series of specific incidents which impelled women, in group after group, to depart and establish their own feminist groups (e.g., see Freeman 1975:56–58), which were small and locally based.

The issue of the influence of New Left causes on the emergence of feminist activism will be addressed more specifically in a later section of this chapter. For now, our interest will be focused on only one aspect of this phenomenon: the importance for movement development of preexisting communications networks. Freeman (1975:48ff; see also Streijffert 1974, for the same argument in terms of Sweden) has argued that for a movement to grow and spread from a series of small cadres to a mass movement, a preexisting communications network, or a set of linkages between local groups, is required. Moreover, the groups linked must be "co-optable"; that is, composed of like-minded people. Two such networks of women who were potentially co-optable to feminism emerged in the early to mid-1960s. Younger, radical women were linked together through their involvement in New Left activities, beginning with the Civil Rights Movement and gaining momentum in the Student Protest and Antiwar movements, and in SDS (Students for a Democratic Society). The older, reformist women were linked by the state and national commissions of the early 1960s, by NOW and other national women's groups which quickly emerged, and by a number of preexisting national organizations comprised mostly of well-educated, white, middle-class, often professionally employed, women. In short, once reborn, the idea of feminism was able to spread swiftly because of the density of networks which linked co-optable women, that had expanded considerably in the first half of the decade. As Freeman herself noted, however, the prior existence of such organizational networks expedites the process of movement development. It is questionable whether their prior existence can be said, in any fashion, to "cause" a movement to emerge.

ECONOMIC TRENDS

Virtually no discussion of the origins of the contemporary women's movement in the United States has ignored a major post–World War II trend: the dramatic increase in the proportion of women, especially married women, and including women with young children, participating in the labor force. Between the war and the early 1970s, the majority of married women shifted their status from full-time homemaker to full-time paid employee. While this was occurring, women's status within the labor force remained essentially constant. Women employed full-time continued to earn 59 cents for each dollar men earned, and women continued to be employed overwhelmingly in a handful of occupations comprised almost entirely of females; that is, to work in highly sex-segregated occupations. These facts have been reviewed by all who have concerned themselves with the emergence of the Women's Liberation Movement.

In earlier sections of this chapter we discussed a series of demographic and educational changes which many have claimed propelled women into the labor force (or kept them there after marriage and even after child-bearing). This "supply-side" logic ignores one simple issue. If jobs don't exist, regardless of whether women want or need them, they are not likely to get them. The dramatic increase in women's employment resulted, first and foremost, from a "demand-side" phenomenon (Oppenheimer 1970). Most noticeably in the United States, but in all highly industrialized societies as well, post-World War II economies have witnessed a dramatic expansion of the tertiary (service) sector of employment. Women are literally "pulled into" these expanding jobs, which mostly required at least a high school degree, if not more education, because they were the only sizable labor pool available to fill them. Since single women were already fairly fully employed, married women with older children first heeded the call in the 1950s. Later, as the need for such labor continued to grow, mothers of young children increasingly were pulled into the labor force as well.

The jobs that have expanded most dramatically in the postwar era have been precisely those that were predominantly filled by women long before World War

II: clerical and secretarial positions, nursing and allied health professions, and while the baby boomers were still young, public school teaching. Low-paying service work in restaurants, laundries, retail establishments, and day-care facilities grew in response to the increasing number of employed wives and mothers, and they too were, and remain, heavily comprised of women. It is little wonder, then, that despite the dramatic increase in the proportion of women employed, the nature of their employment and their relative earnings have remained essentially constant. Although generally ignoring the "demand-side" reasons for women's increased employment rates (for an exception see Freeman 1975:24), scholars concerned with the Women's Liberation Movement have scarcely ignored the fact that women have continued to receive low pay and face very limited opportunities for advancement in the decades since World War II. This continued discrimination is often viewed as more or less of a direct cause of the rise of the feminist movement (Carden 1974:158; Chafe 1977:119–20; Flexner 1975:viii; Guttentag and Secord 1983:33; Lipman-Blumen 1984:205; Yates 1975:3). As Huber and Spitze argued, the rapid rise in female labor force participation, coupled with no change in relative earnings, "made a critical mass of women become aware that the ideology of equal opportunity didn't apply to them. This awareness triggered a new wave of the women's movement" (1983:35; see also Huber 1976:381). Howard (1974:140–41) made a similar observation with respect to expanding female opportunities for work outside the home in nineteenth-century America.

The expansion in married women's labor force participation occurred simultaneously with the postwar ideological development of what has been labeled, since Friedan's 1963 book, the "feminine mystique." The core of this mystique emphasized that women's obligations and contentment rested solely in their roles as wives and mothers; children need full-time mothers, and women can find true happiness by devoting themselves wholeheartedly to their care and to that of their husbands and homes. Several scholars (e.g., Chafe 1977:100–101; Deckard 1983:317; Freeman 1975:25–26; Vogel 1983:3) have noted that this mystique grew up alongside its inherent contradiction: an increase in the full-time labor force commitment of wives and mothers. In the late 1950s and 1960s, the discrepancy grew between idealized femininity and the reality of an increasing number of women's lives, a discrepancy to which the emergence of the Women's Liberation Movement is sometimes attributed (Carden 1974:157–58; Deckard 1983:319).

Freeman rightly argued that strains inherent in married women's labor force participation — the dual work roles discussed earlier, the discrepancy between reality and ideology, and continued sex discrimination — were at least twenty years old by the time the Women's Liberation Movement surfaced. And, at any rate, "social strain does not create social movements; it only creates the potential for movements" (1975:44–45). Again, it is apparent that theoretical transmission mechanisms must be spelled out to link these socioeconomic trends and their resultant strains with the development of consciousness and activism.

Ironically, attempts to explain the emergence of nineteenth-century women's movements often argue the opposite phenomenon: that the early stages of industrialization stripped women in all but the poverty classes of meaningful economic roles, and this resulted in the rise of movement activism. For instance, Freeman saw industrialization as disruptive of the "components of the traditional sex roles," inasmuch as most domestic productive activity was transferred to the factory, and those products (e.g., fabric, clothes, and many processed foods) then had to be purchased with money. Not permitted to enter the labor force, women—especially of the middle class—became totally dependent on their husbands (1975:14; see also DuBois 1978:16,22; Klein 1984:524; O'Neil 1969a:17). In addition, family size was beginning to shrink and household servants were widely available. Bored, frustrated, and feeling relatively deprived compared to their male class peers, such women ostensibly became social activitists in a variety of causes, including women's rights (O'Neill 1969b:chap. 1; Sinclair 1965:introduction). Carden (1974:158) even argued that one of the factors prompting the contemporary movement was the reduction of household duties, contingent upon the rapid postwar development of labor-saving domestic technology, coupled with the professionalization of many volunteer roles. These phenomena presumably resulted in a sense of boredom and frustration for (educated) middle-class women, and therefore in a women's movement.

It appears then, that one argument explaining the rise of women's movements sees them as a result of work overload, the other as the result of boredom because of too few work obligations; one as a result of a too limited role in reality and ideology, the other as the result of a discrepancy between reality and ideology. Both imply, if not state, the importance of women's sense of deprivation in comparison with male class peers as an important cause of women's activism. We concur with this last point and will develop it in more depth in chapter 3.

"CONTAGION" APPROACHES

We conclude with a discussion of an argument, common to all analyses of both the contemporary and the nineteenth-century movements, that we term the *contagion* approach. It is historically accurate to point out that both the contemporary women's movement and its nineteenth-century predecessor arose in eras during which a variety of reformist/radical causes flourished. In chapter 1 it was clear that women's rights arose as an issue when women active in the Abolitionist Movement noted parallels between their status and that of slaves. The Women's Christian Temperance Union (WCTU) and other moral reform movements, along with socialism and other movements for human equality and/or national liberation, also coexisted, and were often intertwined with late nineteenth-century Women's Rights movements. Women's activism experienced a widespread rebirth in the United States in the late 1960s, after a decade of civil rights, student, and antiwar protest. Likewise, women's movements arose at about the same time in Europe, where radical student and pacifist protest had been occurring. Altbach (1984:458) even talked about international contagion, by which the rise of German feminism in the 1970s was seen, in part, as the result of the development of feminism elsewhere, as did Everett in terms of India (1983:20).

The question is, in precisely what ways do the existence of such other movements and protest activities function to impel the emergence of women's movements; in what ways is there "contagion" from one movement, or a general intellectual milieu to specifically women's movements? Many scholars simply assume that such movements emerge as a more or less logical outcome of a generalized questioning of the status quo. Fighting for the rights of others presumably automatically alerts women to their own lack of rights (e.g., Caine 1982:539–40; Carden 1974:151–56; Chafe 1977:96; Deckard 1983:320; Edmondson 1984:1–3; Freeman 1975:27–28; Hole and Levine 1984:533; Howard 1974:144–45; Klein 1984:530; O'Neill 1969a:16; Sinclair 1965:37). No precise mechanisms are delineated to account for how the "temper of the times" results in a specific movement. Apparently, women "catch" the spirit of the times much as one catches a cold, but no analogy to "germs" is presented as a transmission mechanism.

Other, more specific aspects of movement contagion have, however, been suggested by some. In an earlier section we discussed Freeman's (1975) analysis of the importance of preexisting networks of like-minded women for the spread of feminism. From this perspective, connections formed through organizational involvement in other radical/reformist causes serve, at a later time, to transmit feminism. Another approach stresses the organizational, media, and leadership skills acquired by women while working for other causes, which are then available for use on behalf of their own cause (e.g., Deckard 1983:320; DuBois 1978:19,32; O'Neill 1969a:19). A final form of contagion refers to the actual treatment women receive at the hands of the male leadership of other movements (Hole and Levine 1984:534 ff.; Howard 1974:145–46; Huber 1976:371–72; Sargent 1981:xii–xiv; Tolchin and Tolchin 1976:27–28; Yates 1975:6). As discussed in some detail in chapter 1, female activists have most often been treated as anything but equal by their male comrades, and this was no less true of New Left men in the 1960s than socialists and abolitionists a century ago. Many have hypothesized that such treatment sensitizes women to the need for a movement devoted to their own problems. Speaking of a small, underground feminist cadre in the contemporary USSR, Ruthchild (1983:5) cited male underground treatment of fellow females dissidents as a major cause of its emergence. Kaufmann-McCall made a similar point in discussing the rise of French feminism in the late 1960s and early 1970s (1983:283).

In the literature concerning women's movements these separate forms of contagion are not specifically delineated or usually treated separately. Some or all are typically interwoven in a general discussion of the impact of historically prior radical or reformist movements – and especially those in which substantial numbers of women were involved—on the rise of women's movements. In general terms, the contagion process is said to teach women three things, in addition to providing organizational/leadership skills and network formation: (1) to perceive their collective disadvantage relative to males; (2) to locate the source of their problems in social structural phenomena rather than in individual-level characteristics; and (3) to perceive the possibility of structural change through organized, mass action.

The main problem with the contagion approach is that one is left wondering why women active in other causes have often failed to mount a women's movement (or even, in some instances, to become active in existing ones). What is the "vaccine" that prevents transmission of ostensibly contagious ideas? In chapter 1 we noted several examples of movements in which all of the elements just listed were present, but the vast majority of female activists never "caught" a desire to mount a movement on their own behalf—even a light case: the British Reform and Chartist Movements, the Southern Farmer's Alliance Movement, and the Palestinian Arab and Algerian nationalist movements. It is likely that a majority of female black and Chicana activists at most caught a mild case—at least relative to white women. This was the case despite the fact that the Civil Rights Movement is probably the most frequently mentioned "infectious case" from which the Women's Liberation Movement supposedly caught its inspiration in the United States. There is also a deep irony in the fact that feminist scholars employ a contagion approach, inasmuch as it implies that the only way women would think to mount their own movement is to learn why they need one and how to do it from existing, male-dominated movements.

Finally, there is a logical flaw in employing a contagion approach to explain the rise of one type of social movement. As sociologists, we begin with the assumption that it is possible to have a general theory to account for the conditions under which a deprived category—any deprived group—of people will develop a social movement oriented to eliminating its own deprivation, an assumption not shared by all (see, e.g., Edmondson 1984:4). At some point in time in a given society, some such group will emerge in the absence of any other active movements to imitate or from which to learn. In other words, in a specific historical era, some movement has to be "first." This is especially so in that movement activism tends to occur in "waves," with relatively quiet periods in between successive waves of mass sociopolitical activism. It seems reasonable to suppose that whatever general processes explain the emergence of this first movement ought to be relevant to explaining subsequent ones as well—and obviously contagion in any of its forms cannot serve this purpose. This is not to say that social movements do not often occur in clusters historically; obviously they do. It is likely that basic social, economic, and/or political changes often simultaneously impact several groups in a similar fashion, encouraging the rise of several different movements at more or less the same time. Contagion may expedite and help to legitimate movement formation along "latecomers," but that is not the same as saying that the existence of prior or collateral movements is *theoretically* important to explaining the development of women's (or any other kind of) movements. Nonetheless, there are insights to be gained from a contagion approach. In chapter 3 we shall incorporate some specifics from that approach into our theory.

CONCLUSIONS

With the enormous number of changes and events occurring in the 1950s and 1960s in the United States, at a commonsense level it is easy to simply conclude that it is logical that a women's movement emerged when and where it did. The same may be said of the 19th century U.S. movement, and some movements elsewhere. This is what most scholars have done, and then gone on to trace in more detail the history, organizational structure, ideology, strategies, tactics, and/or other issues pertaining to the movement in question. This approach is manifest in a statement made by Pollock. After cataloging the material we have reviewed in this chapter, she wrote, "It was there *inevitable* that women begin to examine their own status [and] . . . roles" (1972:13; emphasis added). We are not arguing that the factors discussed in this chapter are irrelevant. Rather, our intent is to sort through the array of historical particulars to develop a general theory to explain the conditions under which women's movements arise, where and whenever that may be, and the determinants of their size and the scope of their ideological focus. Such a theory will identify which factors are central to explaining the emergence of such movements, which are of minor or historically idiocyncratic importance, and therefore of no general theoretical significance, and which are indirectly influential, based primarily on their impact on central theoretical variables. This is the task of chapter 3.

It is worth noting again that many of the things we have discussed have occurred in other times and places and have not produced women's movements, and especially fully feminist ones. Given the fact that extensive female disadvantage has been a constant for long stretches of time in most parts of the world, and given that at least many of the factors said to have contributed to the emergence of the current wave of feminist activity have existed elsewhere and/or earlier in history, there is still the intriguing theoretical issue of why such movements emerge when and where they do. What, exactly, are the necessary and sufficient variables that combine to produce this, the most comprehensive form of female revolt? What variables function to prevent it? Common sense is not sufficient to understand this phenomenon on an historical and worldwide level; only a theoretical understanding can do that.

3 A Theory of the Emergence of Women's Movements

Social movements represent a specialized form of collective behavior, that is, collective or group mobilization involving behavior that is unconventional. Collective behavior usually involves large numbers of people who share a set of emerging norms and generalized beliefs. It often arises in response to unusual circumstances or in the presence of strains that must be addressed. Fads, panics, riots, and mass hysteria, as well as social movements, represent some of the range of group behaviors under the rubric of collective behavior.

Social movements are the most complex form of collective behavior. Relative to other forms of collective behavior, they are characterized by more organization and a longer duration of existence. Social movements are a response to collectively felt strains and grievances; but in order to sustain their existence, they must rely upon more resources and better networks for coordination, including some degree of leadership. This is not to say that social movements must have a unitary structure or that a single organization speaks for all the participants in the movement. An ongoing group of leaders who articulate goals that are generally concordant is necessary, although different groups and leaders within the movement may advocate different specific goals, tactics, and/or strategies for goal achievement.

The strains that underly the development of social movements are structural in nature: that is, they are inherent in the workings of the social system and representative of the basic power struggles among groups within that system. Smelser (1963) identified as structural strains any ambiguities, conflicts, deprivations, tensions, discriminations, and discrepancies within the social structure. Some theorists have argued that the strains must be essentially of only one kind. We contend, however, that social movements may involve conflicts over any combination of scarce resources, including power, prestige, and property. One widely accepeted definition of a social movement has been offered by Turner and Killian:

> a collectivity acting with some continuity to promote or resist change in the society or the group of which it is a part. As a collectivity a movement is a group with indefinite and shifting membership and with leadership whose position is determined more by the informal response of the members than by formal procedures for legitimizing authority [1972:246].

Sociological theories of social movements have been of two generic types: those which posit that an increase in the level or amount of structural strain must occur in order for a social movement to be mounted, and those which contend that structural strains are ever-present and only a change in the mobilization of resources to mount a movement are necessary before a movement will occur. These two perspectives assume crucial differences in the nature of human nature. Generally speaking, social movement theories that see movements arising out of heightening of strain and tension depict social actors as essentially arational, or even irrational, acting only after they are pressed to do so by strains, grievances, and tensions. The second model assumes that people are more logical and calculating, mounting a resistance to structural strain only when the likelihood of success is relatively high (Jenkins 1983). Finally, the two perspectives differ in the emphasis they place on the role of aggrieved parties in mounting movements. The "strain" theories concentrate on the necessity of movement beneficiaries to mount the movement, while the "mobilization" theories acknowledge the significant roles of entrepreneurs, concerned outside parties, and organizations in creating movements. Jenkins (1983) noted that the theories of collective behavior (see, in particular, Lang and Lang 1961; Smelser 1963; Turner and Killian 1972), mass society (see Katz and Lazarsfeld 1964; Kornhauser 1959; Westie 1964), contagion (see Allport and Postman 1947; Le Bon 1960), and social relativism approaches (including relative deprivation, as enunciated by Geschwender 1964; Gurr 1970; Morrison 1971; Pettigrew 1964; Sayles 1984; rising expectations, as advanced by Davies 1962, 1969; Geschwender 1964; Morrison 1971; and reference groups, as portrayed by Hyman 1942; Kelley 1952; Merton and Kitt 1950; Shibutani 1955; Stouffer et al 1949) are generally part of the first type of social movement theories. By contrast, various forms of resource mobilization theory represent the second type (see, e.g., Gamson 1975; Jenkins 1983; Jenkins and Perrow 1977; Marx and Wood 1975; McCarthy and Zald 1977; Obserschall 1973; Tilly 1978; Wood and Jackson 1982; Zald and McCarthy 1979).

Incorporated in our eclectic model of the emergence of women's movements is an assumption that people are both rational and arational in their actions. Furthermore, we assume that while structural strains are ever-present, reflecting basic power relationships within the society as a whole, changes in the way people are distributed within the social structure and changes in the technology, economy, and political order will heighten some forms of structural strains. In turn, this makes more likely the emergence of social movements, provided that repressing and retarding forces do not make such movements too costly. (We shall itemize such forces as we develop our model.) Finally, we offer a model which sees movements as mounted both by the beneficiaries of movement activities and by individuals, groups, and organizations who are not themselves victims of the deprivations which the movements are designed to redress.

It is part of our assumption that social movements must be mounted by those individuals who are opposed to the existing social order or system of advantage and privilege, and either have been excluded by that system or are conscience adherents (McCarthy and Zald 1977). Social movements are change-oriented, grass-roots actions. Consequently, we preclude state-initiated "social movements" from consideration. Some state-launched social movements are not change-oriented, but are merely demonstrations of mass support for an existing social order. Others may be change-oriented, but they are not grass-roots in origin, and are not mounted by those who have been excluded by the social system.

THE DEPENDENT VARIABLES

Our model of the emergence of social movements has two dependent variables that refer to the size of the social movement and the ideology that characterizes it. We shall attempt to explain both dependent variables in terms of women's movements across time and space. Although ideology and size can be viewed as continuous variables, our theory will attempt only to distinguish gross differences in size and ideology. We therefore conceive of three sizes of social movements and two kinds of ideologies.

Social movements that involve only a small number of people, generally elites among a disadvantaged group, will be termed *incipient* social movements. As a wider range of the grass roots among the disadvantaged participate in the social movement, we shall refer to it as an *intermediate* social movement; and when the size grows still larger, we shall refer to it as a *mass* social movement. No attempt will be made to determine the necessary numerical increase needed to transform an incipient social movement into an intermediate and subsequently into a mass social movement. Recently, Granovetter (1978) has developed a mathematical threshold equation that could prove to be useful in determining the necessary cutting points. Unfortunately, the existing data on the various women's movements we discuss in this work do not permit a precise analysis.

The second dimension we shall examine is the range of ideologies. Again, this should actually be considered as a continuous variable, but given the data at our disposal, we shall view it as a dichotomy. We consider any social movement that challenges only some aspects of the status of the disadvantaged group, but leaves intact the pivotal roles of that group, to be an *ameliorative* social movement. In terms of the current theory, an ameliorative women's movement does not challenge the privileged status of males in the society, but only seeks to make more effective the female's pivotal roles as wife and mother. Thus a temperance movement or even a suffrage movement had as its basic ideology the enhancement of traditional female roles of wife and mother, worker in the home, protector of children, and helpmate of the husband. Such a movement might work to enhance the legal, educational, or even political status of women, but preserved as paramount the women's obligations as wife and mother. By contrast, any social movement that challenges the license and mandate of those with advantage to their right to that advantage, and which seeks to alter the whole range of status and role relationships, including the pivotal roles of the disadvantaged, we shall call *feminist*. More generically, however, one could term such movements *totalistic*. Feminist movements, unlike ameliorative ones, have sought to ensure total social and economic equality for women, thereby altering both the sex stratification and gender role systems.

Presented in Figure 3.1 is a display of our theory of the necessary conditions for the emergence of a women's movement, regardles of size or ideology. The conceptual variables are denoted by twelve blocks of independent variables, in addition to the dependent conceptual variable, movement emergence. Independent conceptual variables are represented by a capital X, with a subscript indicating the particular block; the dependent conceptual variable is represented by a capital Y. It should be recognized that the conceptual variables are all theoretical; they are not observed variables which we can measure. We shall, however, offer some potential operationalizations of these conceptual variables, some of which we shall assemble as a test of part of the model in chapter 6. Other operationalizations will be offered, but data are currently not available to permit their testing.

THE INDEPENDENT VARIABLES

We have already presented our dependent variable, the emergence of women's movements (Y), indicating the two dimensions of size and ideology. We now turn to the definition of each of the independent conceptual (theoretical) variables.

X_1 Structural strain. Smelser (1963) argued that while strains are in themselves not sufficient to provoke social movements, they are a necessary condition. Furthermore, different types of structural strains may lead to different forms of social movements, with distinct goals, ideologies, and strategies. For Smelser and for our theory, structural strains represent the existence of ambiguities, tensions, conflicts, discriminations, deprivations, and discrepancies within a stratified social order. Structural strains represent the ongoing and basic power struggles within a society or between groups (Gamson 1975; Jenkins 1983; Jenkins and Perrow 1977; McCarthy and Zald 1977; Tilly 1978). Structural strains are social facts and exist independent of whether or not their true nature is fully recognized by those who are subject to such deprivations and discriminations. The process by which such structural strains become identified and action is taken to lessen them will be identified in the presentation of other conceptual blocks in our theory.

Some theorists have maintained that the strains must be essentially economic in nature (Marx 1959), while others have cited power as the central element (Dahrendorf 1959; Jenkins 1983). Some have suggested that strains emerge whenever substantial demographic shifts occcur, for instance; during urbaniza-

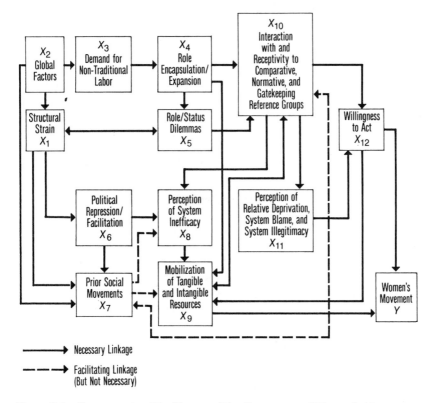

Figure 3.1   Components of the Theory of the Emergence of Women's Movements

tion and industrialization (March 1959; Tilly 1978) or when a previously dominant group has been left behind by such urbanization and industrialization
(Gusfield 1963). However, we contend that social movements mounted by disadvantaged groups may involve conflicts over any combination of scarce resources.

Operationally, structural strain can be depicted by objective differences in
scarce resources between groups: differences in income; occupational deployment (type of work and nature of reward for work); occupational employment
(including rates of unemployment); educational attainment; ability to convert
educational attainment into other valued resources; political power, including
the holding of political offices; legal rights and restrictions; and life chances. In
addition, conflicts over the control of such rights, privileges, and resources provide evidence of the existence of structural strains. Finally, it should be recognized that the inequalities which are associated with structural strain tend to be
legitimated by those with advantage through the use of pejorative hetero-
stereotypes about the inferiority of those without advantage and aggrandizing
auto-stereotypes about the advantaged (Allport 1954; Dworkin and Dworkin

1976; Ehrlich 1973; Myrdal 1944). Thus, an examination of the stereotypes held within a society is a useful index of structural strain.

There are two central points of contention over the nature of structural strains which differentiate many of the theories of social movements. Many theories, including those involving assumptions of social relativism, mass societies, or collective behavior models, assume that the severity and magnitude of strains must change before a social movement occurs. In some instances, the change is toward greater inequality (Gusfield 1963; Marx 1959; Morrison 1971; Smelser 1963), while others note that revolts occur when inequalities are diminishing, thereby creating rising expectations for improvement which outstrip the capacity for the society to meet such expectations (Davies 1962, 1969; Geschwender 1964; Gurr 1970).

A second central point of contention among theories of strain is whether the deprivations inherent in the strains have to be absolute or simply relative. Fanon (1968) pointed to the importance of extreme deprivation in the development of liberation movements among colonized peoples. Similar views of hunger and deprivation characterize the models of revolt by Rudé (1959) and Toch (1965). However, most accept that deprivations need only be relative. That is, the disadvantaged group must have perceptively less of the significant and scarce resources of the society (power, property, and privilege) than the groups against whom they revolt. Wilson has defined relative deprivation as "the conscious experience of a negative discrepancy between legitimate expectations and present or anticipated actuality" (1973:69). For Gurr, who was one of the first to apply relative deprivation to models of social movements, it is "the perceived discrepancy between men's value expectations and their value capacity" (1970:13).

There is good reason to suspect that the relationship between structural strain, as manifested in deprivations, and the emergence of social movements is actually curvilinear. That is, under conditions in which there is no deprivation there are no structural strains as we conceive of them. In such an instance there can be no disadvantaged groups to mount a movement. On the other hand, when deprivations are absolute, despite some claims to the contrary, the deprived tend to withdraw within themselves and cannot be mobilized into a protest group. There are no resources available for mobilization (Jenkins 1983). The classic studies of concentration camp behavior (Bettelheim 1943; Cohen 1953) and studies of severe food deprivation (Brozek 1953) have demonstrated that absolute deprivation makes people more pliable to the desires of their oppressors and even likely to appear autistic, and to hallucinate about food. Thus, somewhere between great deprivation and great equality lie the structural conditions for protest.

It must be acknowledged that there are theories of social movements which do not posit structural strain. Some are psychological theories which see movements as the collective action of people with certain personality characteristics (see Abramowitz 1973; Feuer 1969; Flacks 1967; Keniston 1968; Kerpelman

1972) or interpersonal agitation (Le Bon 1960). Still others advance the presence of entrepreneurs and "agent provocateurs" who stir up protest (Becker 1963; Marx 1974; McCarthy and Zald 1973). However, only when social movements are mounted on behalf of causes not involving deprivations is it possible to claim that there were no structural strains. Entrepreneurs, including professional movement makers, and community organizers most often serve to heighten awareness of actual strains, helping people to recognize the source of the strain and to convert a condition of deprivation into a perception of deprivation. It is essential to recognize that for a social movement to be mounted by the deprived group the structural strains must become experiential, that is, perceived by the group members. During the course of the explication of our theory we shall address the processes by which such a perception comes about, along with other necessary social definitional processes.

X_2 Global factors. These represent the general categories of demographic and distributive shifts which affect all groups in a society by dislocating populations, altering the division of labor, disrupting the operations of a normative order, and affecting such factors as population size, state of the economy, level of technology, and availability of natural resources (see Chafetz, Dworkin, and Dworkin 1976). Among the global forces we see as important to women's movement are urbanization and industrialization. Each has the consequence of concentrating populations geographically, thereby enhancing the interaction of people with similar advantages or deprivations, disrupting traditional status/role relationships, and altering the level of structural strain.

Although social movements can occur without alterations in the intensity of structural strains, changes in the allocation of people within the social structure and geographic concentration of people facilitate the recognition of structural strains. Central to Marx's theory of class consciousness and revolution is geographic realocation and concentration of workers. In his essay, "Eighteenth Brumaire of Louis Bonaparte" (1959), Marx asked whether the peasants could be considered a true class as long as they were isolated from one another on farms. His reply was that they could not become a "class for themselves" (*classe für sich*) until they were brought into the factories by the capitalists and began to discover their common plight and common class enemy. Dahrendorf (1959) identified as one of the two global forces for class consciousness the elimination of geographical and topological barriers which separated quasi-groups (these factors he termed *social conditions of organization*). The other global factor (*political conditions of organization*) we shall examine in another block of our model. Some investigators in the area of race relations have pointed to the significance of racial isolation and ghettoization in the development of the black revolution in America (see, e.g., Blauner 1972; Broom and Glenn 1965; Caplan and Paige 1968; Ransford 1968; Wilson 1980).

Urbanization and industrialization uproot people, concentrate individuals with similar life chances and experiences, and heighten the visible distinctions

between the haves and the have nots. Tilly has analyzed the effects of urbanization and urban density upon political protest in France during the nineteenth
century. He found that net migration to the city, per se, did not produce increased amounts of protest, but that urban density had a very profound effect
upon the size and number of protests (see Tilly 1974:99).

Industrialization also removes people from traditional roles and statuses. Industrialization, with its accompanying relocation of workers into factories, has
been seen as a significant force in the transformation of a quasi-group into a political group (Dahrendorf 1959; Gross 1964; Marshall 1965; Marx 1959; Polanyi
1957; Smelser 1959; Wilensky and Lebeaux 1965; Williams 1960). In the field of
racial and ethnic relations, the combined forces of the urbanization and
ghettoization in northern cities of southern black Americans and their transformation into an urban labor force has been identified as significant for the creation of a significant political voting block and for the development of black protest (see Broom and Glenn 1965; Pinkney 1975; Pitts 1982; Taeuber and Taeuber
1965; Wilson 1980). Grebler, Moore, and Guzman (1970), Maldonado (1982),
and Dworkin (1968, 1972) identified similar factors in the creation of social protest movements among Mexican-Americans in the Southwest. Finally, for
women, industrialization has the potential of moving them into the paid labor
force and thereby increasing the chance that they will have economic power in
family decision making (Chafetz 1980) and a greater control over the economy
(Blumberg 1978; Chafetz 1984; O'Kelly 1980).

Elsewhere, we have proposed that the products of change in the global factors,
such as economic, technological, population, and natural resource changes, affect the demand for labor, as well as the capacity of the traditional labor force,
generally made up of the advantaged group(s), to meet such a demand (see
Chafetz 1978; Chafetz, Dworkin, and Dworkin 1976; Dworkin and Dworkin
1982). Colonialism and warfare often have similar consequences for changes in
status relationships, but for the purposes of this book they do not constitute important variables in explaining the rise of women's movements. The other major
consequences of the global forces for our theory are the decreasng self-sufficiency
of the family as an economic unit; the monetization of foregone family functions,
such that others do them as paid laborers; the accumulation of wealth and the
accompanying growth of the middle class; an increase in leisure time that can be
devoted to nonproduction activities (including social movements); and the geographic segregation of class-based populations. In addition, these global forces
involve a heightening of a demand for goods and services, changes in the pattern
of consumption, and demands for more and better skilled (educated) labor.

Urbanization and industrialization produce a significant embourgeoisment of
a substantial portion of the population. The ideology of this growing middle class
tends to be somewhat more liberal and more sympathetic to the expansion of educational opportunity than does the ideology of any other class. Not having a legitimate claim to privilege that is vested in tradition, as is true of an aristocracy,

the middle class seeks meritocratic criteria for advantage. For them, education is the principal vehicle by which to make such a claim. In fact, as Williams (1960) noted, the middle class is most prone to view education as a cure-all for every social ill. Meritocratic criteria facilitate individualism, personal achievement, and appeals for the rights of individuals over the will of the collectivity (Durkheim 1951). If couched appropriately, even minority group claims will receive a fairer hearing within the middle class than within either the aristocracy or the working class.

The operationalization of the effects of global factor change involves indexes of distributive change such as changes in the percentage of disadvantaged people in the labor force, including the kinds of labor performed (hence, changes in both employment rates and occupational deployment); and in the access to education of that population, and hence its skill level. Additionally, migration of the disadvantaged to urban areas, where they are more likely to be concentrated—even ghettoized—is a significant indicator of distributive change. In the case of women, a substantial increase in their access to educational opportunities and their wholesale entry into work outside of the home (in public work roles) are major indicators of the kind of distributive changes we posit are associated with the emergence of a women's movement. We have previously argued that for a fully feminist movement to emerge, a significant number of married women must be in the labor force, as these women are likely to remain in the labor force during most of their adult lives (Chafetz and Dworkin 1983). Changes in the educational level of women is necessary, too, because education provides necessary insights and skills which, in the presence of continued objective deprivations, can be mobilized into a resource for change.

Migration from farms into cities is also an indicator of a distributive change. City life implies greater propinquity to other women, including women in a paid labor force. Urbanization makes change-oriented reference groups more accessible, consciousness raising more likely, and facilitates access to education and participation in a paid labor force. However, we have argued elsewhere (Chafetz and Dworkin 1983) that suburbanization without labor force participation, where women as homemakers get together in "koffee klatches" to discuss how to cope with children and spouses, does not lead to increased consciousness, and is not a distributive change which would lead to a women's movement (see also Lopata 1971; Oakley 1974).

X_3 Demand for nontraditional labor. A traditional labor force is made up of a category of people who monopolize an occupation or a whole labor market. Nontraditional labor thus is made up of a population normally excluded from that occupation or labor market. Women have often been excluded from either the wage labor market or generally from highly paid, stable, and secure jobs, where mobility to even better jobs is feasible (the so-called primary labor market). Demands for nontraditional labor within the bounds of our theory represent either a demand for females as paid labor when such labor was previously absent, or the demand for female labor in specific occupations or labor markets not previously held by females. It is expected that the demand for nontraditional labor represents an excess of demand for labor over the capacity of a traditional labor force to meet that demand. Employers have preferences for types of workers—workers they feel will be punctual, competent, and not be disruptive to the work force (Arrow 1973; Becker 1971, 1975, 1976; Welch 1975). To the extent that women and other minority populations are believed (in part as a function of stereotypy) not to possess the valued traits, they are excluded from the labor force or from primary labor markets (see Bonacich 1972; Gordon 1972). Thus, it is only when the supply of traditional labor force participants is too low to meet the demand for labor that one might expect employers to seek the labor of nontraditional labor force participants. Dworkin (1980) explained the departure from school districts' practices of recruiting teachers from middle-class origins to recruiting teachers from working-class origins during the baby boom and the challenge of "Sputnik" in terms of the incapacity of the middle class to supply enough teachers to meet the demand.

Operationally the demand for nontraditional labor can be assessed by an examination of changes in the employment and deployment rates of workers. Census data reflecting changes in the proportion of women in the labor force, or the proportion of women in occupations previously monopolized by men are acceptable indexes. Of course, these are post factum observations in which we are inferring that an increase in the deployment rate and employment rate reflects an increase in the demand for such labor.

X_4 Role encapsulation/expansion. Social roles represent the sum of the normatively prescribed behaviors and expectations associated with a position in the social structure (a status). Just as statuses are arranged hierarchically in terms of the amount of power, prestige, and property which accrue to their occupants, roles are hierarchitized in terms of perceptions by others, as well as the role incumbent, of the relative importance of the tasks performed. The system of allocation of rewards in a society (material and nonmaterial)—the stratification system—is inexorably linked to a group's capacity or opportunity to generate scarce resources (goods and services). Groups which monopolize the production of scarce resources exercise considerable control over the reward distribution system, the definitional system (which specifies the abilities of all groups in the society), and control the assignment of groups to roles (see Chafetz 1984).

Because women and racial and ethnic minorities generate fewer scarce resources than do men and racial and ethnic majorities, they are less likely to enjoy the rewards that the latter group enjoys and more likely to be assigned less valued roles. In fact, they may be assigned a more limited number of productive roles than are those in authority. In industrial societies during the previous century women were often precluded from performing many, if not most, work roles which paid wages—a resource that they could use to purchase the requisites for higher status and even more expanded roles. Likewise, racial and ethnic minorities were frequently relegated to labor markets which were poorly paid, unstable, and undesirable. Women as well as racial and ethnic minorities were also expected to provide a pool of unemployed labor to offset inflationary pressures (see Bonacich 1972; Bowles and Gintis 1976; Dworkin and Dworkin 1982; Oliver and Glick 1982). Confinement within a relatively narrow range of typically low status roles constitutes "role encapsulation" for a category of people (e.g., women, blacks, and Hispanics).

The opposite of role encapsulation is role expansion. Here the number and variety of roles available to a group increase. Clearly, the best example of role expansion is found where there are changes in the employment rate or the deployment rate of groups. However, we can also observe role expansion when groups adopt additional nonwork roles, provided that such roles offer new skills which can increase the capacity of the group to acquire expanded or more varied statuses and opportunities. An increase in educational opportunity represents one such role expansion. Likewise, political participation and/or participation in social movement activity which is not specifically a women's movement (e.g., antislavery and temperance movements) represent another type of role expansion. Participating in a social movement mounted by, and on behalf of, a group to which one does not belong provides organizational, communication, and resource management skills. Although incorrect in positing that women's participation in the civil rights and antiwar movements caused women to mount a feminist movement in the late 1960s and early 1970s, those who have argued this (Chafe 1977; Deckard 1983; Firestone 1971; Flexner 1975; Freeman 1975; Kontopoulos 1972; O'Neill 1969a) did make a fundamentally valuable observation. Such prior social movements often provide the base from which leadership skills, communications networks, and material resources are garnered (Jenkins 1983).

One additional benefit of education and/or participation in social movements is that such activities permit individuals to gain access to reference groups which can help to shape attitudes and translate experiences into a rhetoric sympathetic to the development of a social movement on behalf of one's own group. The manner in which such attitudes can be formed and facilitated by reference groups will be discussed later in this section.

It is important to recognize that role encapsulation and expansion involve behavior on the part of deprived group members. This is to be distinguished from the previous construct (the demand for nontraditional labor) which concerns the issue of whether or not individuals will have the opportunity to behave in certain ways. The expansion of a role involves a response to increasing opportunity; the encapsulation of a role involves a rejection or absence of that opportunity.

X_5 Role/status dilemmas. These represent structurally induced contradictions caused by a discrepancy between the socially defined roles performed by members of an ascribed status (such as women), and the emerging roles performed by members of that status. Hughes (1945) depicted such a condition as a status dilemma and suggested that social action might appropriately issue from such dilemmas. That is, as roles are adopted by group members who have not traditionally performed such roles, there emerges a disjuncture between societally defined expectations for such group members and actual role performances. Our theory of social movements is more concerned with the consequences for individuals of lower ascribed status groups performing roles normally assumed by members of higher status groups, although the opposite phenomenon can also occur.

A sociological tradition has explored the manner in which role/status dilemmas create the need for collective social action (see, e.g., the work of Benoit-Smullyan 1944; Hughes 1945; Jackson 1962; Lenski 1954; Olsen 1970). According to this perspective, individuals whose achieved status (i.e., the status attained by personal efforts, including educational efforts) is significantly higher than their ascribed (i.e., the status acquired as a member of a racial, ethnic, gender, or other group into which one is born) face potential dilemmas and contradictions which demand resolution. They must either emphasize their lower ascribed status and perform the roles normally performed by members of that status group, thereby denying their achievements, or they must attempt to change the societal evaluation of their ascribed status, such that it matches their achievement.

Numerous investigators have questioned the assumption that status and role dilemmas automatically lead to attempts to change societal definitions of ascribed statuses through social movements or other forms of activity (Blalock 1967; Kelly and Chambliss 1966; Stryker and Macke 1978, Trieman 1966). Broom (1959) put the case well when he observed that individuals are not always aware that they have status dilemmas, and thus, if they are not conscious of disjunctures between ascription and achievement, they are unlikely to be motivated to act on behalf of such disjunctures. R. Dworkin (1974, 1979) observed that in the absence of reference groups which can serve to translate social structural variables into consciousness, many women may spend all of their lives unaware of their status dilemmas, or act as "queen bees," denying that there are structural barriers since they "made it themselves" (see also Chafetz and Dworkin 1983). We shall address the reference group block shortly.

Operationally, role/status dilemmas can be described through an analysis of the employment and deployment of status groups in the labor market or in education or in any distributive sphere. Role/status dilemmas are present when a distributive sphere is monopolized by a group of one status, but where there is some token or minimal presence of members of another status group in that sphere. Under circumstances of tokenism members of the lower status groups performing roles normally monopolized by higher status groups tend to be stereotyped and isolated within an organizational setting (Kanter 1977). The tokens serve as symbols of their ascribed status group as a whole and their actions and

motives are assessed viz. such stereotypes. Since, as Richter (1956) noted, stereotypes operate both as stipulative definitions and as empirical generalizations, failure on the part of the token serves to confirm the stereotype about the whole
group, while success serves to demonstrate that the individual token is not "typical" of his or her group. Tokens are thus placed in a double-bind situation.
Dworkin, Chafetz, and Dworkin (forthcoming) have demonstrated that in the
case of high status tokens, there is some evidence to suggest that being in a
nontraditional labor market is beneficial for the token's work attitudes. The re-
verse is true for low status tokens, however, reflecting the double-bind in which
such people find themselves.

The presence of role/status dilemmas are most blatant in settings where
people of different ascribed statuses perform the same tasks, but where different
levels of rewards are offered to such individuals on the basis of their ascribed statuses. The presence of such discrimination makes the development of a consciousness all the more easy. We have argued that a necessary condition to feminist movements is a widespread situation of men and women working together,
but in contexts where they receive different levels of rewards (Chafetz and
Dworkin 1983).

X_6 Political repression/facilitation. Within the category of variables identified
by Dahrendorf as the "political conditions of organization" (1959) are those
which indicate the extent to which a political authority permits public assembly
and social protest among its citizenry. As Dahrendorf expressed it, "where a plu-
rality of conflicting parties is not permitted and their emergence suppressed by
the absence of freedom of coalition by police force, conflict groups cannot organize themselves even if all other conditions of their organization are present"
(1959:186).

Severe repression, often characteristic of totalitarian regimes which outlaw
public assembly and social protest, seriously reduces the likelihood that people
will seek to mount a social movement, or even to meet except under the most
clandestine of circumstances. In fact, as the experience of blacks in the United
States in the antebellum South indicated, attempts at public asssembly and social protest were not only severely crushed, but blacks themselves frequently exposed the plots to white overseers (Elkins 1959). Should the level of repression
lessen, however, or should threats of oppression fail to be actualized, then protest will spring up, as both Skocpol (1979) and Dahrendorf (1959) have noted.

With respect to women's movements we propose that the construct re-
pression/facilitation is tripartite. Under the most oppressive of regimes there will
be no movements because such regimes ban freedom of assembly. Thus, where
there are laws against the participation of citizens in social or political protest, we
should expect little protest to exist. Where there are laws which prohibit a particular segment of the population from organizing—for example, laws preventing

women or racial minorities from organizing—we should expect no movements mounted by these groups on their own behalf. Thus a repressive system will be considered one in which the right of assembly and protest are specifically prohibited for some or all members of the populace.

By contrast, an open system may be of one of two kinds. A completely open system may be characterized by no inequalities and therefore no strains necessitating a movement. We would expect to see no movements mounted in such a society—which in the study of racial, ethnic, and gender minorities is merely a hypothetical society, or else we would not be able to speak of minorities (see Dworkin and Dworkin 1982). An empirically demonstrable type of open society would be one in which there are no laws prohibiting the rights of assembly. There may be laws prohibiting certain tactics by groups—such as violent protest and riot—but no laws against assembly and peaceful protest. If the social conditions of organization (Dahrendorf 1959) are present, we should expect movements to occur in such societies. However, if those in control of the society are very obliging and appear to accede to the demands of deprived groups, then social movements would also not be likely to become fully developed. We shall consider a political entity that accedes to enough of the demands of a group to limit the full range of protest of that group to be a co-optive system. Finally, political systems which are neither oppressive nor co-optive are the best candidates for the full development of social movements by deprived peoples. There are few, if any, laws prohibiting assembly and protest, but there is at least some opposition to the demands of the deprived group. In some instances this type of political system is benign; in others, it is a formerly oppressive one which has been so burdened by the vast expenditure of resources required to maintain coercion that it is near collapse. In both of these situations we would expect the full-blown development of social movements, assuming the other conditions stipulated in the theory are met.

In the next chapter it will become apparent that in societies where there is a substantial Protestant population, women's movements emerge more rapidly. It is not our contention that material conditions are created by ideology; rather, we hold that material and social structural conditions are causally primary. However, an existing ideology, or even one created to justify the social relations which issue from the material conditions of life, functions to legitimate and inform public policy. In societies where there is a stress on individualism and meritocratic bases for advantage, political authorities may be more receptive to arguments for minority rights over majority will than in societies without such an ethic. Protestantism tends to foster this type of ideology. In such societies, the political conditions of organization (Dahrendorf 1959) will be stronger than in societies which exclusively stress collective rights over the rights of individuals. Likewise, within socialist and national liberation movements, where the will of the individual or that of a subgroup is subserviant to the will of the collectivity, we would also expect feminism to be retarded.

X_7 Prior social movements. Several writers who have studied the development of women's movements and the emergence of racial and ethnic liberation movements have spoken of the role of prior movements as a source of ideological contagion and consciousness raising. As we observed in the previous section and in chapter 2, there is actually little evidence to suggest that participation in a prior movement automatically makes people aware of their deprivations (see also Chafetz and Dworkin 1983). However, prior movements have several potential effects on the emergence of current movements. From the resource mobilization approach (see especially Gamson 1975; Jenkins 1983; McCarthy and Zald 1977; Oberschall 1973; Rogers 1974) prior movements can be seen as a potential resource for two necessary components of a subsequent social movement. On the one hand, as has been noted earlier, leadership in subsequent movements often spins off from individuals who gained organizational, communication, and management skills from the prior movement. In some instances, those who left movements were dissatisfied because the earlier movements failed to address or appreciate their own group's needs and demands—not because they gained a consciousness of their relative deprivation from the movement. In other instances, economic resources garnered from supporters of prior movements may be transferred to subsequent movements, or at least lists of potential contributors can be obtained. If successful, prior movements can enhance the likelihood of success of subsequent movements by providing a skilled cadre of potential leaders and by serving as an example to the rank and file that desired changes in the social order are possible. It may also make those with advantage more willing to accede to the demands of another group. This, perhaps is one of the benefits that the civil rights movement offered to the women's liberation movement. It is certainly clear that one of the beneficiaries of legislative changes to protect civil protesters, won by the black civil rights movement, were those who participated in the Chicano liberation movement.

But prior movements are not without their potential liabilities to the emergence of subsequent movements. A movement in full swing is likely to so tap both material and nonmaterial resources, that it retards, at least temporarily, the emergence of subsequent movements. Furthermore, if a recent movement has been unsuccessful, especially if it has been suppressed or co-opted by the state, not only will official opposition to another movement be hardened, but clear evidence will be available to demonstrate the absence of the political conditions of organization. The repression experienced by Mexican-American workers attempting to organize in the vegetable fields in California in 1933, including the wholesale deportation of many Mexican-Americans who could not prove their U.S. citizenship, effectively stopped any attempts at union organization and civil rights activism for nearly a whole generation (see Dworkin 1968, 1972; Estrada, García, Macías, and Maldonado 1981; McWilliams 1949).

X_8 Perception of system inefficacy. As we shall see, reference groups can provide the necessary sense of distributive injustice, inform the individual of the systemic nature of that injustice, and create definitions of system illegitimacy. However, it does not automatically follow that once the members of a group of individuals have such raised consciousnesses that they will act against the structural inequality. In fact, as Riger (1977) noted in her study of consciousness-raising groups, the initial response to the perception of system blame and system illegitimacy is anger, frustration, and despair. After all, if one comes to the realization that the source of one's dissatisfaction and deprivation is the entire society and all of its institutions, one is likely to be overwhelmed. What is additionally necessary is the development of a perception that collective social action has the chance of being successful. Certainly reference groups play a role in providing that awareness. However, there must be objective data which can be pointed to, that supports a notion that the system has "clay feet." Resource mobilization models specify this as a necessary element in the rational calculus that determines when a movement is to be mounted. In Skocpol's (1979) analysis of peasant revolts, evidence of system weakness was a necessary precondition for social action. In political systems wracked by war and economic instability, which weaken the potential of political oppression of movements, the likelihood of revolts increases profoundly. In more open societies, where it is normative for dissatisfied groups to coalesce into voluntary associations (Morrison 1971), there still needs to be some evidence that an attempted protest will be successful. Benson (1971) examined the causes of the Black Power Movement and concluded that the failure of the federally created community action programs convinced blacks that even when the system attempted to be egalitarian and supportive it managed to fail. This convinced the activists that only they could attack their own problems and that the social system was incapable either of helping or hurting their cause. Paige (1971) observed that an essential element in the belief system of black ghetto riot participants was a conviction that the agencies of social control were ineffective.

In one sense, the best operationalization of objective system inefficacy is post factum evidence that a social movement was not suppressed, subverted, or co-opted. However, Skocpol (1979) and Durkheim (1951, 1964) have each suggested alternative indexes. If there is widespread dislocation of the agencies of social control caused by wars, inflation, depression, or other economic crises, there may be objective evidence that the system will be unable to react. Of course, this is true only if there is a sufficient amount of disruption of governmental functions that the agencies of social control cannot be mobilized.

The perception of system inefficacy must be precisely that: a perception. Objective conditions facilitate such a perception, but the conjoined effects of reference group definitions and objective facts are needed here. System failure to suppress a prior social movement is likely to be the fuel for such a definition. Likewise, the failure of a program attempted by system authorities to ameliorate strains represents another item of fuel for the definitional process. Evidence that a belief in system inefficacy is present can best be obtained through an analysis of the rhetoric of the movement. If movement leaders amd movement entrepreneurs point to the failings of the social system and comment upon the weakness of those in authority, then there exist data on the perception of system inefficacy.

X_9 Mobilization of tangible and intangible resources. The defining attribute of deprived groups is that they possess less power, property, and prestige than do advantaged groups. Resource mobilization theorists have been quick to point out that minorities and other deprived groups are unlikely to be able to amass the capital necessary to mount a movement on their own—at least at the mass level. It should be noted, however, that as women increase their participation in the labor force, their access to resources, and consequently a women's movement's potential resource base, increases. Movements need such tangible resources as capital and facilities in order to gain attention and forcefully to communicate their message. Movements also need intangible resources such as access to the media, supporters, conscience adherents (who are not members of the deprived group but can be mobilized to work for the group), networks of communication, technically skilled labor to organize, manage, and address legal issues, and of course, large numbers of volunteers. For the purpose of our theory, we shall not include the mobilization of deprived individuals as part of this theoretical block. That massive resource is covered in the progression of blocks X_3-X_5, and X_{11} and X_{12}.

Evidence for tangible and intangible resources can be garnered by inspecting budgets of organizations, mass media coverage, communications between groups, and interlocking directories of supporters listed on organizational letterheads. In the absence of such data, estimates of participation rates by supporters who are not members of the deprived groups may be of use.

X_{10} Reference groups. A central element in many of the social relativism theories of social movements are reference groups which are seen as the transmission mechanism between structural strains and individual awareness. Reference groups represent individuals and groups of individuals that a person knows, or knows about, who serve as role models, or antimodels (Francis 1963), or standards of judgment and comparison in the formation of attitudes and the creation of actions. Reference groups have been identified as performing three central functions in attitude and behavior formation. They perform a comparative function, in that people come to assess their own advantages or disadvantages relative to that group and conclude whether or not they ought to feel relatively satisfied or relatively deprived. Reference groups also serve a normative function, in that group members reward or punish the actions of individuals and thereby maintain conformity to group expectations. Finally, reference groups serve as gate-keepers, controlling access to new roles and new statuses for individuals.

The first two functions of reference group were identified with the work of Hyman (1942), Kelley (1952), Merton and Kitt (1950), Stouffer et al. (1949), while the third function was identified with the studies of Shibutani (1955).

Reference groups are likely to interpret the social conditions, beliefs, and actions of individuals differently. Thus, in our theory it is necessary that we examine the particular reference groups relative to the functions that they might be expected to perform. We can imagine at least two general categories of reference group relevant to our analysis: reference groups composed of members of an individual's own status group (women) and reference groups composed of members of a status group other than one's own—and, in particular, one made up of a higher status group (men). For disadvantaged groups, including women and racial and ethnic minorities, the first type of reference group would consist of other women or other members of one's own racial or ethnic group, while the second type of reference group would consist of men or members of the racial or ethnic majority. If a member of a disadvantaged group principally interacts with, or principally observes, in-group members, social comparisons will only be with individuals who are likewise disadvantaged. However, interactions and comparisons with members of higher status out-groups mean that relative disadvantages may become more obvious (see Abeles 1976; Pettigrew 1971).

A different set of conditions applies when reference groups serve normative and gate-keeping functions. Here, interactions principally with out-group members mean that the norms, expectations, and stereotypes that have served to maintain the status differentials will be reiterated. By contrast, the normative and gate-keeping functions performed by members of one's own group may be less likely to reinforce the status differentials between the groups. (This is not to deny the possibility that some members of one's own group may enforce and advocate norms which maintain deprivations. Such individuals might be thought of as having "false consciousness.")

The leadership of a social movement makes up some portion of the internal normative and gate-keeping reference group. Such individuals had previously come to embrace a necessary sense of group consciousness and other factors to be discussed later on in this theory.

X_{11} Perception of relative deprivation, system blame, and system illegitimacy. Incorporated within this block are perceptions about one's social condition, attributions about the source of blame for that condition, and a conclusion based upon these perceptions and attributions. Relative deprivation is a perception that in comparison to members of another group one is disadvantaged. Relative deprivation is the conscious recognition of the structural strains and role/status dilemmas of which we spoke earlier. For relative deprivation, as well as other variables in this block to operate, individuals must come to recognize the nature of the stratification system and its contradictions and inequities, unlike the variables enumerated in previous blocks, which could exist while individuals were blind to their existence. Social relativism theories link together the comparative functions of reference groups and the perception of relative deprivation. Much of our understanding of the construct relative deprivation came from the large body of research conducted by Stouffer and his associates (1949) during World War II. Some of the clear examples of relative deprivation (as well as of the comparative functions of reference groups) are represented by the following findings. Among enlisted men, married men with children to support felt more dissatisfied with military life than did single men, and when such married men compared their army experiences with those of their civilian friends (who had not been drafted), they reported that they were victims of an injustice. By contrast, black Americans from the South reported greater levels of satisfaction with army life than did black Americans from the North, or white Americans. The southern blacks reported that they were better off socially and economically in the army than they had been at home, and felt relatively advantaged.

Riger (1977), Freeman (1975), and R. Dworkin (1982) have noted that when individuals recognize relative deprivation they most frequently become bitter and angry. Consciousness-raising groups serve to provide such a sense of relative deprivation. Anger per se, however, is not likely to lead to action or even to attributions of blame. In fact, as Merton (1968) observed, socialization systems often encourage people to interpret relative deprivations as personal failings, rather than as structurally induced problems. The old maxim "If at first you don't succeed, try, try again" specifically removes the locus of blame from the social structure or groups outside of one's own and places the onus on the individual. Personal failure is seen as a product of personal inadequacy. System blame then runs counter to many a social ethic. System blame is the recognition that the source of one's disadvantage—one's relative deprivation—is within the very stratification system itself. An exploration of the rhetoric of disadvantaged groups provides evidence for a perception of system blame. As long as members of a disadvantaged group explain their deprivations in terms of their lack of effort, lack of caring, luck, or the superior abilities of those with advantages, system blame is absent. Such observations by women with limited employment opportunities as "I really didn't want a career outside the home," or "Men are just better as managers," or "I didn't get the job because it wasn't in the cards" all deny system blame. National opinion surveys can also be indicators of system or self-blame, especially if such surveys include items from such efficacy scales as the locus of control measure developed by Rotter (1966). In such a measure items which demonstrate an internal locus of control (the respondents see themselves as personally responsible for their own destinies) or a specific type of external locus of control (where luck or fate is evoked), manifest an absence of system blame. However, where such surveys denote a view that corruption or discrimination account for relative deprivation, then system blame is present.

Blumer (1978) has observed that even if individuals feel deprived and that the social system is the source of such deprivation there is little reason to expect that they will be motivated to social action. In fact, in his theory of social unrest, those two conditions are said only to produce individual dissatisfaction, and perhaps, collective dissatisfaction. Dissatisfaction, however, is likely to be accompanied by a belief that "even if the system is not perfect, it is the best one we have." For a social movement to develop, Blumer argued, there must be a perception that the system of rewards and the social structure which insures such a system of rewards, is illegitimate. That is, there must be a perception that those with advantage do not have a license and a mandate to such advantages. Thus, the third construct in the block of social definitions and perceptions is that the relative deprivation and the system which insures its existence, are not proper and right. Durkheim (1953) once observed that what makes the normative system operative is not simply that it exists or that is is expedient and functional, but that people see it as right, correct, and in fact, the only possible arrangement. The perception that the structure is illegitimate and that those with advantages do not have a license and mandate for such advantages means that people see alternative and preferable normative orders. Of course, the perception of illegitimacy need not be directed at the entire social order or the central values of the society—this might be true only in cases of revolution, as Smelser (1963) suggested. Rather, the perception might instead be about the norms, or rules of conduct; rewards; and expectations, regarding a part of the social order. Many reform movements, as Smelser (1963) maintained, have such a focus. The rhetoric of a deprived group is an indicator of a perception of system illegitimacy. Attribution theory in social psychology has long demonstrated that people tend to attribute the successes of others to luck and their own successes to skill (Shaw and Constanzo 1970). As long as advantages of elites or other groups who are not deprived are seen by deprived groups as based upon luck, or as the elites might maintain, on skill, the legitimacy of the distribution system will not be challenged. However, once a rhetoric emerges which perceives the advantages of such groups as wrong and immoral, then there is clear evidence of a perception of system illegitimacy. Again, general social surveys with an analysis of the responses of deprived peoples can be a source of data on system illegitimacy.

X_{12} Willingness to act. This is simply the decision of disadvantaged individuals to mount a movement or to participate in a movement for their group's benefit. It is a social psychological assessment that comes when individuals recognize that the attainment of group goals will coincide with the attainment of their own personal goals and that the costs of participation are less than the expected benefits or the cost of nonparticipation. Participation in a movement or a movement organization, including contributing tangible or nontangible resources, joining in marches, signing petitions, joining organizations, all represent outcomes of such decisions to act. In the absence of survey data on willingness to act as Klandermans was able to collect during his study of a unionization movement in the Netherlands (1984), sometimes the results of the decision are the only data available. It is possible to rank order the levels of willingness to act by asking individuals to specify the amount of time, effort, and resources they would dedicate to a movement.

LINKAGES BETWEEN CONSTRUCTS:
AN EXPLICATION OF THE THEORY

We begin the presentation of the linkages between constructs with the assumption that because we offer a theory of social movements on behalf of disadvantaged groups, and women in particular, structural strain will be taken as an existing condition. That is, women as a disadvantaged group possess at least two of the conditions of minority status—they have less power than do men and are thus pejoratively treated (Dworkin and Dworkin 1982). Additionally, our theory, as a theory specifically of women's movements, posits the necessary presence of two of the global forces discussed earlier: urbanization and industrialization. Under the conjoined conditions of urbanization and industrialization there emerge several necessary phenomena, including (a) an increase in the division of labor; (b) a decrease in the capacity of any family unit to produce all or most all of its necessary goods and services for economic survival, including "the displacement of major female functions outside the home" (Freeman 1975:14); (c) the monitization of labor such that "the major female functions had to be paid for in cash" (1975:14); (d) a further increase in economic surplus, and hence wealth to heighten the demand for still further goods and services; (e) an increase in the size of the middle class, including merchants and managers in the production and distribution system; (f) an increase in leisure time, especially among the middle class; and (g) a concentration of populations and a geographic aggregation of people with similar advantages or deprivations (propinquity).

Linkages between Global Forces, Structural Strains, and Demand for Nontraditional Labor

1. The greater the levels of industrialization and urbanization of a society (as represented by the proportion of the population in an urban wage labor force), the less the self-sufficiency of the family unit and the more the displacement of major women's functions outside of the home.

2. The greater the level of industrialization and urbanization of a society, the more economic functions performed by members of the society will be monetized (become wage labor activities).

3. The greater the displacement of women's economic functions, the less the economic power of women and the greater the structural strain to which women are subjected (discriminations, deprivations, and disadvantages).

These three propositions hold that industrialization and urbanization disrupt divisions of labor within the family thereby making many female roles performable by paid labor and thus making some of women's work less indispensible. Chafetz (1984) has argued that the status of women and their access to control over their lives varies directly with their capacity to generate valued economic resources. As Freeman (1975) noted, one of the functions performed by women which was displaced during the Industrial Revolution involved the manufacture of clothing. With less control over the production of valued goods and services, and the presence of alternative sources for such goods and services, the status of women decreased and the commensurate disadvantages experienced by women increased.

4. The greater the level of industrialization and urbanization of a society, the larger the size of an economic surplus, the larger the size of the middle class, and the greater the amount of leisure available to members of that class.

5. The greater the economic surplus and the greater the monetization of labor to produce goods and services, the greater the demand for additional goods and services and the greater the capacity of those with wealth to purchase such goods and services.

The consequence of increased levels of industrialization and urbanization is the accumulation of additional wealth, not only to purchase more goods and services, but to produce better quality goods and services. However, improvement in the quality and quantity of goods and service necessitates an educational system to improve skill levels. Furthermore, those who provide the most valued goods and services in a monetized economy, and those who manage the distribution of such goods and services, accumulate greater levels of capital than those who do not. The capital, in turn, is translatable into demands for even better goods and services, as well as heightened levels of education. With heightened levels of leisure time and education come improved communications skills, organizational skills, and increased participation in voluntary associations.

6. The greater the demand for goods and services, the greater the demand for additional labor.

7. The greater the demand for additional labor, the less the capacity of a traditional labor force (in this case, males) to satisfy that demand for labor.

8. The less the capacity of males to meet the demand for labor (barring technological innovations that can reduce the demand for more labor), the greater the demand for participation of a nontraditional labor force, specifically, females.

These propositions maintain that increases in the demand for labor have taxed the capacity of the males to provide all the labor. In the early days of industrialization, work was labor intensive. The demand for labor was sufficiently high that some tasks, usually undesirable ones, were offered to nontraditional laborers. Bonacich (1972) observed that labor castes often evolved in which especially skilled and valued work was monopolized by majorities (usually white males) and other work, which was not as valued, was taken over by minorities, including women. Where the work was unpleasant but could not be performed by women and children, immigrant labor was brought in to do the work, as in the case of Oriental labor used to build the transcontinental railroad in the 1860s, or Mexican national labor to harvest crops from World War II through 1960 (under the Bracero bill, the name applied to the public law passed by Congress which enabled the use of such Mexican laborers). When such minorities attempted to gain access to jobs dominated by high-priced labor, exclusionary practices were evoked, including the demand for union shops or restrictions on immigration (see Bonacich 1972).

In later stages of industrialization work demands greater levels of skill and more work is done by machinery, which offsets the muscle strength advantage of males. Access to education to provide such skills initially was denied to women, except for middle class women whose life-styles and leisure permitted and necessitated conversational skills and at least a modicum of education to provide intellectual stimulation for their children. As the demand for skilled labor increase some educated women met that demand, but usually at lower skill levels and for less pay than their education warranted.

Linkages between Demand for Nontraditional Labor and Role Encapsulation/Expansion

Increasing the demand for nontraditional labor usually results in the development of labor castes, namely, labor force roles which are monopolized by men as distinguished from those performed chiefly by women. Urbanization and industrialization combine to concentrate a labor force in which interaction among individuals with similar life chances and relations to the means of production is intense, not only at work, but, given residential segregation, during nonworking hours as well. With an expansion of wealth and an unequal distribution of that wealth, housing patterns emerge such that middle-class individuals are segregated together and away from the working class. As Mack (1954) observed, the same patterns of segregation and limitations on interaction are found in the workplace.

Greater demands for quality goods and services not only increase the demand for labor, but will tend to escalate the price of such goods and services. Such an escalation can tax the ability of the middle class to compete for those goods and services as long as only middle-class men are in the paid labor force. Pressures tend to emerge to increase the participation of middle class women in the labor force.

9. The greater the demand for nontraditional labor (here, female labor), the greater the participation of women in work roles outside the home and the less the role encapsulation of women in solely wife/mother roles.

10. The greater the demand for nontraditional labor in labor force roles demanding skill, the greater the educational attainment of women and the greater the capacity of women to expand their roles beyond that of wife and mother.

11. The greater the cost of goods and services demanded by the middle class, combined with an incapacity by many middle-class men to pay for those goods and services, the greater the participation of middle-class women in work roles outside the home and the less the role encapsulation of middle-class women.

Central to many theories of the emergence of women's movements, and especially the most recent movements, has been the wholesale participation of married women in a paid labor force (Chafe 1977; Chafetz and Dworkin 1983; Deckard 1983; Freeman 1975). Not only does participation in a paid labor force permit women to make a contribution to the family income, but their increased economic resources also often results in increased family decision-making power. Furthermore, with such a role expansion women gain an increasing capacity to purchase the services of others to assume some of the housekeeping and especially food preparation and child-care duties associated with the wife/mother role. In turn, this expands the jobs available to other women, especially from the less educated strata of the society.

Linkages between Role Expansion and Role/Status Dilemmas

As long as women primarily perform unpaid labor roles as wives and mothers, and less valued labor force roles (due to labor castes which allocate men to higher paid and preferred jobs), they control only a limited amount of the economic resources in the family and the society. Men therefore are loathe to accord women equal control, including control over the definitions of their abilities, status attributes, and appropriate roles. The definitions of women's ability and appropriate work will thus be in conflict with their expanded roles, thereby creating role/status dilemmas.

In order to maintain their dominance within the economic sphere, and hence control in the family, men will tend to define women who value their labor force roles more highly than their wife/mother roles as pathological. In fact, Freeman (1975) pointed to the rise of the psychoanalytic movement as specifically a means of making women feel guilty about their labor force roles, which reduce their total dedication to the wife/mother roles.

Status dilemmas, as we noted earlier, involve a disjuncture between ascribed and achieved statuses. As a relatively low ascribed status, females who face such a discrepancy will inevitably have a lower ascribed than achieved status. Such women will have achieved a relatively high status role only through perseverance, skill, and the expenditure of considerable resources, material and psychic. Pressure by men on such women to abandon the higher achieved status and conform to expectations associated with the ascribed status will mean the abandonment of hard earned rewards and costly investments (Hughes 1945; Olsen 1970).

Yet, it is likely that men will engage in such pressure, as they seek to maintain a monopoly over the higher rewards associated with their status (Bonacich 1972). Under such pressure women may feel anger, frustration, and even rage, similar to that expressed by blacks encountering such role/status dilemmas, as reported by Grier and Cobbs (1968).

13. The more public (i.e., nondomestic) roles that women perform, the more likely will they perform roles normally monopolized by men.

14. The greater the number of nontraditional roles (labor force and other public roles) that women perform, the greater the likely disparity between societally prescribed female roles and the actual roles performed by women.

15. The greater the disparity between the societally prescribed roles for women and the actual roles performed by them, the greater the likelihood of negative sanctions directed at women by men.

16. The greater the disparity between the societally prescribed roles for women and the actual roles performed by them, the more will men expect women to resolve the disparity by ceasing the performance of nontraditional roles, thereby emphasizing the women's ascribed status over, or to the exclusion of, their achieved status.

17. The more that men negatively sanction the performance of nontraditional roles (labor force or other roles) by women and the more that men expect women to emphasize their lower ascribed status over their higher achieved status, the more frustrated and angry will women become.

During an initial phase of the "desegregation" of a role/status by women there may be vehement resistance on the part of men. The racial analogy to this occurred during the early years of school desegregation where crowds attacked a token group of black children on their way to white schools (Greenblatt and Willie 1980). On the other hand, resistance may take the form of snide comments and "water cooler humor," as reported by Kanter (1977) regarding the experiences of token females in male-dominated corporate offices. The perception by the high-status group (e.g., men) of the magnitude of the threat to their status by lower-status group members (e.g., women) is a significant determinant of the nature of the reaction (Useem 1980). The more members of the lower ascribed-status group involved, the greater the likelihood of perceived threat, and therefore the more vehement the reaction. The U.S. Supreme Court and the federal district courts had mandated desegregation of the public schools. Thus the small number of black children coming to Central High School in Little Rock, Arkansas, in 1957 was seen as only a vanguard of a much larger wave of black students.

There is, no doubt, a tipping point in any situation involving high-status and low-status groups, where a further increase in the number of lower-status members has the consequences of flight and abandonment of roles by the higher-status group. Armor (1980) has documented the magnitude of white flight from public schools occasioned by the influx of large numbers of black students to those schools. Likewise, as the number of women in public school teaching increased to a tipping point in the early years of this century in the United States, teaching began to be defined as a female occupation and the prestige of that occupation thereupon declined (Dworkin 1980; Lortie 1975). Once a role is monopolized by the lower-status group, or course, we can no longer speak of such individuals as occupying nontraditional roles or as having role/status dilemmas.

It is not expected that the resistance of higher-status groups to the entre of lower-status groups will often lead the latter to abandon their efforts. The demands of the high-status group would be honored if the overall demand for labor diminished, or if the capacity of the traditional labor force to meet that demand improved. In such instances, the lower-status, nontraditional labor force participant would be removed from the role, not voluntarily exit it. This is what happened in the aftermath of World War II when a million women were laid off to make room for returning veterans, despite the expressed desire of most to continue their work.

Linkages between Role Expansion, Role/Status Dilemmas, and Reference Groups

Some status dilemma approaches, such as those offered by Hughes (1945), Lenski (1954), and Olsen (1970), would argue that the model, as we have developed it to this point, would be sufficient to account for the emergence of a change-oriented consciousness on the part of a deprived group such as women. That is, the combined effects of the global forces, structural strain, distributive reallocation, and demands for nontraditional labor, role expansion, and role/status conflicts, create the necessary structural conditions for individuals to be readied for a social movement. However, we believe that there is an abundance of evidence that unless deprivations are experienced and defined within a particular frame of reference, people are not likely to define their condition as problematic and seek to redress their deprivations. Otherwise we could neither explain the relative infrequency of women's movements, nor the fact that even today many working women are resistant to the call of feminism. We would also not be able to account for the sporadic nature of black protest in this century in America or why so many black Americans continue to support institutions which advantage whites.

18. The greater the expansion of the roles of individuals into nontraditional domains, the greater the likelihood of interaction with groups offering divergent definitions of the social structure and of one's appropriate place in that structure.

19. The greater the number or degree of role/status dilemmas the more likely will one interact with groups offering divergent definitions of the social order and of one's place in that order.

20. The greater the role expansion, the greater the likelihood of interaction

with external comparative reference groups (groups other than one's own, which one uses to compare one's rewards, advantages, and disadvantages).

21. The greater the magnitude of role/status dilemmas, the greater the likelihood of interaction with external comparative reference groups.

22. The greater the role expansion, the greater the receptivity to internal normative and gate-keeping reference groups (particularly, members of one's own group who likewise have expanded their roles, encountered role/status dilemmas, and have been defined as a threat by higher status external groups).

23. The greater the magnitude of role/status dilemmas, the greater the receptivity to internal normative and gate-keeping reference groups.

Expansion of roles, especially the inclusion of nontraditional roles, means that one interacts with people from a wider range of groups. Since, to a significant degree, people interpret social reality on the basis of definitions of the situation offered by their own group (Hyman 1942; Kelley 1952; Merton and Kitt 1950), interaction with members of diverse groups means interactions with diverse definitions of the situation. Higher-status groups, especially those who see their status as threatened by the encroachment of lower-status groups, are likely to look for inadequacies in the lower-status group, define such inadequacies in terms of inherent weaknesses in such groups (stereotypes), and deny the existence of discrimination (Allport 1954; Ehrlich 1973; Myrdal 1944; van den Bergh 1967; Westie 1964). By contrast, interaction with members of one's own group is likely to be associated with more negative imagery of the outgroup (in this case the higher-status group, or males) and explanations for deprivations which do not blame the victim (Dworkin 1965; Loomis and Dworkin 1976; Maykovich 1972).

Linkages between the Interaction with and Receptivity to Reference Groups and Consciousness Formation

Earlier we noted that there are three functions performed by reference groups—comparative, normative, and gate-keeping. We also suggested that internal reference groups (members of one's own group and especially such members who have also experienced role expansions and role/status dilemmas) are likely to interpret reality differently than members of an external reference group (members of another group, including one whose status is threatened). It is our contention that so long as deprived people compare their status to that of other deprived groups they will not sense that they are relatively deprived. Von Eschen, Kirk, and Pinard (1976) found that black Americans who were isolated from interaction with whites tended to be less likely to think of themselves as a deprived group and thus were less involved in civil protest. Likewise, R. Dworkin (1979) found that women who were unsupportive of feminism were least likely to be in the labor force or to consider themselves as members of a deprived group. Conversely, Pettigrew (1964, 1971) noted that much of the impetus for black involvement in a civil rights movement came when some southern blacks came North to white universities and discovered that their own education would not buy them the same level of job opportunities as their white classmates. Much of the civil rights activism of the 1960s was mounted by middle-class blacks who interacted with whites and came to expect that they too deserved that which whites took for granted.

24. The more women compare their own rewards, advantages and deprivations with those of other women, the less likely are they to come to realize that they are relatively deprived. However, the more that women compare their rewards, advantages, and deprivations to those of men, the greater the probability that they will realize that they are relatively deprived.

Of course, for a sense of relative deprivation actually to occur one must find that external comparative reference groups are receiving more rewards for their efforts. If there is actual equity, then a sense of relative deprivation is unlikely. However, we need not worry that women will often be in contexts of opportunity and reward parity with men. The sociology of work literature is replete with evidence that minorities and women are less well rewarded for performing the same tasks (see Almquist 1977; Chafetz 1978; Dworkin and Dworkin 1982; Grebler, Moore and Guzmán 1970).

For a shift of comparative reference groups (from internal to external) to occur in the case of women, the role expansion and role/status dilemma must involve work settings in which women and men work together doing relatively similar tasks; that is, there must be desegregation at the unit of the work place. As long as the sexes work in different roles and in different parts of a building, such that women and men do not normally interact (as might happen if the women are segregated in the steno pool, or where women are placed in management positions over only other women) then a shift in reference group is not likely. "The context must necessarily demonstrate that the world, and hence the rewards of males are not categorically distinct—not another universe—from those of women" (Chafetz and Dworkin 1983:32).

The recognition of relative deprivation is likely to result in a sense of frustration and anger (Forward and Williams 1970; Geschwender 1964; Gurr 1970; Paige 1971). However, depending upon the normative and gate-keeping reference groups, the anger will either be turned outward or inward. Since higher-status groups (e.g., males) are interested in protecting their relative advantage, it is in their best interest to interpret relative deprivation as due to the inadequacies of members of the deprived grops (e.g., females). Thus, if women who sense a relative deprivation turn to males for an explanation of their problem, they are going to be assured that their rewards are commensurate with their skill levels and that if only they worked harder they would receive greater rewards. It has not been uncommon for such men to appeal to a woman's sense of fairness in accepting the relative deprivation, considering that a man had a family to support and, after all, she was working only for "pin money" or for some sense of self-gratification (Freeman 1975).

25. The more the interaction with, and receptivity to, internal normative and gate-keeping reference groups, the greater the likelihood that one will come to evoke system blame for one's relative deprivation. However, the more the interaction with, and receptivity to, external normative and gate-keeping reference groups, the greater the likelihood that one will evoke self-blame for one's relative deprivation.

This is especially a problem for women, because among the strongest bonds women form is with men through marriage (Rossi 1964). Thus, men are likely to serve as one's normative and gate-keeping reference group for married women.

As Morrison (1971) has observed, the likelihood of receptivity to definitions of self-blame offered by external reference groups is diminished as one increases interaction with internal normative and gate-keeping reference groups. After all, self-blame is plausible if only a few members of a group are relatively deprived. However, if an entire category of people is deprived, then an argument of individual culpability seems less credible than an argument for wholesale discrimination. As individuals who are relatively deprived turn to one another for an explanation of that deprivation, and to fix blame, they develop a rhetoric which makes increasingly less plausible any interpretation other than system blame. It is the constant retelling of atrocities and fixing of blame which characterizes consciousness-raising groups and which fosters definitions of system blame.

As we observed earlier, the recognition of system blame is likely to be overwhelming. If the source of one's relative deprivation is the entire society, what can one do but feel helpless? We shall address this shortly when we introduce the linkages with system repression and system inefficacy. However, another result of a sense of relative deprivation is to attempt to rationalize the strengths of the social order. As Blumer (1978) contended, relative deprivation and system blame are unlikely to lead to activism as long as people feel that the social order, while imperfect, is the best one possible. Only if internal normative and gate-keeping reference groups offer counters to this argument can we expect a sufficiently changed consciousness that individuals will be willing to act to effect change. Here too, reference groups recount atrocities and wage arguments that the advantages of privileged groups are illegitimate, along with the entire system of resource distribution. In such instances the license and mandate accorded to privileged groups is doubted and symbolically withdrawn.

The normative and gate-keeping reference groups transform a sense of relative deprivation into a sense of both system blame and system illegitimacy through a blitz of rhetoric, the recounting of atrocities, persuasion and, especially in more recent times, the use of mass media campaigns. All such actions involve what Klandermans has recently described as "consensus mobilization" (1984:586). We suspect that some of the processes present in models of emotional contagion (heightened suggestability, heightened stimulation, and homogeneity of experience) noted by Allport and Postman (1947) are operative here. The result is that a full sense of consciousness is developed and willingness to act is plausible. Through such interaction, Blumer (1978) observed, dissatisfaction becomes social unrest – the necessary social psychological element in the mounting of a movement.

26. The greater the interaction with internal normative and gate-keeping reference groups, the greater the likelihood that one will define the license and mandate of those with advantage (e.g., males) as illegitimate and the greater the likelihood that one will define the social order as illegitimate.

What remains problematic is whether individuals, even with raised consciousness, will join a movement or support an embryonic movement. Klandermans put the problem quite succinctly when he noted "that persons have to decide to participate at a point when they do not know whether others will participate" (1984:585). Yet willingness to take risks is necessary for the survival of the movement, or even for its emergence. If a significant number of people are convinced that the movement will fail, or that others will not join, then the probability that a movement will be mounted is quite low. Likewise, if a significant number of people feel that they have little to contribute and that there will be plenty of people available to participate, then they, too, can doom an effort to mount a movement.

Social movements seek group goals, rather than goals for specific individuals. Yet, as Olson (1968) and some other resource mobilizaton theorists have observed, individuals are expected to participate in a movement for the good of the group with the hope that some benefits will trickle down to them personally. Rational individuals will not participate, and thereby doom a movement, if they believe that the collective benefits (benefits which a movement seeks on behalf of an entire category of people, such as all women) will not accrue to them as individuals, or will accrue at such low levels that personal expenditures of time, money, and other resources will be greater than potential personal gains. The combined perception that one will not have enough to contribute, that the movement will succeed without one's participation, and that one would be likely to receive fewer rewards than the amount of effort demanded by the movement, have been identified as the "free-rider problem" (see Jenkins 1983; Klandermans 1984; Olson 1968).

One benefit which could motivate people to participate, even if individuals' returns relative to their investments in movement activism are not likely to be very great, is the positive affect and comradeship which is part and parcel of movement participation. The positive affect offered by a normative and gate-keeping reference groups may be a reward in and of itself. Likewise, the desire to do something may be a sufficient motivator of some individuals. The combined benefits of comradeship and a sense of doing something may be the central rewards for "conscience adherents" – individuals who join even through they are not members of the deprived group and will gain no increase in tangible benefits (e.g., male feminists).

27. The more that internal normative and gate-keeping reference groups can demonstrate to individuals that movement goals are attainable, that tangible benefits can also accrue to individuals, that their personal participation is essential, and that personal costs will be exceeded by personal benefits (material gains, status gain, comraderie, or self-image enhancement), the more likely will such a reference group motivate individuals to participate.

Structural Linkages That Minimize the Cost of a Social Movement

Our theory to this point has attempted to explain how individuals come to recognize that they are relatively deprived, evoke system blame and system illegitimacy for such deprivations, and may be also motivated to participate in a movement. However, our theory must address two additional key problems. We need to explain how reference groups can effectively answer the question that if it is the system that is to blame, what can solitary individuals, or even small groups, do to alter the system? Additionally, we need to account for how small collectivities of individuals involved in social action recognize that they are not alone. That is, how does a national movement evolve out of individual and small group actions?

To answer the first question, we need to explore the linkages between global forces, structural strain, system openness/repressiveness, and the perception of system inefficacy. It will be recalled that a repressive political order, which prohibits voluntary association and makes illegal the coalescence of protest groups, effectively stiffles the development of social movements (Dahrendorf 1959). Likewise, we argued earlier that if a political order accedes to enough of the demands of movement activists to make it appear to participants that they have attained their goals, this also stiffles movements. With the appearance that one has won, there remain few reasons to motivate people to continue to join a movement. Only if the political authorities are relatively benign (and do not forbid coalitions) and sufficiently resistant (not acceding quickly to some of the demands of the movement) will a movement develop.

As already noted, extreme deprivation of a group is usually associated with inactivity. Not only is this true because group members have few resources to mobilize and because such individuals tend to turn inward when severely deprived, but such deprivation is usually maintained by a political authority which prohibits collective action by them. Such was certainly the case for American blacks in the South during slavery (see Elkins 1959; Stampp 1959). In the absence of any deprivation, social movements on behalf of deprived groups would, by definition, not be needed or likely to emerge. Only when deprivations are sufficiently great to make credible claims of discrimination, but not too great to stiffle group formation, can movements emerge. Therefore we make the following proposals:

28. The greater the deprivation of a group, the less likely is that group to mount a social movement to end that deprivation. However, in the absence of any significant structural strain (deprivation), social movements are not going to be mounted either.

29. Social movements are unlikely to emerge in political systems that prohibit political activity on the part of deprived categories of people.

30. Social movements are unlikely to survive if political systems easily acceed to some number of the movement's demands.

Any force which changes the level of repression of a group or which makes political authorities less able to ban collective action, will, of course, facilitate the rise of a social movement. As Skocpol (1979) pointed out, warfare and major economic crises (elements of global forces) can be sufficiently disruptive of a government that it fails to govern. In fact, any destabilizing force may have the consequence of reducing the capacity of a political authority to ban the coalescence of groups. We can modify proposition 29 by noting the following:

31. The less effective a political authority is at repressing and banning political activism, the more likely will social movements emerge.

32. The less effective a political authority is at repressing and banning political activism, the more will individuals come to realize that the costs of their participation are diminishing relative to the potential benefits of participation.

Proposition 27 covers the logical outcome of proposition 32. To the extent that political repression is a cost of participation, a diminuation in that cost will lead to an increase in the likelihood of an individual participating, as well as an aggregation of individuals participating in a movement.

Linkages between Structural Strain, Global Forces, Political Repression, and Prior Social Movements

The same global forces that, in the United States, created demands for nontraditional labor and thus the impetus for a women's movement previously had created the conditions that encouraged a black civil rights movement. For instance, some have noted that the rise of the civil rights organization CORE (Congress of Racial Equality) occurred soon after A. Philip Randolph of the International Brotherhood of Sleepingcar Porters threatened a march on Washington. That march was proposed to demand fair employment for blacks, given the manpower shortages occurring in the United States during the beginning of World War II (see Meier and Rudwick 1973; Pinkney 1975).

A society that discriminates against one minority is likely to discriminate against others. Thus, the propositions we have offered to account for the emergence of a women's movement may be evoked to account for the prior emergence of other social movements on behalf of some deprived group(s).

We contend that a prior social movement is not a necessary condition for the emergence of other social movements. Women did not become aware of their relative deprivations through participation in the civil rights movement or in the antiwar movement. This is not to say, however, that a prior social movement cannot be useful to a subsequent one. The former can provide organizational skills, communications networks, economic resources, the mobilization or conscience adherents, lists of donors, and a host of resources which can be used by a subsequent movement. McCarthy and Zald (1973, 1977) and Jenkins (1983) have argued that the leadership for a current social movement may come from people who were conscience adherents in a prior movement.

If one movement is still in full mobilization, however, it may retard, rather than facilitate the emergence of another movement. Large-scale movements tap enormous amounts of resources, thereby limiting the resources available to a second movement. As we saw in chapter 1, many socialist and national liberation movements urged women to abandon, at least temporarily, their demands for women's rights until the "larger issues" of workers' or nationalists' rights were addressed. Prior social movements may also effectively block the emergence of other movements if they were unsuccessful or if they were repressed. Such prior failures demonstrate the high cost of mounting subsequent movements. In part because of the successful repression of the labor movement mounted by Mexican-Americans in the 1930s, an entire generation of Mexican-Americans was reticent to try again. Only when economic conditions were ripe and a new generation of leadership had matured did a National Farmworker's Organization and a Chicano Movement emerge in the 1960s.

33. The more successful a prior movement has been in attaining its goals, the more willingly will a disadvantaged group support a subsequent movement.

34. The more a movement drains resources from a collectivity, the less likely will additional movements emerge until the former movement has reached a conclusion.

Linkages between Political Repression, Prior Movements and the Perception of System Inefficacy

Political authorities which have been successful in repressing groups convey to others how powerful and effective the social structure is. Bettelheim (1943) documented the effectiveness of the Nazis in limiting protest in concentration camps for political prisoners during the late 1930s, due to the fact that people perceived the social system as unassailable. Evidence of the inefficacy of the U.S. government to stop student protest during the Antiwar Movement encouraged greater activism (see Wood 1974). Conversely, the successful completion of a social movement can make subsequent movements easier by demonstrating the openness of the system and/or enhancing the perception of its inefficacy in preventing change, as well as by providing resources.

35. The greater the magnitude of repression of a group by the political authorities, the more will people perceive the system as unassailable.

36. The less a political authority is able effectively to repress a social movement when it tries, the more will people come to perceive the political system as ineffective.

37. The more successful a prior movement has been in attaining its goals despite resistance by political authorities, the more ineffective will people come to perceive the system.

Linkages between Role Encapsulation/Expansion, Prior Social Movements, and the Mobilization of Resources

As we have seen, social movements depend upon the mobilization of resources from conscience adherents. In addition, the disadvantaged always provide substantial intangible resources for their own movement. As they increase their labor force participation and/or alter their labor force deployment, the disadvantaged increase their capacity to provide material resources as well. The likelihood that either will actually donate such resources to a movement is dependent upon evidence that such resources will be utilized effectively (Klandermans 1984).

38. The more successful a prior social movement has been in attaining its goals, the easier it will be to mobilize resources from conscience adherents and utilize networks for a subsequent social movement.

39. The greater the role expansion among women, the more able they are to contribute resources to their own movement.

Linkages between the Perception of System Inefficacy, Reference Group Interaction and Receptivity, and Personal Willingness to Act

Evidence that the political authorities and the social structure itself have "clay feet" provides the necessary fodder for reference groups for their retorts to those who have been overwhelmed by the recognition that the source of their deprivation is the whole social structure (Riger 1977). When people realize that goals are attainable through collective action, then the probability of gain through movement participation becomes sufficiently high that people are willing to be mobilized.

40. The greater the perception of the inefficacy of the social and political systems, the more will internal normative and gatekeeping reference groups point to such inefficacy in their attempt to mobilize participants.

41. The more deprived individuals come to define as ineffective in preventing change the very system that has caused their relative deprivation and that they have come to define as illegitimate, the more will such individuals be willing to be mobilized into a social movement.

Linkages between Reference Groups, Tangible and Intangible Resource Mobilization, and Willingness to Act

Within the ranks of the normative and gatekeeping reference groups are the leaders of a social movement. Such individuals are composed of the vanguard of the disadvantaged whose middle-class status, educational attainment, skills, networks, and group consciousness were established earlier. Many may have participated in prior social movements, but almost all have encountered role/status dilemmas due to the disjuncture between their ascribed and achieved statuses. A myriad of studies of minority civil rights leaders, women's movement leaders, and leaders of other disadvantaged groups have shown them to have most of the attributes of elitehood, but denied such elitehood because of their ascribed status. Studies ranging from the *Report of the National Advisory Commission on Civil Disorders* (1968) on leadership in ghetto violence, to assessments of the leaders of early civil rights movements (Meier and Rudwick 1973), and assessments of the characteristics of feminist leaders (Freeman 1975), to studies of the women involved in the Abolitionist Movement (Hewitt 1984), all support this assessment.

The tasks to be performed by the leaders are manifold. Not only must they interpret and define the situation of their disadvantage to their sisters, but they must mobilize the myriad of resources which are needed to mount a movement. They must impact media, mount a campaign for funding, exploit existing communications networks, and establish new networks. It is not uncommon for such leaders to emerge from university settings or from corporate settings—where organizational tools may be at their disposal. In the nineteenth century they frequently relied upon the resources of family wealth or their husband's, brother's, or father's organizational resources (Hewitt 1984). They were often effective in persuading their male relatives to support them.

42. The more that leaders drawn from normative and gate-keeping reference groups can persuade conscience adherents of the legitimacy of their claims of deprivation, the more effective will these leaders be in mobilizing tangible and intangible resources.

Haines (1984) has recently examined the consequences of extremist factions within a deprived group in garnering support for more moderate leaders of that deprived group. He explored how tangible resources were mobilized during the period of the Black Civil Rights Movement (1957–70). Haines noted that as activism became more radical and violent, dollar contributions from whites to moderate civil rights groups escalated. It has long been recognized that riots encouraged federal funding of bureaucratically stalled projects. Freeman (1975) noted that the bargaining power of the National Organization for Women (NOW) was enhanced by the activities of fringe radical, lesbian, and socialist groups.

43. The more extreme the demands of one faction of the deprived group, the more will conscience adherents and other outsiders consider the demands of

leaders of core (central and moderate) groups to be legitimate and reasonable.

44. The more radical the ideologies and actions of extreme factions of a deprived group, the more will conscience adherents and other outsiders provide tangible and intangible resources to the more moderate core of the group.

There is a cumulative, circular, social interaction associated with the linkages between leaders, the mobilization of tangible and intangible resources, and the willingness of deprived group members to act. The effective appeals for resources mounted by a leadership buoy the confidence of those leaders, who in turn can mount better appeals to their less motivated sisters. The heightened enthusiasm of the following provides additional proof of the viability of the new movement to outsiders, which may encourage even higher levels of resource contributions.

45. The greater the magnitude of tangible and intangible resources provided by conscience adherents, the greater the willingness of deprived groups to act, and vice versa.

When we completed the part of the theory which accounted for individual perception of deprivation, we voiced two issues. The first was how people realize that participation in a social movement will net them desired gains, especially given the systematic nature of their deprivation. We believe we have addressed that issue. We can now turn to the second issue. Recall that it deals with the manner in which social movements made up of small cells of activists aggregate into more national movements. Since social movements need some level of coordination, the haphazard and independent development of many local units is unlikely to be able to attack a systemic problem, such as the deprivation of a whole social group.

Our model to this point has satisfied four of the five conditions for social movement development specified by Morrison (1971). There exist (a) "a large population experiencing the relative deprivation;" (b) "close interaction, communication, and proximity" among actors; (c) "high role and status commonality [such that] it is more difficult to interpret a blockage as due to individual causes;" and (d) "a stratification system with clear strata boundaries and visible power differences" (1971:684–85). Additionally, there must exist "the presence of much voluntary association activity in a society," making likely the idea of a structural, organizational solution to the felt deprivations (1971:685). This, however, is likely to lead to the emergence of several organizations, generally local in scale, to address and protest the problems. A national social movement necessitates broader scale communication between units and the active participation of more cosmopolitan entrepreneurs. Of course, attention-focusing events, especially if well covered by the mass media or other forms of communication, not only heighten the sensitivity of more members of the deprived group, but also alert isolated movement-oriented groups to the possibility of coalition. Thus, the Montgomery bus boycott of 1955 signaled a call to action on the part of preexisting local black groups throughout the South. The storming of the Bastille alerted the underclasses in France to action. In some instances, although we cannot speak of this as the beginning of the movement, the state actually heightens sensitivity toward a problem. Thus, when President Kennedy organized the Presidential Commission on the Status of Women in 1961, a significant sensitizing phenomenon was in the making. However, only if the groups then take the initiative to organize can we speak of the development of a social movement. The spin-off of the presidential commission was the National Organization for Women. NOW, in turn, began to work with local consciousness-raising groups to expand its national membership and to transform local action into a movement (Freeman 1975). Of course, other cosmopolitan organizations emerged over the course of the women's movement, each with somewhat different ideologies and/or strategies, and they too, are considered part of the movement. As we shall see in the next two chapters, in many instances national organizations do not develop. In their absence, however, dense communications networks and a plethora of coalitions may serve the same purpose.

We thus maintain that the same general force which transforms personal dissatisfaction into system blame and group awareness at the local level, operates to transform the disparate awarenesses of subgroups into collective, national awareness: communication between reference groups. What transforms a number of isolated groups into a mass movement, or what transforms groups of system-blaming individuals into an incipient movement, is a network of communication (see Zald and Ash 1966, for a discussion of how the nature of such communication can affect the survivability of movement organizations). The presence of a medium of mass communication certainly speeds up the time needed for groups, each having independently arrived at a sense of relative deprivation, system blame, and system illegitimacy, to recognize that they are not alone. However, prior to the advent of such mass media, communication between such groups was still possible, albeit slower. In essence, the collective decisions on the eve of the American Revolution emerged out of networks of communication, both in group meetings, such as the Union of Albany and other formal organizations, as well as through the letters sent between groups via the Committee of Correspondence.

46. The greater the mobilization of tangible and intangible resources and the greater the communication between individuals and groups that have already developed consciousness and willingness to act, the greater the likelihood of the emergence of a social movement.

THE DETERMINATION OF THE SIZE AND IDEOLOGY OF MOVEMENTS

The theory we have offered explains the process by which social movements, especially women's movements, emerge and are mounted. It has focused upon both the factors which create a consciousness and a decision to act on the part of members of disadvantaged groups, and it explains how structural factors are conjoined to translate individuals' motives and decisions into collective action. Among the blocks of constructs several are pivotal in permitting us to explain and predict the ideological scope and size of social movements created by and for disadvantaged groups generally, and women in particular. Most significant among these blocks are the global forces of industrialization and urbanization and the demand for nontraditional labor, accompanied by role encapsulation/expansion, role/status dilemmas, and reference groups.

Increases in the global factors of industrialization and urbanization elevate the level of wealth, the size of the middle class, and demands for skilled and educated labor. In the presence of sex stratification and gender differentiation, the initial demand is for a better educated male labor force, but nonetheless the level of female education tends to increase with industrialization and urbanization. The reduction of functions within the household, previously part of women's responsibilities, combined with an increase of leisure, result in increased levels of middle class female involvement in nonwork public roles, such as voluntary associations and social movements (excluding women's movements). This results in a heightened probability that these women will use their husbands as an external comparative reference group in terms of educational attainment and efficacy in attaining sociopolitical goals. In turn, a sense of relative deprivation emerges. Ameliorative women's movements, such as those which sought increased educational opportunities and suffrage for women, do not challenge the economic domination of women by men, or even the expectation that women would principally be wives and mothers. Rather, such ameliorative movements have sought to reinforce traditional gender roles by insuring that men would support their families. Furthermore, such movements have often had as a goal the protection of children from perceived evils. Even education for women has been sought in order to maintain family stability and make women better able to raise and teach their children. We shall explore these issues more fully in the next chapter.

In a sense, ameliorative movements never questioned the continued role encapsulation of women. The changes they sought were seen as mechanisms to allow them to do a better job in their encapsulated role under new socioeconomic conditions. As long as married women, especially middle-class ones, were out of the labor force, they could make few demands for social equality with men. They could only insist that men uphold their roles as husbands, fathers, and chief providers. Only when women's economic power made possible their survival and the survival of their children in the absence of male support or beneficence, could women mount a social movement to challenge the systems of sex stratification and gender role differentiation; that is, a feminist movement.

We have seen that social movements are rarely, if ever, mounted by the most oppressed. In fact, the plethora of evidence from civil rights, women's, and national liberation movements suggest that the more advantaged among a deprived group are the first to become activists. The most deprived often do not have necessary educational and organizational skills to be effective in communicating their woes. Thus, the creation of a middle class is necessary for any type of women's movement, as we shall be describing in the ensuing chapters.

It is central to our theory of women's movements that the ideology of such movements is contingent upon the nature of the role encapsulation/expansion of women. If urbanization and industrialization have created a middle class for whom principally educational and political role/status dilemmas exist (to the exclusion of labor force role/status dilemmas), and husbands serve as the external comparative reference group, then only an ameliorative social movement will emerge. If, however, the demand for nontraditional (here, female) labor expands the roles of married middle-class women to include labor force roles, and role/status dilemmas involve men and women working physically together but within a labor caste system which disadvantages women, then male coworkers become the external comparative reference group and a fully feminist women's movement can emerge.

The numbers of women experiencing role expansion, role/status dilemmas, and the other blocks of constructs determine the magnitude of the social movement. The larger the percentage of middle-class, educated, married women in settings where they experience a role expansion, but not in the paid labor force, the larger the size of the ameliorative women's movement. By contrast, the larger the percentage of middle-class, educated, married women in the paid labor force, with males as a comparative reference group, the larger the size of the feminist movement. As we indicated at the beginning of this chapter, and as we shall reiterate in subsequent chapters, our assessment of the cutting points between incipient, intermediate, and mass will always be crude.

CONCLUSIONS

It is essential to recognize that the theory we have presented is one which attempts to account for the emergence of social movements on behalf of deprived groups in general, and women in particular. Except for the linkages between prior social movements and other independent constructs, the linkages are all necessary conditions; they must be met for a social movement to emerge. However, once such a movement emerges, its particular size and ideology are contingent upon the magnitude of the effect of the blocks of constructs. In the absence of a substantial level of industrialization and urbanization, such that the size of the middle class remains relatively small and the educational level of women is low, only an incipient movement is possible. Such a movement would be launched by that minority of urban women who are middle class and relatively well educated. With an increase in the scale of the urban middle class would come first an intermediate and finally a mass women's movement. The pivotal construct for the emergence of a specifically feminist movement is the large-scale entré of married women into the wage labor force. When only single women participate in the labor force, they tend to perceive their work roles as temporary. As such, their role models are married women who are not in the labor force. Therefore, males do not constitute a comparison group. As large numbers of married women enter or stay in the labor force, they are likely to perceive employment as a major, lifelong role and a male comparison group becomes more feasible. As the proportion of married female labor force participants increases, the size of feminist movements changes from incipient to intermediate to mass.

Before we begin the series of case studies that constitute much of the remainder of the book, a note of methodological caution is warranted. It is impossible to compile comparable information concerning the number of societies reviewed in the next two chapters. Furthermore, the inherent difficulties involved in cross-cultural comparisons are seriously compounded as we go back in historical time. All historical data are biased to some degree by what contemporaries chose to record, how they recorded it, and what has been preserved subsequently. Some data are unavailable because they were never collected or recorded. Some are unavailable in English and/or in this country. Even census data, which has been routinely collected in most societies (at least in the West) for at least a hundred years, are not directly comparable from one society to another, or even across time in one nation. For instance, as Deacon (forthcoming) demonstrated for Australia, different methods of defining "work" and "labor force participation" used in census enumerations have led to substantially discrepant statistics concerning women's labor. Arizpe (1977) and Chincilla (1977) spoke of an "informal economy" in Latin American societies, where women are street vendors, domestic employees, and bar girls, which are not formally enumerated in government statistics, thereby biasing estimates of women's labor force participation.

The logic of our theory would entail a comparison of the socioeconomic trends characterizing societies that experience a women's movement with those in which not even an incipient one emerged. This, however, cannot be done. Scholars, especially historians, do not, as a rule, publish accounts of the absence of a phenomenon. Therefore, if we find no discussion of a movement in a given society, we cannot know if no movement existed, or if no scholar writing in English has gotten around to studying one that did exist, especially when incipient movements are in question. We leave to others the future task of testing our ideas in times and places where there is good reason to know that no movement existed on behalf of women — regardless of size or ideology.

Given the absence of many kinds of data needed to test our theory, biases in much of the materials that are available, and problems of comparability where seemingly similar data exist cross-culturally, our case studies cannot be said to constitute a critical test of our theory. The purpose of the ensuing chapters is twofold. On the one hand there is a paucity in the existing literature of comparative studies of women's movements, especially comparisons of many parts of the world and in different times. These chapters are an attempt to begin the task of directly comparing and demonstrating the prevalence of such movements. On the other hand, we hope to present enough information pertinent to our theory to lend credibility to it.

In light of the preceding caveats, what follows are a series of hypotheses for which substantial cross-cultural data are available. It is clear that data pertaining to many of the theoretical variables, including all of the social-psychological ones, are not available cross-culturally for the range of cases we shall examine. We begin our hypotheses with those which predict movement size, follow with those pertaining to movement ideology, and conclude with some suggestions concerning the interaction between the two.

Size

1. The greater the level of urbanization, the larger the size of the women's movement.

2. The greater the level of industrialization, the larger the size of the women's movement.

3. The higher the average educational level of women, the larger the size of the women's movement.

4. The greater the proportion of the population that is middle class, the larger the size of the women's movement.

5. The greater the number of women who participate in roles monopolized by men in the recent past (i.e., the greater the role expansion), the larger the size of the women's movement.

6. The greater the levels of repression or co-optation of movement goals by male authorities, the smaller the size of the women's movement.

Ideology

1. The greater the proportion of married women in the labor force, the more likely a women's movement will develop a feminist ideology.

2. The greater the proportion of women labor force participants working in male-dominated occupations, the more likely a women's movement will develop a feminist ideology.

3. The greater the proportion of women labor force participants working in high-status occupations (i.e., those most conducive to role/status dilemmas), the more likely a women's movement will develop a feminist ideology.

4. The more similar the educational achievements of the two sexes, the more likely a women's movement will develop a feminist ideology.

Interaction

We predict that the modal large (intermediate or mass) ameliorative women's movement will arise in societies characterized by the following traits: (a) relatively high levels of urbanization and industrialization, hence a substantial-size middle class; (b) a relatively high level of female education, which nonetheless does not equal that of males in their society; (c) a low proportion of married women, especially middle class, in the labor force; and (d) a government which is neither highly repressive, nor unduly sympathetic to women's demands. A small (incipient) ameliorative women's movement will arise in societies characteried by (a) relatively low levels of urbanization and industrialization, therefore a small middle class; (b) a relatively poorly educated female population; and (c) a low proportion of married women, especially middle class, in the labor force.

A large feminist movement will typically arise in societies in which (a) the levels of urbanization and industrialization are very high, thereby creating a substantial middle class; (b) the educational level of women approaches parity with that of men; (c) the proportion of married women, including middle class, in the labor force is high. Finally, small feminist movements will tend to occur in societies which (a) are moderately urbanized and industrialized; (b) have a moderate proportion of married women, especially middle class, in the labor force; and (c) have male and female educational levels approaching parity, but less so than where large feminist movements emerge.

4 The First Wave: Women's Movements of the Nineteenth and First Half of the Twentieth Centuries

Most European societies, as well as the United States, experienced more or less extensive women's movements in the closing decades of the nineteenth, and first decades of the twentieth centuries. Many countries throughout the rest of the world also did, especially after the turn-of-the-century. This chapter concerns itself with these movements. In the next chapter we will explore contemporary women's movements in a number of societies. For each case examined in these two chapters, we will focus our attention on two central issues, to the extent that relevant information is available:

1. How extensive was the movement's *appeal* to women in numerical terms? Was it a small, incipient movement or did it attract the allegiance of a larger number of women as an intermediate or mass movement? Were activities centered in one or a few small groups or were they more widely dispersed?

2. How broad was the *ideological focus* of the movement? Did it raise issues concerning the fundamental gender role and sex stratification systems as they were manifest in several different social institutions? Or did it accept the gender role status quo and seek only ameliorative changes, designed to expedite essentially traditional role fulfillment? As a corollary, did the leaders and followers share an ideology, or was there a fully feminist leadership whose appeal to its followers was based on a considerably more narrow, ameliorative set of issues?

In chapter 6 we will treat all these case studies as a sample and test some of the ideas developed in chapter 3 using quantitative data.

In this chapter, among other movements, we will discuss those in the United States and Great Britain in the nineteenth and early twentieth centuries, and in the next chapter the contemporary U.S. movement. The existing literature on these three women's movements is vast, detailed, and readily accessible. In view of that, we will keep our discussions relatively brief and sharply focused on the issues just raised. Many of the remainder of the cases examined in both chapters suffer from the opposite problem: a paucity of available literature. Those discussions will therefore also be relatively brief. We make no claim that these accounts are a comprehensive history of any of the movements discussed or that we have identified all women's movements that occurred in the past century and a half.

THE UNITED STATES

Some scholars speak of two women's movements in nineteenth-century America: an early one, which began in 1848 with the Seneca Falls Convention and lasted until some time after the Civil War, and a later one, which began in the closing decades of the nineteenth century and ended with the ratification of the Nineteenth Amendment in 1920 (e.g., Chafe 1977: chap. 4; Kraditor 1965: chap. 1). Others consider this entire time as constituting one movement (e.g., DuBois 1978; Flexner 1975:70; Hole and Levine 1984). Regardless, most agree upon the beginning and end points. We shall examine both early pre-Civil War appeal and ideology, and later, turn-of-the-century ones. It should be noted that there were a handful of feminists in the decades before the 1848 convention, including the fiery Grimké sisters, but they acted as individuals and in no way can be considered leaders of even an incipient feminist movement (see Flexner 1975:24ff). Likewise, feminists and a few, small organizations, such as the relatively radical National Woman's Party (see Patterson 1982; Ware 1981: esp. chap. 1), continued in existence after 1920 and until the reemergence of movement activity in the late 1960s, but they were all but invisible to the rest of the society (Banks 1981:149-50; Deckard 1983:284-87; O'Neill 1969a:88; chap. 5; 1969b: chap. 8; Sochen 1973). Indeed, Howard (1974:139) pointed out the irony that 1920 witnessed not only final ratification of the suffrage amendment, but organizational efforts for the first Miss America contest, objection to which was to help reignite a woman's movement nearly half a century later.

In the years before 1848, vocal feminists had raised their voices, especially within the Abolitionist Movement (see chap. 1). Other women, involved in various reform movements, had also begun to develop an awareness of their disadvantaged status (Berg 1978: chaps. 8, 9). As Flexner noted, however, ". . . there were workers here and there hewing away at prejudice and law; but they were scattered and isolated from one another. . . . What was needed now was a sharp impetus—leadership and, above all, a program" (1975:71; see also DuBois 1979, for a discussion of "proto-feminism" in the 1820s and 1830s, and Melder 1977: chap. 8). The Seneca Falls Convention provided such an impetus. The "Declaration of Principles" presented at that convention, and signed by 69 women and 32 men, presented facts which "ranged over every aspect of woman's status," and called for general sexual equality (Flexner 1975:75, 77; see also O'Neill 1969a: document 2). It basically paraphrased the Declaration of Independence. While the convention represented no abrupt discontinuity in the gradual evolution of feminist thought, it did represent the beginning of a self-consciously feminist movement which subsumed a variety of heretofore rather discrete issues.

Suffrage for women was the least agreed upon issue of the entire convention, only carrying by a narrow majority (Hole and Levine 1984:536-37). It was never to become a central demand of pre-Civil War feminists (Flexner 1975:146). The main focus of the early feminists was legal reform. In most states, married women's status was defined on the basis of English Common Law, under which it was assumed that the husband and wife were legally one person—him. Married women had no rights to property, to custody of their children in case of divorce, even to their own earnings. They could not sign contracts or serve on juries. Another major focus of feminists was equal educational opportunity. Oberlin had just opened its doors to women, but by and large, higher education for women still meant seminaries, where the main instruction centered upon becoming a "lady." Likewise, the early feminists called for equal opportunity in the workplace—especially trade, commerce, and the professions (Sinclair 1965: 61). In fact, a Seneca Falls resolution called for raising the wages of their own domestic servants (Paulson 1973:42–43). The issue of women's employment opportunities became increasingly more salient as educational opportunities for women rapidly expanded, especially in the Midwest, in the ensuing decades. Other issues addressed by pre–Civil War feminists included:

1. Dress reform; an end to the constricting attire of female apparel; for a while, many feminists took to wearing bloomers as an expression of their stance on this issue

2. Physical fitness and exercise for women, to combat their frail health and lack of vigor

3. The negative image of women portrayed by established religions

4. The sexual double standard; men's "promiscuity" was attacked by most (Sinclair 1965:38), while a few even espoused "free love" (O'Neill 1969a:28)

5. Equality between marital partners (O'Neill 1969a:25–27; Sinclair 1965:47)

6. The right of women within marriage to refuse sexual activity with their husband (O'Neill 1969a:42)

7. The stereotype of "the lady" which, under the guise of chivalry, kept women confined to a narrow, domestic world (Sinclair 1965:120–23).

In short, feminists in this era raised issues concerning every major social institution: law and the polity, the economy, the family and sexuality, religion, education, as well as cultural definitions of femininity as tied to the concept of "the lady" and to physical restraints on activity. They must be considered as ideological radicals, whose concerns ranged broadly over myriad aspects of the entire sex stratification and gender role systems (Hole and Levine 1984; see also Hersh 1978; Melder 1977: 154–56). They were, by any definition, truly feminist in their ideology—if not always in their own personalities and behaviors. Sinclair argued that while decrying the image of ladyhood, most of these feminists were themselves ladies.

> The early feminists rightly saw how the role of the lady had enslaved American women. Yet they themselves only felt free when they were playing the part of ladies. They never came to terms with this anomaly, and thus feminism in the nineteenth century remained largely a middle-class and ladylike business [1965:109].

We shall see that this was to have far-reaching consequences for the post–Civil War movement. The feminists represented a new type of middle-class woman: relatively well educated, having taken advantage of the educational reforms beginning in their own youths, and experienced in employment outside the home, even if only for a few years. Examination of the biographies of 51 first-generation feminist-abolitionists by Hersh (1978: chap. 4; see also Paulson's description of the signers of the Seneca Falls Declaration 1973:36) revealed that 15 (29 percent) were Quakers, 29 (57 percent) grew up in middle- to upper middle-class families, while only 4 were raised in relative poverty, and all "were remarkably educated for women growing up in the mid-nineteenth century" (1978:133). While only 2 graduated college and 6 others attended medical school, 41 (80 percent) were "known to have acquired above-average educations" (ibid.), usually through private tutors and attendance at female seminaries where they received "a good classical education." Only 3 were known to have received little formal schooling. Finally, "at least half" (1978:135) taught for some part of their life, usually before marriage.

While their ideology was broad, their movement was not. No formal, feminist organization developed in the prewar years. After Seneca Falls, feminists held conventions in many towns and cities, almost annually (for a discussion of these see Melder 1977: chap. 10). As we noted in chapter 1, they often met concurrently with abolitionist conventions, to which they remained attached. Loose steering committees existed in the interim, but that was the extent of their organizational development (Flexner 1975:83), excepting a few state and local organizations (Melder 1977:153). Initially, they were confined to a few cities in the East, but by the decade preceding the war, feminism had spread to the growing towns of the West, including Ohio, Indiana, Pennsylvania, and upstate New York (Flexner 1975:81). Feminist ideas made no inroads in the South at this time (1975:79). In toto, feminists were not numerous. "Against every lady for reform in principle—whether extreme or mild—there was one bitterly opposed . . . and ten who were generally opposed out of indifference and absorption in their households" (Sinclair 1965:109). Its appeal was restricted to relatively well-educated, middle-class, white urban women, and only a minority of those. On the more narrow issues of legal reform in the property and guardianship rights of married women, and educational opportunity for women, support was more extensive. These reforms were perceived as serving the interests of conservative, wealthy families which were concerned about the ability of their daughters to maintain their own inheritance. In fact, in prewar years, the most progress for women by far was achieved in those two areas (Deckard 1983:247; Sinclair 1965:86ff), but such progress was often achieved in the absence of any feminist pressure (Banks 1981:36).

In general, we must conclude that feminism before the Civil War was an incipient movement. An ideology of feminism was well-developed, and an adequate leadership cadre existed. Followers numbered only a few, however.

The feminist leaders who emerged in the years before the Civil War were exceptionally long-lived; many did not die until the waning years of the century (e.g., Stanton, Anthony, and Stone). The decades after the war witnessed a gradual shift in ideology and a substantial increase in followers, as new leaders (most notably Carrie Chapman Catt) came to replace the old (Kraditor 1965:xi).

In chapter 1 we discussed the split between feminists and abolitionists that occurred over the Fourteenth Amendment wording, which included males only. The feminists had few sympathizers, however (Flexner 1975:148). In 1868 a feminist newspaper, *The Revolution*, was founded in New York City. It concerned itself with the full range of issues raised before the war, as well as the injustice of the Fourteenth and Fifteenth amendments (1975:153-54). By this time, feminists had become aware of the central importance of the vote as a tool if they were to achieve their general goals. However, in 1869 the women's movement split into two rival organizations: the National Woman Suffrage Association, led by Stanton and Anthony, and the American Woman Suffrage Association, led by Stone, Blackwell, and Livermore. The American began its own newspaper in Boston, the *Woman's Journal*. The two groups were to remain separate for twenty years. Basically, the Natonal maintained its radical orientation to a broad range of feminist issues and pushed for a national constitutional amendment. The American was far more conservative in orientation and, in an attempt not to alienate "influential sections of the community," did not raise issues pertaining to organizing working-class women, divorce, or religion. It concentrated on state-level campaigns for suffrage (some of which were successful in the West) but paid only lip service to a federal amendment (1975:154-56). The American even disassociated itself from a new Women's Declaration issued by the National in 1876, which was far less "strident" than that of 1848 (1975:174-75). They also disavowed Stanton's feminist *Woman's Bible*, published in the 1890s (Hole and Levine 1984:540; Sinclair 1965:198).

There was, in Flexner's words, a "steady trend" by the movement in the conservative direction, during the last twenty years of the nineteenth century (see also O'Neill 1969a:72). This paralleled a general social phenomenon, as growing fear of immigrants and radical working class agitation overtook the middle class. The feminist leadership became increasingly comprised of wealthy women and the professionally employed, and

> along with increased means . . . came greater influence and prestige. Twenty years had seen a profound change of public attitude. Woman suffrage was not yet generally accepted, but it was no longer considered the province of eccentrics and crackpots [Flexner 1975:224; see also Deckard 1983:265].

It is also interesting to note that in a study of 26 major suffrage leaders from 1890 to 1920, Kraditor (1965: appendix) found that they were considerably better educated, especially at the college level (62 percent), than the average woman of the time (1965:281). Moreover, nearly two-thirds had been employed some time during their lives (1965:282).

In 1890 the two organizations reunited, the old radical wing losing virtually all its influence in the process. Ideologically, the women's movement had become the Suffrage Movement (Hole and Levine 1984:540). We saw in chapter 1 that the Women's Christian Temperance Union (WCTU) argued for the vote on the basis of the moral superiority of women and on their need to defend the home. Pacifist women too argued that female suffrage would reduce the probability of war because of women's supposedly more gentle and humane nature. Other suffragists argued for the vote because of women's inherent interest in schools and in protective legislation for women and children (Flexner 1975:309). In short, the new ideological focus stressed the traditional roles of women and saw suffrage as a tool in pursuit of their traditional values, as well as a means by which to improve the moral tone of national life (Allen with Allen 1974:126: O'Neill 1969b: chap. 2). As Sinclair put it, "All sort of suffragists, outside of the radical fringe, were guilty of hallowing the virtues of motherhood at the expense of the free and single woman" (1965:239). In addition, most suffragists were racist, and northerners chose to support southern women's desire to restrict the enfranchisement of women to whites (Allen with Allen 1974: chap. 5; Flexner 1975:316–18; Jacoby 1975:129). Fear of blacks, workers, and especially immigrants, led many to argue for male and female suffrage restricted to the propertied and educated Sinclair 1965:236, chap. 22; see also O'Neill 1969a:73; 1969b:69ff). Despite such prejudice, many black women were active in the suffrage struggle (Allen with Allen 1974:160).

Working-class women had been most concerned with their pay, hours, and working conditions. We saw in chapter 1 that some attempted to organize unions or join the men's unions in pursuit of these goals, efforts that largely failed. After the turn of the century, they increasingly turned their attention to protective legislation and therefore to the need for women's suffrage (Flexner 1975:267). The Women's Trade Union League led the way in this, uniting feminist, suffrage, and working-class issues (see chap. 1; Jacoby 1975). From the vantage point of a later generation, protective legislation is often perceived as having served to "protect" women from a variety of good employment opportunities. From the perservice of women who suffered under the deplorable working conditions of the turn of the century, however, it was very progressive. On this issue most suffragists agreed, although some did perceive it as likely to further handicap working women (O'Neill 1969a:91).

Ideologically, the decades after the Civil War witnessed a transformation from a feminist movement, concerned with a broad set of issues, to an ameliorative movement concerned almost exclusively with the very narrow issue of women's suffrage (Banks 1981:135). The ideology underpinning the call for suffrage was traditional, mostly reiterating notions of women's greater morality and concerns for home and children (see O'Neill 1969b: chap. 2). Focus shifted from women's natural right to suffrage to the beneficent social effects which women's suffrage would entail (Kraditor 1965: chap. 2; O'Neill 1969a:72–73). This narrowing of focus and increasing ideological conservatism, in turn, resulted from, and further impelled the involvement of, a broad cross-section of American women in the movement. As feminism evolved into suffragism, an incipient movement became a mass movement. Radical feminism became the preserve of a small group of "bohemian" women, centered in Greenwich Village, and a small group of socialist feminists (Sochen 1973:19–23, chap. 2).

Where no feminist organizations per se existed in prewar days, the decades between the Civil War and the passage of the Nineteenth Amendment witnessed the growth of suffrage organizations, and especially of an alliance of other women's organizatons active in pursuing suffrage, in addition to the two already discussed (see O'Neill 1969b: esp. chap. 5). We have seen in chapter 1 that the huge WCTU actively worked for suffrage under Willard's leadership, in the process making it acceptable to conservative, religious women. So too did the Association for the Advancement of Women, founded in 1873 (Flexner 1975:116). The Women's Trade Union League was very active in pursuing suffrage (see chap. 1). The growing number of women's clubs, eventually united into the General Federation of Women's Clubs, formed in 1890, and having about 1,000,000 members by 1910 (O'Neill 1969a:48), along with charitable, missionary, church, trade-union, settlement house, and educational groups of women, began to support suffrage (Flexner 1975:179). The Grange threw its support to women's legal and political equality after 1885, as did the Association of Collegiate Alumnae, founded in 1882. In 1872 a short-lived Equal Rights Party was formed which endorsed a woman for president of the United States. Feminist newspapers sprang up in San Francisco, Portland, Oregon, and Utah (1975:162–66). In 1908 the New York Suffrage League was formed and soon had 19,000 members. A host of similar organizations rapidly grew up around the nation (1975:261–62). The Women's Political Union was organized in 1907 to attract working-class women to the cause (Sinclair 1965:300). A petition to Congress in 1909–10 fell far short of its goal of 1,000,000 signatures, but did get over 400,000. In 1915 500,000 signed such a petition, and in 1917 1,000,000. Thousands of women took part in various marches. In 1916 the National Woman's Party, later renamed the Woman's Party, formed in states where women were enfranchised, to work for suffrage elsewhere. It had as many as 40,000–50,000 members (Deckard 1983:277). On the eve of World War I, women representing all aspects of American life—rural and urban, industrial and farm workers, middle and working class, housewives and the professionally employed, supported women's suffrage (Flexner 1975:299).

Together, the National and the American Woman's Suffrage Associations probably numbered less than 10,000 in the 1870s (Sinclair 1965:194). The reunited group numbered but 17,000 in 1905 (Deckard 1983:277). At the turn-of-the-century, temperance women outnumbered suffragist women by 10 to 1 (1965:22). As DuBois put it, "The WCTU commanded an army . . . while woman suffrage remained a guerrilla force" (1975:69). O'Neill added, "For every active suffragist there were a hundred women engaged in club work, education, charity, and various reforms" (1969a:33). But by 1917 an estimated 2,000,000 women were members of the National American Woman Suffrage Association (Kraditor 1965:7), and countless millions others were involved in, or at least supported, the suffrage campaign; it had taken over from temperance as the major women's movement (Sinclair 1965:226).

In the nineteenth and early twentieth centuries the United States was not ready for a mass movement which questioned the entire gender role and sex stratification systems. A full range of radical feminist issues were publicly proclaimed, but they mostly fell on deaf, if not hostile ears. As Kraditor stated:

> The women suffrage movement had no official ideology. Its members and leaders held every conceivable view of current events and represented every philosophical position. Although they all agreed that women should have the right to vote, they disagreed on why they ought to have that right [1965:vii].

Only in narrowing the issue to suffrage and embedding the logic of this reform in traditional definitions of women's domestic and moral roles was a mass following achieved (Sochen 1973: chap. 1).

GREAT BRITAIN

The nineteenth-century British women's movement was relatively narrowly focused on suffrage and legal reform throughout most of its history (O'Neill 1969a:29–30). Starting with the 1792 publication of *A Vindication of the Rights of Women* by Mary Wollstonecraft, there were many British feminists, including several prominent males (e.g., John Stuart Mill). The various socialist ideologies, groups, and movements so common in nineteenth-century Britain often included feminist ideas, many quite radical and comprehensive (Rowbotham 1976: chaps. 8, 9). Yet a separate feminist movement, organizationally distinct from socialism, failed to emerge except around the issues of women's suffrage and legal reforms in divorce, child custody, inheritance, and property rights. Women also worked for better educational opportunity for their sex, but as an isolated issue—as they had in the early nineteenth-century United States. In general, Great Britain was several decades behind the United States in providing educational opportunities for women and in many areas of legal reform. However, middle-class and aristocratic women had partial, local voting rights by the middle of the nineteenth century. Also, beginning a few decades before their U.S. counterparts, British women had been publicly active in reform causes, such as the Reform and Chartist Movements discussed in chapter 1, and the Anti-Corn Law League and Antislavery Movement. As in the United States, many of the early feminists were active in antislavery groups and came from Quaker families (Banks, 1981:23–24; Paulson, 1973:21–22).

The conservative and ameliorative ideology of the turn-of-the-century U.S. movement characterized the entire history of the British movement, which began somewhat later than its U.S. counterpart (Banks 1981:33; Bouchier 1983:13). There were brief stirrings of activity in the late 1840s, but not until the late 1860s did it become even an incipient movement. The mass movement phase coincided with that of the United States, momentum developing rapidly after the turn of the century (O'Neill 1969a:30). Because of the ameliorative nature of the movement, and like the U.S. case, victory after World War I all but spelled the end of the women's movement in Britain.

A tiny handful of British women raised the issue of women's suffrage early in the nineteenth century (Banks 1981:33, 118). Recall that in the United States suffrage was the least agreed upon proposal at Seneca Falls and was not to become a central issue until after the Civil War. In Britain, the late 1840s and early 1850s saw the founding of "small female suffrage organizations" in Manchester and Sheffield. However, they remained local and "soon lapsed" (O'Neill 1969a:22; Sinclair 1965:280). Just as the word *male* had been introduced for the first time in the U.S. Constitution only with the Fourteenth Amendment, so in Britain was the vote explicitly denied females (not that most were actually permitted to vote earlier) with the First Reform Bill, passed in 1833, which extended the vote to middle-class males. In both cases, some degree of organized women suffrage activity followed upon these explicit denials of what had only been implicitly understood.

The 1850s and 1860s witnessed middle-class female activism for a series of reforms in the legal position of women, focused especially on the need for a Married Women's Property Bill (which was eventually passed in 1882). The *Englishwoman's Journal* was published by a small group of women, and it included in its concerns expanded educational and occupational opportunities for middle-class women, as well as property law reforms for married women. In her discussion of nineteenth-century British feminism, Caine (1982; see also Banks 1981:34 ff; Banks and Banks 1964: chap. 3) talked of a feminist movement at this time. Yet, she pointed out that these legal reforms were pursued separately by a series of organizations which lacked formal linkages (1982:539). Despite the lack of ties, they may be said to have constituted a reform *movement* in that there was an underlying theme of "full adult status" for women through equality before the law. However, those involved accepted the traditional division of the sexes into separate spheres, and legal reforms were sought "to enable women more adequately to carry out the role prescribed for them within the Victorian middle-class domestic ideal" (Caine 1982:544; see also Paulson 1973:26). They attempted neither to change "consciousness" nor to mobilize women "on a mass scale." Throughout the entire span of the British movement, including the mid-nineteenth century, most of the participants went to great lengths to appear and act like "ladies" (see Billington 1982:668–69). In our terminology, the activists of mid-century constituted an incipient ameliorative movement.

It was not until the late 1860s that organizational work began again in the struggle for female enfranchisement, after which it was continuous until victory in 1918. In the 1860s the London-based Women's Suffrage Committee was founded. In 1868 Lydia Becker organized the Manchester Women's Suffrage Committee, in which 5,000 women were soon involved. This was quickly followed by the formation of similar groups in Bristol and Edinburgh. These local groups were loosely federated under the National Society for Women's Suffrage (see Banks 1981: chap. 8). Becker edited a newspaper, *Woman Suffrage Journal*. In 1869 petitions totaling 61,475 signatures were presented to Parliament (Rosen 1974:9). However, activism was never very widespread and, with only a "few and occasional helpers," Becker almost single-handedly "kept the question of woman suffrage alive in England for the next twenty years." She found some support among female factory workers, as well as among a few middle-class and aristocratic women (O'Neill 1969a:71; Sinclair 1965:280–82).

From the 1860s to the 1880s a series of constitutional setbacks occurred in the struggle for female enfranchisement (Rowbotham 1976:50), which eventually served to galvanize more middle-class women. In 1889 the Woman's Franchise League was formed, which was concerned with the rights of married women, especially the vote, but including equality with males in divorce, child custody, and inheritance (1976:50; Rosen 1974:17). The Pankhursts, about whom more will be said shortly, were involved with forming this group. In 1897 the conservative National Union of Woman's Suffrage Societies was founded, which published the journal *The Common Cause*; its leader was Millicent Fawcett. This group, "which was about the same in social membership and policy as the National American Woman Suffrage Association" in the United States, pushed for female suffrage confined to the middle class (Sinclair 1965:383; see also O'Neill 1969a:86). In the same year, over a quarter of a million signatures appeared on a woman suffrage petition to Parliament (Strachey 1968:287).

Radical women, including socialists, raised a full range of feminist issues in the last years of the nineteenth century, concerning the economic structure and women's employment, the family and sexuality, as well as law and suffrage. Reforms of all kinds were proposed, particularly designed to benefit working-class women. As we saw in chapter 1, however, except for those women who renounced the socialist movement to focus on issues of their own sex, women's rights, including suffrage, remained a low priority among socialists (see also Banks 1981: chap. 4). Those who did depart socialism for the most part became associated with the rather narrowly focused suffrage movement. Banks concluded that although the socialists were the most "whole-hearted" feminists of any groups, they had the "smallest part to play in nineteenth century feminism" (1981:58). Of the pre-World War I era Rowbotham wrote: "Feminism in this period was diffuse, inchoate and contradictory. It was not a clearly worked out ideology" (1976:90). In the milieu of Victorian England, which was even more conservative than the United States at that time (Sinclair 1965:283), nonsocialist women were reluctant to raise many issues pertaining to the family and sexuality (see Rowbotham 1976:51). For the most part, they steered clear of association with the nascent family planning movement (Banks and Banks 1964: chap. 7). Like their U.S. counterparts, they did however press for an end to the double standard by arguing that men should be more chaste and cease to frequent prostitutes (Banks, 1981: chap. 5; Billington 1982:667–68).

At the turn of the century, a new boost to the suffrage cause came with the creation of the Women's Social and Political Union (WSPU) in 1903. Emmeline Pankhurst, along with her daughters Christobel and Sylvia, split from the Labour party in anger over their refusal to work actively for woman's suffrage, bringing with them many socialist women (Rowbotham 1976:81; see also chap. 1 of this book). They introduced the extremely militant tactics for which the British suffrage movement became known, although only the WSPU, among a number of suffrage organizations, employed them. The WSPU attracted factory girls and professional women, while other suffrage organizations "pressed more quietly for votes for women chiefly in middle class circles" (Sinclair 1965:285). A number of suffrage groups existed by this time, including the Women's Freedom League, the Women Writers Suffrage Union, the Northern Men's Federation for Women's Suffrage, the National Union of Women's Suffrage Societies, the Catholic Women's Suffrage Society, the Free Church League, the Jewish League, and the Scottish Churches League (see O'Neill 1969a:86; Rowbotham 1976:89; Strachey 1968:320). Despite the militancy of its tactics, the WSPU was ameliorative in its demands, and eventually turned its attention to courting conservative, aristrocratic women and the Tory party. Sylvia Pankhurst broke with her mother and sister and formed the East London Federation of Suffragettes. This group continued the original Pankhurst commitment to socialism and feminism, by working for a variety of reforms on behalf of working-class women and children, as well as suffrage.

The militant tactics of the WSPU created widespread publicity for the cause, encouraging many women to join it, and especially the more moderate groups (Lance 1979:52; Sinclair 1965: 286–87). The moderate wing of the movement was united under the National Union of Women's Suffrage Societies, led by Fawcett. In 1910 alone it added 60 new branches (Strachey 1968:320), and between 1909 and 1913 it quadrupled its membership (Morgan 1975:125). In one suffrage demonstration, a march from South Leeds to Hunslet Moor led by Emmeline Pankhurst, 100,000 people were involved (Rowbotham 1976:79). Weekly strategy meeting attendance of the WSPU went from 200 to 1907 to 1000 in 1908, while circulation of its official organ, *Votes for Women*, increased from 2000 in 1907 to 35,000 in 1910. During 1907 "the number of new [local] branches rose from 47 in February to 70 in August." And on June 21, 1908 participation in a female suffrage march to Hyde Park was estimated at up to 500,000 (Lance 1979:57–58; see also Rosen 1974:104).

Like the United States, as suffrage became a mass movement in the early twentieth century, it attracted women from all backgrounds, with very differing motives for wanting the vote, and very differing political views. A minority were ideological feminists. While it was largely a middle-class phenomenon, "support from working-class women certainly existed, despite the policy of courting upper-class women after 1907" (Rowbotham 1976:79). As in the United States, many middle-class women publicly pursued various moral and social reforms, including temperance, and often viewed the vote as a tool for that purpose (Banks 1981:122), although they were highly conservative in their definitions of women's domestic role and "proper sphere" (Holton 1979a, b). Others, especially working-class women and socialists, wanted the vote as a weapon to use in the struggle to ameliorate the employment-related problems and poverty that were the lot of industrially employed women (see Liddington and Norris 1978). Like their American sisters, many British women perceived protective legislation for working women as the only viable solution to their problems (Banks 1981: chap. 7, 123). Still others undoubtedly saw enfranchisement as a necessary step in the general emancipation of women. Finally, as in the United States, despite the existence of radical feminists espousing ideas concerning virtually all aspects of socio-cultural life, no underlying ideology of feminism unified suffrage activists, especially during the mass movement stage in the years prior to the ultimate success of their efforts (see Banks 1981:149; Harrison 1978:238). With so many, and sometimes conflicting motives prompting commitment to the cause of female suffrage, it is not surprising that unity evaporated with success. A mass ameliorative movement and an incipient feminist one characterized the years from the last few decades of the nineteenth century through World War I in Great Britain.

CANADA

In Canada, it is questionable whether women ever proceeded beyond the incipient stage to develop a mass movement on their own behalf. Moreover, even more so than in Britain, the movement was conservative and ameliorative throughout its relatively brief history. The same political and legal handicaps under which women belabored in the United States and Britain characterized Canadian women of the nineteenth and early twentieth centuries (Gorham 1976:28–29). For Canadians, however, it would appear that these inequities were eventually resolved (to the extent they were elsewhere) almost in the absence of widespread female complaint, and with the active support of a large number of influential and socially elite males. As Bacchi noted (1983:3), the Canadian suffrage movement began late and succeeded easily.

The suffrage movement in Canada was comprised primarily of a series of provincial-level organizations, only loosely federated at the national level. Typically, "a small group of devoted workers" (Cleverdon 1950:11) in one or two of the major cities in each province constituted the movement. Much more so than in the United States and Great Britain, influential males, including many Protestant clergy, much of the liberal press, and major labor and farm organizations, were highly active in the cause. Even more than in the United States, the WCTU not only provided many Canadian suffrage leaders, but constituted a very important source of organized suffrage activity. It "was often at work [on suffrage] many years before any full-fledged woman suffrage organization appeared on the scene" (ibid.). In addition, the National Council on Women, founded in 1893 as an umbrella organization for women's social and moral reform organizations, eventually became actively involved in the suffrage movement. It was by far the largest and most influential woman's organization in Canada (1950:12). In all, explicitly suffrage societies constituted a tiny minority of groups and organizations active in the pursuit of the franchise for women.

Although a few Canadians attended women's rights conventions in the United States as early as 1852, there was no organized activity until 1876, when Dr. Emily Stowe began the first suffrage society in Toronto. In fact, that organization was originally "disguised" as the Toronto Women's Literary Society, and it was not until 1883 that its real purpose became public, when its name changed to the Toronto Women's Suffrage Association. This group of less than 100 members accomplished relatively little. In 1889 it again changed its name to the Dominion Women's Enfranchisement Association, which despite pretensions as a national organization, remained more or less a Toronto-based one (Gorham 1976:32). Stowe's daughter, Dr. Stowe-Gullen, the first female physician trained in Canada, assumed the leadership of this group upon her mother's death, and in 1907 changed the name again to the Canadian Suffrage Association. In 1914 a second, highly conservative national organization emerged, the National Union of Woman Suffrage Societies of Canada, which also had its roots in Toronto.

Between 1877 and 1918, the date women won the national franchise, 22 provincial-level suffrage organizations sprang up across Canada (see Cleverdon 1950). They all were comprised of members of both sexes, and in some cases males led them. At their height, they had but about 10,000 members, comprising 0.2 percent of the adult population of Canada (Bacchi 1983:3). Bacchi compared this to the United States, where at the height of the movement 2,000,000 people, or 3 percent of the adult population, belonged to suffrage groups (1983:83).

Before the second decade of the twentieth century, the issue of women's suffrage met with widespread apathy. In Nova Scotia, a suffrage society began in 1895 and disbanded within a year, not to resurface until 1915. New Brunswick had a small one from 1894 until 1902. In Manitoba, a suffrage group of Icelandic immigrants emerged in 1870 and remained active, while an English-speaking group both formed and died in 1894 (Bacchi 1983:27–28). In British Columbia, the WCTU managed the issue in the absence of any suffrage organization until 1910 (1983:27; Cleverdon 1950:209). Prince Edward Island had no suffrage activity whatsoever (Cleverdon 1950:198), nor did Newfoundland until after World War I (1950:209).

In 1910 the National Council on Women officially endorsed woman's suffrage, giving impetus to the movement. By 1916 Toronto alone had 8 suffrage organizations (Bacchi 1983:32). A 1909 petition to the Ontario Parliament contained over 100,000 signatures (1983:34). In the second decade of the century the provincial Grain Growers Associations and various labor organizations took up the issue (1983:chap. 8), often forming women's auxiliaries to work on it (Cleverdon 1950:78). Prior to and during World War I, Canada experienced a suffrage movement that bordered on the mass level in appeal, although organizationally it was not distinct from a plethora of other groups. A distinct movement on behalf of women's rights simply never went beyond the incipient stage.

Bacchi (1983) argued that the small suffrage movement of the nineteenth and early twentieth centuries was at least led by feminists with an agenda for women that went beyond suffrage. Stowe and her daughter, Stowe-Gullen, were equally active in efforts to expand educational and employment opportunities for women, and they argued for equality within marriage and for the right of married women to pursue careers. However, their followers were more conservative, and after 1914, when the National Equal Franchise Union split from the Canadian Suffrage Association, the conservative, ameliorative bent of the movement was even more apparent (1983:39). In all, feminists constituted "a rather insignificant tributary to the mainstream" (1982:578), and were "isolated and unpopular" (Bacchi 1983:11).

Supporters of women's suffrage were, first and foremost, conservative, Anglo-Protestant members of the urban upper middle class, whose chief priority was strengthening the family through social and moral reform. The vast majority "emphasized mothers' contribution" to home and family, which was defined as very important, and "demanded political recognition on these grounds" (Bacchi 1983:11). They wanted no change in traditional gender roles (1983:24). Their chief slogan was "home protection" (1983:33), and the ballot was seen as a means to that end. In this they differed not at all from their counterparts in the United States and Great Britain (Gorham 1976:25). Given this orientation and the heavy involvement of males in the Canadian movement, Bacchi concluded that "the suffrage movement was less a 'woman's movement' than an attempt on the part of particular men and women, predominantly urban professionals and entrepreneurs, to supervise society" (1983:123). Presumably, women were interested in reforming laws pertaining to child protection, health, temperance, protective labor legislation for women, and in peace (Cleverdon 1950:10-11). Most did not even support issues of expanded educational and occupational opportunity for women (Bacchi 1983:3).

Bacchi studied 156 female and 44 male leaders of Canadian suffrage organizations. She found that 60 percent of these women were employed outside the home, mainly as professionals such as lawyers (39 or 25 percent), educators (23 or 15 percent), and physicians (19 or 12 percent). The housewives were married to professionals or businessmen, and the male leaders were similarly employed, with the addition of a number of clergy and members of Parliament. They were very well educated, as might be expected given their occupations. Among the women, 33 percent had an M.A. degree or higher, 17 percent a B.A., 13 percent went to normal school, 12 percent to "ladies colleges." They were virtually all Protestant, mainly Methodist, Presbyterian, and Anglican, and unlike the United States and Britain, Quakers comprised but 1.4 percent. Nearly two thirds were active in reform or charitable organizations, including 25 percent active in temperance (Bacchi 1983:4–7). They differed little from their U.S. counterparts discussed earlier.

After federal suffrage passed in 1918, provincial suffrage for women was passed everywhere but in Quebec in the ensuing few years, resulting in the end of the movement in most of Canada. Quebec had the longest suffrage campaign in Canada, not ending until success in 1940. The Canadian women's movement remained tiny compared to its United States and British counterparts. For the issue of suffrage alone, it bordered briefly on a mass movement—but not in all parts of Canada. It is likely that an ideologically broader feminist movement did not even reach the incipient stage.

NEW ZEALAND, AUSTRALIA, AND FINLAND

In the two societies which were first in the world to fully enfranchise women, the former British colonies of New Zealand (1893) and Australia (1903), women's movements were relatively small and experienced rather easy success. In New Zealand, organized suffrage activism began with the formation of the WCTU in 1885. Despite a membership of only 600, it spearheaded the campaign for suffrage and for other reforms for women in the ensuing decade. In 1891 it received the backing of women's labor unions for the suffrage issue (Grimshaw 1972:49), and in 1892 it provided the initiative for the formation by nontemperance women of Women's Franchise Leagues in a number of cities (1972:50, 109). Although it appears that relatively few women belonged to organizations working for suffrage and reforms in the status of women, in 1892 over 20,000 signatures appeared on a suffrage petition, and in the next year 30,000, or 25 percent of the adult female population, signed such a petition (1972:49, 86–87; see also Blackburn 1971:234–35; Paulson 1973:127–28). That year women were enfranchised.

When the various provinces federated as Australia in 1901, in some (e.g., South Australia and Western Australia) women were already fully enfranchised, and in all, women were partially enfranchised. Within two years of unification, full suffrage was extended to women in all parts of the new nation, without much ado. The suffrage struggle, such as it was, existed at the provincial level during the decade of the 1890s. In the 1880s and 1890s women's suffrage organizations formed in all of the provinces (Summers 1975:350), and were especially active in the more populous areas of Victoria and New South Wales (Blackburn 1971:231; Paulson 1973:125). They were comprised almost entirely of middle-class women (Summers 1975:353). The WCTU, which arrived in Australia in 1881 and had chapters in all provinces by 1887, was also active in the suffrage campaign (1975:351). In 1891 the Victorian WCTU was able to garner 30,000 signatures on a women's suffrage petition (Evans 1977:60). Besides suffrage, these organizations sought a series of legal reforms in the status of women, much like those sought in other English-speaking nations, and manifested special interest in abolishing the sexual double standard by requiring male monogamy and abolishing prostitution (Summers 1975:11).

In both nations, the basis upon which women's suffrage was sought was the same as in the United States and Great Britain: the ballot was to be

> a means of increasing woman's efficiency in imposing good, moral values upon society. . . . The suffragists expressed no desire to upset traditional sex roles but promised to extend the familial influence into politics to make society more temperate and moral [Bacchi 1982:576; see also Summers 1975: chap. 11].

In general, sympathetic male politicans made moot a movement for women before one could get beyond the beginning stages (see Evans 1977:62). At least relative to other nations, no "genuine feminist movement" (Paulson 1973:122) emerged in these two nations. This interpretation is disputed for New Zealand by Grimshaw (1972) and for Australia by Summers (1975). However, they offer no data to demonstrate that a woman's movement of any substantial size emerged in either nation.

The Finnish experience was similar to that of Australia and New Zealand. Finland was ruled by Russia, but only in 1899 did the Russians impose their laws on Finland. This, in turn, sparked a general nationalist movement by the Finns, and in 1905 they won the right to their own constitution. Prior to this, Finnish women had organized into two associations, the Finnish Women's Association (1884) and the Union of Women's Rights (1890). Both were cultural and moral reform groups comprised of upper- and middle-class women (Edmondson 1984:117–18). They raised the issues of higher education for women, married women's property rights, and an end to state-regulated prostitution (Evans 1977:87). They raised the suffrage issue for the first time in 1879 when the Women's Association petitioned the Diet, and then again at a meeting of 1,000 women in 1904. When the Finns received autonomy from Russia the next year, the Marxist Social Democrats, who had been most active in the fight against Russia, were a highly influential party. They had been committed to universal suffrage, so, when some women agitated for the right to vote, one of the first things the new Parliament did when it met in 1906 was to give it to them (Edmondson 1984:118–19). Once again movement activism was rendered moot virtually before it could begin, by sympathetic, powerful males.

NORWAY

There is very little written in English about the Norwegian women's movement in the era under discussion. It would appear that an incipient movement did develop, beginning in the 1880s, which was largely ameliorative in focus and which lasted somewhat beyond the winning of full female suffrage in 1913.

The woman's issue was first raised throughout Scandinavia by feminist novelists during the 1850s (Paulson 1973:98; Rasmussen 1982:648). No organized activity emerged, however, for another 30 years. Middle-class women began to organize for social reform purposes with the 1884 founding in Oslo (then Kristiania) of the Norwegian Association for the Rights of Women (Blom 1982:569). During the next 20 years housewives organized their own associations which, along with other female reform groups, united under the National Council of Women in 1904. None of these groups were feminist (1982:569–70), and apparently none ever worked for woman's suffrage.

At the same time, feminists and socialist women were also organizing, and both of these branches supported suffrage and reforms in the rights of women. In 1884 the Norwegian Feminist Society was founded to seek improvement in the educational and occupational opportunities of women and to better the legal and personal status of married women. It tentatively supported suffrage for women at the local level as well (Rasmussen 1982:649). Three years later it began a feminist bimonthly journal, *New Frontiers*. Meanwhile, in 1885 the Norwegian Suffrage League was formed in order "to see the suffrage issue moved to center stage" (ibid). In the ensuing decades it resembled very closely its U.S. counterpart, with which it was in touch and which it sought to emulate (ibid.). In 1892 a WCTU-sponsored society was established in Norway as well (Evans 1977:83).

The result of the activity of these groups was that several hundred sympathetic persons, among them leading professionals and politicians, signed petitions supporting the goals of the Norwegian Feminist Society (Rasmussen 1982:649). It appears that feminism and the more ideologically limited suffrage movement won only "the support of a minority of Norwegian women." Although influential enough to win suffrage for women earlier than all but three other nations (Australia, Finland, and New Zealand), in terms of numbers, Norway never had much of a movement (Blom 1982:571). Moreover, both liberal feminists and socialists agreed that the chief responsibility of married women was the home and care of children, and neither fought for the right of such women to work (1982:573). Based on this scanty evidence, we conclude that Norway experienced at most an incipient, ameliorative women's movement.

SWEDEN, DENMARK, AND ICELAND

In the closing decades of the nineteenth century, Sweden, Denmark, and Iceland all witnessed the emergence of relatively large, ameliorative women's movements. In general, by the 1870s women in these three societies had a variety of rights and opportunities denied women elsewhere, including better educational opportunities, extensive employment rights for single women, and some limited political rights. Available literature on these movements is confined to one source (Evans, 1977). What follows is therefore only a brief description of each.

Sweden

In the 1870s Sweden experienced a temperance movement, along with the establishment of the Association for Married Women's Property Rights, founded in 1873. Since Swedish women already had a limited, municipal franchise, this organization not only worked to influence the legislature (with little success), but also on encouraging women to vote in local elections. An organization oriented chiefly to economic and educational opportunities for women and to charitable causes was begun in 1885. Suffrage (at the national level) became the central women's issue with the founding of the Swedish Woman's Suffrage Association in 1902. By 1907 it had over 10,000 members in 127 branches, and by 1912, 13,000 members in 187 local associations. A 1907 women's suffrage petition contained 142,000 signatures (all information taken from Evans 1977:71-75). These numbers should be seen within the context of national population figures. At the turn of the century there were only 1.7 million females over the age of 15 in Sweden (Mitchell 1975:60; computed by authors from data provided).

Denmark

The organized women's movement in Denmark dates to 1871 with the founding of the Danish Women's Association. As in Sweden, it focused on economic opportunities, especially for married women. But by 1883 it numbered only 500 members. The association was internally torn over the issues of opposition to state-regulated prostitution and women's suffrage. As a result, two new organizations spun off: the Danish Women's Progress Association (1886) and the Danish Women's Suffrage Society (1888). By 1890 the movement in general was endorsing temperance, sexual purity, and women's suffrage. However, the suffrage society never grew beyond 200 members and dissolved in 1897, at the same time that the Progressive Association also fell apart. In 1898 yet another organization was founded, the Danish Women's Associations' Suffrage Federation, followed in 1900 by the National League for Women's Suffrage. By 1910 the various women's movement groups collectively numbered about 30,000 members, in a society with a female population of less than 1,500,000 (all information taken from Evans 1977:76-81).

Iceland

The Icelandic Women's Association was formed in 1894 to press for educational and economic rights for women. In a country with a population of only 50,000, by 1895 this organization was able to garner 2200 signatures on a petition. In 1907 the Icelandic Women's Rights Association was founded and focused on political rights for women. Within a year it numbered 400 members in 5 branches, and soon gathered 12,000 signatures on a female enfranchisement petition (all information taken from Evans 1977:89–90).

In all three countries, total population was quite small, and therefore, despite total numbers of activists that appear small, they constituted a significant proportion of their respective populations. We therefore conclude that all three nations experienced intermediate to mass movements. The focus of these movements seems to have been the same as that of other Western European and North American societies, namely, ameliorative, focusing on education, moral reform, political rights, and legal reforms especially in the rights of married women.

HOLLAND AND BELGIUM

The two nations of the Lowlands experienced very different histories in terms of women's movements. The available material is very limited and what follows is a brief description of each, taken from Evans (1977:134–35).

Holland

Dutch women mounted an active suffrage movement just after the turn-of-the-century. In 1894 the first Dutch female physician founded the Association for Women's Suffrage. By 1909 it numbered 6500 members in 62 local branches, grew to 100 branches with 10,000 in 1911, and 14,000 members in 108 branches by 1913. A separate Dutch Association for Women's Suffrage, founded in 1907, numbered 4800 members in 62 branches in 1913. At the turn of the century, the Netherlands numbered but 1.7 million females over the age of 15 (computed by authors from data in Mitchell 1975:53). We therefore conclude that, as in the three nations just discussed, the Dutch experienced a movement of intermediate proportions.

Belgium

Unlike Protestant Holland, Catholic Belgium failed to develop even an incipient women's movement. Liberals and left-wing Belgians feared that women would "swell the clerical vote" and even socialists failed to back women's suffrage. In 1910 the only suffrage group, the Feminist Union, had a total of 117 members in three branches.

FRANCE

Feminism, both as an ideology and as activity in the pursuit of that ideology, had a longer history in France than virtually any other society. Yet an organized movement appears to have existed only from the 1860s to the outbreak of World War I, and it is not clear that the movement can be considered as ever having become mass in appeal. While clearly of very broad and diverse ideology, French feminism was unlike other movements of this era considered to this point in relegating suffrage to minor importance. Perhaps partially as a result, French women did not receive the vote until 1944. The English literature concerning this movement has concentrated on socialist-feminism, and we could find relatively little material on the middle-class branch of the movement. In fact, the available literature emphasizes French feminist thinkers and writers far more than movement organization and activity.

French feminism dates to the French Revolution of the turn of the nineteenth century. During the Revolution, in 1790, a number of women's political clubs were formed because females were excluded from male revolutionary clubs. The next year witnessed the first feminist magazine, which proclaimed the equality of the sexes. The clubs were suppressed by the government in 1793. During the entire first half of the nineteenth century a number of prominent female writers propounded feminist ideas (Robertson 1982: chap. 19). The 1830s witnessed another flurry of feminist activity, concurrent with general social upheaval. The *Women's Tribune*, a feminist-proletariat paper, was founded in 1832, but banned two years later. Between 1836 and 1838 the *Women's Gazette*, a moderate, middle-class feminist publication, argued for the right of women to petition the government for reforms. During the 1830s and 1840s, feminism was primarily intertwined with, and advocated by, a number of utopian socialist groups, such as those associated with Fourier, St. Simon, and Cabet (Paulson 1973:47, 53–54). The next round of specifically feminist activity occurred during the revolutionary upheavals of 1848, when the first feminist daily, *Women's Voice*, appeared and advocated woman's suffrage, along with equality in civic privileges, property rights, education, employment, marriage, and even armed service obligations (Robertson 1982:288). A number of revolutionary feminist clubs also appeared. Within a few months, with the cessation of the Revolution came the repression of feminist activities (this chronology of events taken from Marks and Court-ivron 1980: introduction 2). In short, each wave of French revolutionary activity brought with it a flurry of feminist activism, which was quickly quashed by the authorities in the aftermath of revolution. No organizational continuity linked these separate outbreaks.

Organized feminism began as the Second Empire was beginning to crumble in the late 1860s (Boxer 1982). In 1869 a magazine, *Women's Rights*, was founded which argued for legal rights for women. In that same year, the League for Women's Rights began, under the leadership of Deraismes, but it "awakened no great interest" (Boxer 1978:76). The year 1871 saw the establishment of the Third French Republic as well as the Women's Union, which was oriented to organizing working women into syndicates (unions), and was led by the socialist-feminist Mink. These two organizations represent the two divergent branches of French feminism which were to continue up to World War I. A third, explicitly suffrage organization also appeared under the leadership of Auclert (1982:553), in 1882 (Evans 1977:129). Feminists in all three branches were agreed on the need to remove the educational, economic, and legal disabilities of women. Furthermore, they were all republicans (i.e., antimonarchists) who were therefore also anticlerical. Except for the suffragists, most opposed female enfranchisement because of the highly religious, hence promonarchy stance of the majority of French women (see Boxer 1982:553). It was not until 1896 that the demand for woman's suffrage even appeared on the agenda of the frequently held feminist congresses (1982:554).

In 1874 the government forbade public discussion of women's rights as "subversive and immoral" (Robertson 1982:344). When, in 1876, the Society for the Amelioration of the Condition of Women was founded, it was met with general apathy. In response to 17,000 circulars it sent out, the organization received only 2 responses (1982:345). Organized feminism languished during the rest of the 1870s and 1880s. In 1889 new life was breathed into it by two successful conferences on the rights of women, which called for a variety of legal reforms and equal pay for teachers (1982:345). Robertson claimed that the "popular woman's movement in France could be said to have been . . . launched at this time" (1982:345). During the next decade a feminist theater was formed and a women's daily paper, *La Fronde* (1897), began, reaching a circulation of 200,000, and advocating issues of legal reform and voluntary motherhood (1982:345). Ironically, several Catholic feminist organizations favoring woman's suffrage organized in the 1890s, and they mobilized more support for this issue than any other branch of the movement (Boxer 1982:554). But of the "numerous feminist associations founded" (1982:554) up until 1914, most continued to emphasize reforms other than suffrage.

After the late 1890s, middle-class feminists and socialist-feminists began to come into manifest conflict (Boxer 1982:554). Despite seeming support for sexual equality, in fact late nineteenth century French socialists were deeply divided over the "women question." At any rate, there were no more than about 1000 female members of the unified Socialist Party, or 3 percent of the total membership

(Boxer 1978:78-79). When some of these women organized in the late 1890s into the Socialist Feminist Group, they received no support from the party (1978:75). Most female socialists, like their comrades elsewhere, subordinated their feminism to their socialism (see chap. 1 and Boxer 1978:79). In 1901 the Union of Socialist Women of the Seine was formed and began a journal, *Socialist Women*, but it had "difficulties in attracting women." By 1905 socialist-feminist groups were defunct (1978:94, 96).

The middle-class feminist movement directed its energies toward such issues as married women's rights to their own earnings, to testify in civil suits, and authority over their own children; some advocated female suffrage. They also argued for paternity suits by unwed mothers, equal penalties for adultery, and the abolition of legalized prostitution. In pushing for such reforms they were able to win "considerable support from a large proportion of middle- and upper-class French women, and several parties in the Chamber of Deputies," and by 1900 feminism was "fashionable" among educated bourgeoisie (Boxer 1978:95; 1982:554). They won several of the reforms they advocated. These feminists were well educated, often Protestant, either employed as teachers, or were well-to-do ladies (1982:554). They also demanded equal employment opportunities, inasmuch as they were well-educated and sought professional opportunities denied them. This became the crux of their increasing conflict with socialist-feminists, who demanded protective legislation for working women, inasmuch as their concern was for exploited industrial workers. In fact, the Socialist Party wanted to raise the wages of male workers to a level where their wives could leave the labor force to care for the home and family (1982, 1978). The result was that virtually no working-class support for feminism developed (1978:106), and no movement for women that crossed class lines ever emerged (1982:556).

At one time or another, French feminists raised issues pertaining not only to legal reform and suffrage, employment and educational opportunities, but also to religion, sexuality, the family, in short, to every major social institution. Feminist writings advocated free love; equality within marriage, including sharing domestic work; and birth control. Some even argued for drafting women into the armed services. In the range of issues considered, they were ahead of women in most other nations (Robertson 1982:349-50, 281).

In the absence of data concerning numbers of organizational members, petition-signers, and marchers, we are unable to determine whether it became a mass feminist rather than an incipient movement. Boxer argued that it "remained less a movement than a mosaic of leaders and groups divided by class, religion and personal rivalry" which was "estranged from the majority of Frenchwomen" (1982:551). However, it was she who stated, as quoted earlier, that at the turn-of-the-century feminism was "fashionable" in the educated middle class. Several pieces of information suggest that the movement was somewhere between incipient and mass, and certainly smaller than movements in the United States and Great Britain in terms of the relative proportion of women involved.

Robertson (1982:329) explicitly stated that there was less feminist agitation in France than in England or Germany. Socialist women, not to mention socialist-feminists, were very few in number during the entire time in question, as we noted earlier. Liberal feminists were described as mostly Protestant, but as a Catholic nation, few French were Protestant. It is likely that France had a significantly smaller relative proportion of well-educated, urban, middle-class women, namely, the type of women found in women's movements, than the United States or Britain, an issue to be explored in chapter 6. So, even if it was fashionable among them, their relative numbers might have been insufficient to have constituted a mass movement. Moreover, the liberal branch was heavily ameliorative in focus, demanding primarily reforms in the legal status of women. Boxer called their ideology "familial feminism," by which they "sought to achieve 'equality of difference' or 'equivalence' based on a clearly defined sexual separation of spheres" (1982:554). We conclude, therefore, that France experienced a truly feminist movement, which was incipient for most of its history, and possibly midway on a continuum of incipient to mass in the two decades before World War I. However, as in other nations, as the movement grew in appeal, the ideology narrowed and became more strictly ameliorative.

RUSSIA

Unlike most Western European nations and the United States, at the turn-of-the-century Russia had just begun to industrialize; its populace was still overwhelmingly comprised of peasants. Moreover, neither sex had any political rights under the autocratic czarist government. The status of Russian women, however, barring the serfs, was in almost all respects similar to that of their Western counterparts (Edmondson 1984:11). Probably because of the considerably less developed socioeconomic and political condition of Russia, unlike many of the European and North American countries, Russian feminism was, for the most part, inextricably bound up with broader issues of human rights and general social liberation (1984:9–10). Russian feminism, which was ideologically relatively broadly focused, never reached the mass movement phase before the 1917 Revolution. It was manifest in two relatively distinct factions: within the radical and socialist movements, which we discussed in chapter 1, and as "bourgeois feminism" (see Edmondson 1984 for a detailed discussion of this faction).

After the Bolshevik coup, the party organized local women's groups called *zhenotdel*. Their purpose was to educate and "emancipate" women throughout the Soviet Union. Stites (1980:26 ff.) defined the period of their existence as a continuation of the prerevolutionary feminist movement. He therefore dated the end of the movement at 1930, when Stalin abolished the *zhenotdel*. Stites also pointed to similar organizations and "feminist movements" in post–Communist Revolution China, Vietnam, Cuba, and Yugoslavia (1980:27). Others (e.g.,

Edmondson 1984:169; Lapidus 1977) have defined the end of the feminist movement in Russia as concurrent with the Bolshevik coup, as do we. After their
coup, Bolsheviks faced the need to win from the masses of women "their active
support for the October revolution and mobilize them behind official Bolshevik
policy" (Heitlinger 1979:56). Lapidus (1977:137) argued that in the USSR, sexual
equality "has meant an equal liability to mobilization." The *zhenotdel* were the
mechanism for such state and party mobilization of women before 1930. Although they probably did help in the overall process of emancipating Russian
women (see Heitlinger 1979; Stites 1980),

> because Soviet political institutions have been designed to inhibit the aggrega-
> tion and representation of group interests at the societal level, the responsive-
> ness of the Soviet leadership to the special needs of women has not . . . been the
> result of autonomous, organized action by women on their own behalf [Lapidus
> 1977:137].

By *definition* a social movement is a "grass-roots" phenomenon, organized by
interested citizens rather than by the political authorities of a nation. We therefore will not include in this book a discussion of government- or party-organized
groups designed to mobilize, to educate, or even to fight for the rights of women.
We are not arguing that such groups fail a litmus test of "feminist"; they may or
may not depending on the case. Rather, we contend that they are simply not social movements. Therefore, for our purposes, the feminist movement in Russia
ended with the Bolshevik coup.

The woman's issue surfaced in Russia in the 1850s, just after the disastrous
Crimean War (Edmondson 1984:10; Lapidus 1978:27; Stites 1978:chap. 2). At
that time there was general social agitation, especially oriented to ending serf-
dom (which was done in 1861). Included as part of this agitation were women's issues, especially pertaining to educational and occupational opportunities. During the following decade, many daughters of the wealthy became publicly active
in one of two different movements. On the one hand, there were the radical anarchist and nihilist groups discussed in chapter 1. Women were very active in
these, especially the Chaikovskii Circle, The People's Will, and the Pan-Russian
Social Revolutionary Organization. These women were highly unconventional
and sought their own personal and economic independence. However, they ultimately sacrificed their feminism completely to the general radical movement
(Engel 1978, 1980; see also Stites 1978: chap. 5).

Other women in the 1860s became involved in organizations which advocated
educational opportunities for women, especially at the higher levels, and for professional employment opportunities as well (Edmondson 1984:15; Lapidus
1978:28; Stites 1977:56; 1978 chap. 3). They were also involved in a variety of
charitable activities, through which their sympathies for the poor were developed. Because of this, they were sympathetic to the more radical groups and
women, although not directly allied with them (Stites 1980). Since men were not
yet enfranchised in nineteenth-century Russia, the specific issue of woman's suf-

frage was not raised, and at the end of the century, "feminism in Russia remained largely apolitical" (Edmondson 1984:20; see also Lapidus 1978:27). Moreover, substantial educational and occupational gains for women in the 1880s and 1890s led many women to abandon feminism altogether (Edmondson 1984:20).

In the nineteenth century, Russian women were legally barred from membership in organizations that were other than philanthropic or educational in purpose. A group of St. Petersburg women, many feminist, organized the Russian Women's Mutual Philanthropic Society in 1893. While its more radical members soon departed, this group was to prove important to the feminist cause in ensuing years (see Edmondson 1984:20–21). In the first few years of the twentieth century, a number of "small 'women's mutual aid societies' and educational or philanthropic associations" were established in provincial towns, but these were not involved in political protest (1984:31). An avowedly feminist newspaper, the *Women's Herald*, was begun in 1904, but it had a "negligible" impact on the public. In addition, most activist women rejected it because it put specific feminist demands, such as equal pay, maternity benefits, and issues of male dominance, ahead of more general issues of human liberation (1984:29). In general, in the years 1900–1904 "the development of the women's movement did not match the expansion of political acitivity in society at large" (1984:27). Indeed, in 1904 "a number of women came to St. Petersburg . . . in search of active women's groups which would serve as a nucleus for a political union" (1984:31). They found only the Philanthropic Society.

The Revolution of 1905, which resulted in limited male suffrage and the establishment of a Parliament (the Dumas), also sparked a renewed and invigorated feminist movement. Indeed, Stites (1978:191) claimed that there was no women's movement before 1905. Early in 1905, a petition, signed by 150 St. Petersburg women demanding female suffrage, began "a flood of demands by women for political rights" (Edmondson 1984:5). In February 30 people in Moscow established the All-Russian Union of Equal Rights for Women, a group which soon oriented itself to larger issues of liberation for all Russians (1984:36). By the end of April, this rapidly growing group was in contact with 18 other such groups around Russia. The Union held a national congress in May where, besides suffrage, they endorsed other feminist demands such as equal rights for peasant women in future agrarian reforms, coeducation at all levels, legal equality of the sexes, admission of women to all occupations, protective legislation for women workers, and the abolition of special laws concerning prostitution (Stites 1978:199–200). By the fall of 1905 the Union had 54 local groups and "several thousand" members, by 1907, 80 branches and 12,000 members (Evans 1977:121). The Union gained support for women's suffrage from various labor and peasant groups which also sprang up during 1905. The Philanthropic Society also became active in petitioning for women's suffrage and for other feminist issues. The Union competed with the socialists in trying to recruit female factory workers and domestic servants; neither was very successful. Throughout the year, the Union also supported a variety of broad reform issues, but was torn by internal dissension between those who put feminist issues first and those whose priority was general liberation (Edmondson 1984:40–47; Stites 1977). The feminists lost control in October 1905, after which "there was often little time for feminist propaganda" (Edmondson 1984:51). Nonetheless, in 1906 a schism occurred and the radical and socialist women departed the Union. Besides the Union and the Philanthropic Society, 1905 witnessed activism by other, newly formed women's groups. The specifically feminist, less leftist Women's Progressive Party was formed, and published the only feminist journal in Russia between 1905 and 1907. In turn, the All-Russian League of Women split off from that group.

Despite all this organizational activity, in 1905–6 feminists failed to establish their concerns "as one of the burning issues in Russian life"; they had but "slender" support (Edmondson 1984:53, 60). Two petitions for woman's suffrage in 1906 garnered 4000 and 4500 signatures, respectively (1984:63), while a 1907 petition from all over Russia had about 20,00 signatures (1984:79). At that time the population of Russia was in excess of 125,000,000 (Department of Commerce and Labor, 1909). Women therefore failed to gain suffrage when the men did in the aftermath of the revolt, and within a few years the return of police repression almost totally silenced the movement. The Union, which was the most dynamic of all the groups, never expanded beyond the "urban intelligentsia," despite major efforts to do so. The feminists were for the most part urban, middle class, well-educated, and often professionally employed (Stites 1977:58), not unlike their counterparts elsewhere. However, most urban, educated Russian women were never drawn to feminism (1978:231). In the years before World War I, the remaining women's groups became less generally radical and more focused on women's demands than they had been in 1905. The Russian League of Equal Rights for Women was the primary organization, but it never numbered more than 2000 members, usually about 1500, and had but four local chapters (Edmondson 1984:133; see also Stites 1978: chap. 7). It was a rather cautious organization which stayed away from political issues, rather emphasizing the need for legal reforms on behalf of women (Edmondson 1984:136).

The Social Democratic Party, consisting of both the Bolsheviks and the Mensheviks, began its growth with the 1905 Revolution. As we saw in chapter 1, they were committed to sexual equality in principle, but it was a low priority and it was assumed that the end of class inequality would automatically "solve" women's problems. An increase in industrial workers who joined the party after 1905 resulted in a decrease in the proportion of middle-class intelligentsia, and in turn, the proportion of female members. In 1917 only 14.3 percent of party members were female, and by 1922 that had declined yet further to 8 percent (Lapidus 1978:39). When, in 1907, the famous socialist feminist, Aleksandra Kollontai, tried to organize working women by establishing the Society of Mutual Aid for Women Workers, 300 members were attracted, only 10 of whom were working women (Clements 1979:46). She received little support or encouragement from Bolshevik or Menshevik leaders before the Revolution.

The last gasp of the feminist movement in Russia occurred as the Revolution was dawning. In 1917 the newly established Constituent Assembly called for civil equality but ignored the issue of sex. The League of Equal Rights protested and organized a march of 40,000 women (in a nation of about 180,000,000 people; Department of Commerce and Labor 1920). Women were hastily enfranchised, after which the avowedly feminist Republican Union of Democratic Women's Organizations was formed to pursue further change (Edmondson 1984:165–66). Edmondson (1984:172) argued that Russian feminists were not simply suffragists but were deeply interested in such issues as the rights of women within the family, including divorce law, sexual relations, child upbringing, education, and the fundamental nature of the sexes. "They saw education, employment and civil and political rights as a means of establishing their autonomy" (1984:172–73). The issue soon became moot, however, as the Bolsheviks dispersed their organizations and closed down their journals. Little is known of what happened to the women themselves (1984:169).

Given the immensity of Russia on the one hand, and the numbers cited as organizational members or petition-signers, on the other, we conclude that prerevolutionary Russia never experienced a mass movement on behalf of women (see Stites 1978:227 for a comparison with women's movements elsewhere). One might have developed in the aftermath of the 1905 uprising, but the return of police repression, if nothing else, was an effective deterrent. Likewise, one might have developed after the 1917 Revolution, but for the Bolshevik coup. However, chapter 6 will provide information that points to the low probability of mass feminist movement activity in Russia at either time. For the most part, the issues pursued were those of legal reform and, for a brief period, political equality. Often radical in their ties to revolutionary groups and movements, nonetheless the demands made specifically on behalf of women were basically ameliorative after 1905.

GERMANY

Turn-of-the-century Germany experienced both the most well-developed feminist movement within socialism and the most timid and conservative middle-class women's movement of any European society. A thoroughly feminist ideology probably never appealed to more than a small minority of activist socialist women, and therefore did not go beyond the incipient stage. A more ameliorative ideology, focused on educational opportunity, legal reforms, and issues of male sexual morality, but not on women's suffrage, probably reached a mass movement level. German class and religious antagonisms were so great that the two branches of the women's movement never cooperated and no unified movement on behalf of women emerged (Stephenson 1975:25).

Like France, several of the German states experienced revolutionary upheaval in 1848, and part of the activism was feminist (Robertson 1982:372). During that year, a short-lived feminist newspaper was founded by Luise Otto in Saxony, as were numerous "democratic women's associations" or "women's educational associations." By 1850 they had been repressed by the police, and laws were passed in most German states prohibiting women from attending political meetings or from joining political organizations. These laws were to remain in effect until 1908 (Gerhard 1982:562).

The middle-class women's movement in Germany may be said to have begun six years before German unification, when Otto founded the General German Women's Association (ADF) in Leipzig in 1865 (Evans 1976:24; Stephenson 1975:13), and called the first women's conference in Germany. The purpose of that organization was to create educational programs for girls, especially the poor. Otto wanted to see young females raised with a sense of courage and independence, and she also wanted the development of "feminine" jobs appropriate for women (Robertson 1982:375). By 1877 the organization numbered between 11,000 and 12,000 members (1982:375). At about the same time the ADF was founded, a group called *Letteverein* was also, and it too was dedicated to creating educational and occupational opportunities for women (1982:377). These early women's groups were quite timid in that they not only failed to advocate equal political rights for women, but they also failed to advocate legal changes in the rights of women, until 1876. At that time the ADF first petitioned for the rights of married women to control their own property and income, to have authority over their own children, and to enjoy a legal status independent of their husbands (Evans 1976:25). In general, their aim was not sexual equality; they accepted the traditional stereotype of women as subordinate and motherly. They wished to enoble, rather than reject that role (1976:26).

In the 1880s the women's movement, which was little more than a charitable and social welfare movement, was "numerically weak, fragmented and conservative" (Evans 1976:30). In 1894 the Federation of German Women's Association (BDF) was founded, comprised of 34 organizations of all sorts. It rapidly became the major German women's association, numbering 50,000 members in 65 organizations in 1895, and 70,000 members in 137 organizations in 1901 (1976:37). Most of its constituent organizations were social welfare and charitable in purpose. At the same time, the Women's Association Reform was established, to pursue equal educational opportunity, and in the ensuing few years a number of other groups of like purpose sprang up. The feminist newspaper *The Women's Movement*, founded in 1895, advocated equal rights for women in many fields. As the 1890s wore on, the BDF gradually became more radical, meaning that it adopted such positions as opposing legal brothels, demanding an end to the sexual double standard through greater male chastity, and reforming women's prisons. Such positions characterized the conservative branch of most other European and North American women's movements of the time. Around the turn-of-the-century the more radical women of the BDF left to form the Union of Progressive Women's Associations. Not until 1902 was the women's suffrage issue supported in any fashion by the BDF. In that same year the German Union for Women's Suffrage was born, which allied itself with the Union of Progressive Women's Associations. They sought the vote not as an end in itself, but as a means to bring about a variety of social and moral reforms, such as temperance, peace, child protection, and the end of prostitution (1976:72, 76). While smaller, it differed little from the major U.S. and British women's suffrage groups of the time.

In 1908 it became legal throughout Germany for women to organize politically. The Suffrage Union, which in 1908 numbered but 2458, grew to 10,000 by 1914 (Evans 1976:93). Evans estimated that the entire suffrage movement numbered only about 14,000 in 1914, including about 10 percent males. It "was in no sense a mass movement" (1976:96). Internacine battles led to two splits within the Suffrage Union, and on the eve of World War I, the movement was in a state of total disarray (1976:100).

In general, the major turn-of-the-century issue for middle-class women's groups was state-regulated prostitution. Some feminists were advocating free love, and they were thus led to raise questions concerning the concept of illegitimacy, the nature of marriage, and of divorce law. In 1904 these women formed the League for the Protection of Motherhood and Sexual Reform, which in 1908 numbered 3726 members in 10 local chapters (Evans 1976:120 ff.). They supported abortion, contraception, and generally advocated women's control over their own bodies (1976:138). The middle-class women's movement polarized over this issue, with the League and the BDF opposing one another. The BDF ultimately won, further increasing the conservative nature of the German women's movement (1976:131–37). The radical organizations within the movement, the League, the Progressive Women's Association, and the Suffrage Union, all gradually declined.

Meanwhile, by 1908 the BDF numbered 150,000 members, and by 1912 it claimed to represent 500,000 women, although Evans (1976:193) claimed it was probably about 280,000. It was now "officially committed to the 'improvement of the female sex in economic, legal and spiritual matters' " (1976:146). Concretely, it supported: (a) reform in the Civil Code in the direction of equality within marriage, including the demand that the husband be obliged to give a portion of his income to his wife for her personal use; (b) an end to state-regulated prostitution and the sexual double standard; (c) equal and fully coeducational opportunities for women; (d) equal pay and promotion opportunities and an end to all employment restrictions on women (e) equal admission to all governmental jobs, to juries, and to the legal profession; and (f) equal suffrage "in order to secure their rights in other fields" (1976:146–47). Despite this rather broad agenda, many of the constituent organizations of the BDF did not support any or many of these demands; they remained social-welfare and charitable in focus and conservative in membership. Priorities were set by the BDF on the most moderate demands, excluding suffrage. Moreover, the BDF increasingly subscribed to doctrines of racial superiority, and thus to the central role of German women in producing and raising numerous "superior" babies (1976:164–66). Robertson concluded that "only a minority of German women . . . took part" (1982:389) in the middle-class movement to bring about reforms in status of women.

As the war was ending, in 1917 the BDF launched a major campaign for female suffrage. In 1918, largely through the efforts of the socialists (SPD), women achieved the vote in the new Weimar Constitution. The BDF continued to exist until the Nazis abolished it in 1933. It became increasingly nationalistic, emphasizing women's role within the family and as baby-producers, and stressing the differences between men's and women's nature (Evans 1976: chap. 8). With suffrage won, the more radical groups disbanded, leaving only the BDF, which returned to its traditional social-welfare emphasis. By 1931 it claimed 1,500,000 members, although Evans (1976:245) estimated it probably had about 750,000. At any rate, it had lost its vitality and had trouble attracting young women (Stephenson 1975:26). Evans concluded that "as soon as the BDF ceased to be an unrepresentative minority movement and began to gain a measure of mass support, it ceased to be truly feminist" (1976:274).

Parallel to, but separate from, the middle-class women's movement was socialist-feminism, as expressed within the SPD (see chap. 1). While rejecting the label "feminist," socialist-feminist women, under the leadership of Clara Zetkin and Lily Braun, raised a full range of issues concerning the role of women in every social institution, including the family (see Quataert 1979, 1978; Thönnessen 1973). In 1906, before it was legal for women to participate politically, only 1.7 percent of SPD members, or 6460 women, were members. In 1908 this jumped to 5.5 percent (29,458), in 1914 to 16.1 percent (174,751), and after the war in 1918 to 28.3 percent (70,659) (Thönnessen 1973:116). In 1891 the SPD feminists began their own newspaper, *Equality*, whose circulation was 23,000 in 1905, 94,000 in 1911, and 141,115 in 1913 (1973:57). Clearly, the number of German women involved in, or exposed to, socialist-feminism was substantial, relative to other European nations. As Quataert stated: "In terms of sheer numbers, Germany had the largest Socialist women's movement by far. Its feminist plank was the most progressive" (1979:229). Unlike the middle-class women's movement, the socialist-feminists actively worked for universal suffrage for both sexes, from the early date of 1875 (1979:93). They especially parted ways with the middle-class movement over the issue of women's employment. As elsewhere, the socialists demanded protective legislation for women, while middle-class women espoused equal treatment and opportunity for both sexes (Robertson 1982:382). As we saw in chapter 1, after 1908 when women were permitted to join political organizations, the SPD abolished its separate women's organizations, and with them the autonomy of socialist-feminists. The feminist rhetoric of the party was never matched by action, and at any rate, by definition, women's problems received no priority because they were to automatically disappear when class differences were abolished. In addition, "latent and overt antifeminism and the persistence of traditional family norms and sex-role expectations in the working class hindered the efforts of female activists to mobilize working women and wives of male socialists" (1979:160). After World War I the socialists became increasingly revisionist and less committed to women's issues, encapsulating female activists in their own domains, such as welfare issues (Thönnessen 1973: chap. 6).

Like France and Russia, feminism was stymied in nineteenth-century Germany by political repression. The middle class and socialist wings never cooperated, as was the case in France. Although the middle-class women's organizations in Germany were relatively large, it is questionable whether the majority of members supported official reform positions on most issues concerning women's status and rights. At any rate, the issues which received official endorsement were quite conservative—even timid—relative to such movements elsewhere. Likewise, the SPD had a substantial female following by the second decade of this century, but the extent to which most of those women subscribed to the feminism of their leaders is questionable. Combining the two branches, it is likely that by the second decade of the twentieth century Germany experienced a mass movement on behalf of women's rights. However, a broad feminist ideology was probably confined to a handful of socialist-feminist leaders who, at any rate, subordinated their feminism to the class struggle. Therefore, we conclude that feminism was incipient during this era of German history, and the mass movement, if indeed it reached mass proportions, was fundamentally ameliorative. Neither branch of the women's movement appears to have survived in a distinct and viable form much beyond World War I.

ITALY AND THE AUSTRO-HUNGARIAN EMPIRE

The available literature on women's movements in Italy and Austro-Hungary is not only sparse, but oriented to socialist-feminism. In neither case could we locate any data which could give an idea of the scope of movement activity, other than the number of female socialist party members. There is enough evidence to assert that in both nations socialist and middle-class women's movements did emerge in the time period of concern in this chapter.

Sexual equality was part of the rhetoric of the Italian Unification Movement of the first half of the nineteenth century. Women were very active in that movement and many were feminists (Robertson 1982: chap. 27). During Mazzini's short-lived Republic in 1848–49 there was even a partly feminist women's newspaper. Nonetheless, the new civil code written after unification placed women in the same subordinate position they held elsewhere in Europe. Many women objected to it and in 1867 some petitioned the new Parliament for suffrage (1982:433–34). A feminist newspaper, *La Donna*, was published from 1868 to 1888, and in the 1890s a series of small, local feminist leagues developed in major

Italian cities (La Vigna 1978:167). By the turn-of-the-century, Milan had its own feminist journal and there was a Catholic feminist journal. A National Council of Women was formed in 1903, and in 1905 the National Committee for Women's Suffrage was organized. These organizations were mainly confined to the north of Italy, and remained "pitifully small." In 1907 only 600 people signed a women's suffrage petition (Evans 1977:136). The first national congress of Italian feminists was held in Rome in 1908. Catholic, liberal, and socialist feminists attended and fought with one another, with the result that no concrete program, no unified ideology, and no effective organization emerged (La Vigna 1978:167). Within the Italian Socialist Party, feminist issues were generally sacrificed to the proletariat cause (1978), as we have seen elsewhere in Europe. Robertson concluded about the Italian movement:

> it seems that Italian women tended to fall into extreme categories. Some were heiress to a long tradition of scholarship and personal involvement at the very highest levels. Others, the majority, were less exposed to modern ideas than those of other nationalities. Their women's movement was small and ineffective because of the inertia of the mass [1982:453].

As a footnote, Italian women received the vote only after World War II.

The Austro-Hungarian Empire also experienced a small, middle-class women's movement, beginning in 1893 with the founding of the General Austrian Women's Association. This organization was dedicated to "supporting greater rights for women, but [believed] . . . that women had a special civilizing mission" (Evans 1977:95). While it advocated the vote for women, it stressed nonpolitical issues. It was led by Rosa Mayreder, who advocated androgyny, but her influence was "limited to intellectuals" (Lafleur 1978:219). In general, it "failed to generate much support" (Evans 1977:95). The largest part of the movement was comprised of the Catholic Women's Organization, which supported protective legislation for working women, but felt that women's proper place was in the home (Lafleur 1978:220). Among the Austrians, no female suffrage organization was ever formed (Evans 1977:94). The enormous diversity of national, linguistic, and religious groups that comprised the pre-World War I Austro-Hungarian Empire resulted in separate, parallel, but generally uncooperative women's groups. While often pursuing women's rights, they had as their first priority nationalistic goals (Bohachevsky-Chomiak 1980). In the 1890s and early 1900s a number of Ukranian and Polish women's groups held rallies and petitioned for suffrage, sometimes even cooperatively. Czech women also organized in the first decade of the twentieth century, again with strong nationalistic priorities (Evans 1977:96). At the same time Hungarian women organized the National Council of Women, which united 104 organizations by 1913. Its main efforts were directed at temperance and at other moral reform issues; suffrage received virtually no support (1977:99). However, Jewish-Hungarian women, organized separately, did support suffrage. In 1912 they held a rally attended by about 10,000 people (1977:101). In fear of jeopardizing universal manhood suffrage, the prewar Socialist Party offered no support for women's rights, especially after 1907, despite extensive activism by socialist-feminists (Bohachevsky-Chomiak 1980; Lafleur 1978:220). In 1910 there were 15,000 female members of the Socialist Party, although how many subscribed to feminist ideas is not known. Women gained suffrage after World War I with the establishment of the Austrian Republic. From then until the Nazis abolished the party in 1934, the Austrian socialist women's movement was "one of the largest, most active and most innovative in Europe" (Lafleur 1978), women numbering 165,000, or 29.7 percent of the party in 1925.

It would appear, then, that like France, Russia, and possibly Germany, middle-class women's movements remained small in Italy and Austro-Hungary. It was ameliorative in Austro-Hungary, although possibly more fully feminist in Italy. Socialist-feminism was equally or even more limited in appeal, except possibly in Austria after the war.

CHINA

The relative position of women in nineteenth-century China was substantially worse than in any society discussed to this point. Footbinding was still practiced by all segments of society; Chinese women had no role in the choice of marital partner and, once married, were under the total control of their in-laws. In addition, they suffered from educational, legal, and economic handicaps at least as severe as those of their Western counterparts.

While it is inappropriate to speak of a women's movement in that century, there were some precursors. In the mid-nineteenth century the Taiping Peasant Rebellion included demands for sexual equality. Where it won control, footbinding was banned, women were given governmental positions, and 40 women's armies, each numbering 2,500, were established. However, the male leaders did exploit many of the female activists – sexually and otherwise – and at any rate the Imperial Army soon defeated the rebellion (Croll 1978:39–41). In this same era, in some southern provinces small groups of young women (numbering about 10 each) came together in communal sisterhoods "specifically designed to challenge their traditional fate of marriage" (1978:43). The 1890s witnessed a reform movement by male intellectuals, who perceived part of China's "backwardness" as the result of women's suppressed status. They called for the end of footbinding and for education for Chinese females. In 1892 the first Unbound Feet Society formed, a movement which eventually numbered 10,000 members (1978: chap. 3). However, such societies were largely comprised of "foreign ladies and government officials," along with the male reformers; rarely were Chinese women involved, and those who were tended to be the wives and other relatives of male activists. Moreover, they were strictly urban, and confined to the gentry and official classes (1978:50). After the turn-of-the-century, new schools, mostly Christian, rapidly developed for women in the urban areas of China. These schools became feminist hotbeds, with many early activists coming from the ranks of their teachers. They published a number of feminist and nationalist magazines (1978:56–58). However, their circulation was limited to "the small percentage of urban literate women" and "very little attempt was made to organize women around their own special oppression" (1978:58–59).

The first decade of this century was a time of intense nationalistic activity to overthrow the Manchu Dynasty and to rid China of foreign dominance. The women of the new schools joined revolutionary societies in large numbers, even fighting in their own battalions. However, victory and establishment of the Republic in 1911 brought no legal or political gains for women. The result was the emergence of an organizationally distinct women's movement.

During the early years of the Republic, a number of Chinese women's organizations sprang up, including the Chinese Women's Franchise Association, the Chinese Women's Co-operative Association, and the Chinese Suffrage Society, which was deliberately modeled after the British movement. While the activities of these groups were rather narrowly confined to the goal of gaining suffrage for women, their stated goals covered a broader range of reforms: improved educational opportunity for women; an end to footbinding, concubinage, prostitution, and child marriage; an elevation of the wife's status and rights within the family; and equal political rights (Croll 1978:70–72). Croll argued that "their activities were more conspicuous than widespread"; that these organizations were "limited in range of membership [to a] narrow social group of the wives and daughters of reformers and revolutionaries and the students and teachers of the new schools" (1978:72). They were based in the major cities of Peking, Shanghai, Canton, and Tientsin, and "neither urban-working nor peasant women were involved" (1978:72). Moreover, a 1912 law restricted the right of women's organizations to participate in any change-oriented discussions or activities, and by 1913 the suffrage organizatons were experiencing government repression (1978:77–78).

After 1916, male reformers and revolutionaries again became active in what is called the May Fourth Movement. In their call for modernization they included proposals for sweeping changes in the institution of the family and an improvement in the status of women; seeking an end to the sexual double standard, footbinding, and arranged marriages; and advocating birth control and political rights for women. They mounted a general attack on the Confucian ideal, which included substituting notions of individual rights and liberties for loyalty to family and tradition, and thereby liberating women as well as men from ages-old constraints (Croll 1978:81–88; Johnson 1983:27–28). Women quickly became involved in this movement, especially in the girls' schools and in universities (which were opened to females in 1920). They formed "study societies" which focused heavily on women's issues, revived the women's press, and in 1922 even opened their own bank in Peking (Croll 1978:93–95). Women's rights organizations were founded in several cities between 1919 and 1921, and in some provinces they were successful in gaining women's suffrage (e.g., Hunan, Guangdong, and Zhejiang). And, as we have seen elsewhere, the WCTU also became involved in issues of women's rights, particularly in Shanghai (1978:96–98; see also Andors 1983:16–17; Johnson 1983:31–33). Apparently, however, the number of women involved remained small. Croll spoke of marches and demonstrations numbering 1,000 (or fewer) participants, and a petition signed by 500 (1978:97–98). The central demands were still suffrage and an end to concubinage which "hardly seemed relevant to the majority of women. Indeed, the suffragettes complained of the lack of interest in their cause" (1978:102). They remained isolated from rural and working-class women, the latter of whom were increasingly organizing and striking for better wages and working conditions during the 1920s (1978:106; Andors 1983:18).

By the mid-1920s the women's movement had split into two groups: those who turned to the Communist and Nationalist Parties to pursue sweeping socioeconomic change, and those who, like middle-class women elsewhere, focused on suffrage, a few legal reforms for women, self-help, and social welfare projects (e.g., the YWCA, the WCTU, the National Council of Women, and various women's business and professional clubs) (Andors 1983:17; Croll 1978:110). By 1927 the two branches were totally isolated from one another (Croll 1978:114).

From its inception in 1921, the Chinese Communist Party (CCP) had as a part of its party platform the emancipation of women. In 1923 it established a Women's Section to recruit women for the new movement and it published a number of magazines for women. By 1925 female membership stood at 100,000, and had tripled 2 years later (Crolls 1978:118–121). Likewise, the *Goumindang* or "Nationalist Party" (GMD) had established a Women's Department and the two worked very closely together beginning in 1923. Indeed, Johnson (1978:45) argued that the GMD was more actively feminist than the CCP at that time. For both, however, revolution and a unified China were first-priority issues. As we have seen repeatedly, issues of priority made for an uneasy alliance between the feminists and party officials. Also as elsewhere, the male rank-and-file (in this case mostly peasants) resisted feminist demands. It appears that throughout the history of both parties, male officials sought to mobilize women to their cause, which had top priority, stressing women's emancipation primarily as a handy recruitment tactic, much as we saw in the case of Russia. Nonetheless, working cooperatively, the CCP and GMD organized 1,500,000 women into their the women's branches by 1927 (Johnson 1978:45).

In 1927 the two parties split violently, with the GMD controlling most of China. In the next three years it brutally suppressed not only CCP members, but all outspoken feminists, who were automatically assumed to be Communists. Its 1928 Code excluded women from politics. Some legal reforms were made to ameliorate the status of women, but the family remained "patrilineal and patrilocal," education for women was to be restricted to the preparation of women for wifely and maternal duties, and certain jobs were closed altogether to women (Croll 1978:154–56). By the 1930s the party was emphasizing the basic differences between the sexes and advocating a return to the ideals of "maternal love and wifely devotion" (1978:157–61).

In 1927 the majority of feminists had chosen to stay with the GMD and to settle for limited reforms. Their women's movement was dead. The few CCP feminists who survived GMD persecution spent the next 20 years mobilizing women in the areas under CCP control, and working to improve their social, legal, and economic statuses. But first priority was always party survival and this meant that women's issues were often sacrificed or ignored (see Andors 1983:23; Croll 1978: chap. 7; Johnson 1978: chap. 5). Nonetheless, because of the work of the feminist Communists, by 1943 the CCP Women's Associations numbered 2,500,000, by 1946 7,000,000, and on the eve of party victory in 1948 20,000,000 (Croll 1978:220). As in Russia, after the final victory of the Communist Party an All-China Women's Federation was established by the party to mobilize women and to promote party policy, but Andors (1983:30) concluded that this was not a "feminist group."

In general, then, the 1910s and 1920s witnessed the development of a relatively small, urban women's rights movement which "was perhaps too small, too isolated, and too naively reformist to be a real women's movement" (Johnson 1983:42). In our terminology, it was an incipient, ameliorative movement. In the 1930s and early 1940s the CCP was able to organize a truly mass movement of women, but feminist issues were not high in priority and were rather used by party leaders as needed to expedite the recruitment and commitment to party policy of females.

JAPAN

The Meiji period of Japanese history, which spanned the years 1868–1912, was a time of official commitment to the modernization and Westernization of that nation. Traditionally, the status of Japanese women was similar to that of their Chinese counterparts. Within the change-oriented milieu of the early Meiji period, an incipient women's movement emerged in the 1880s, only to be silenced by the government for nearly thirty-five years. It reemerged in the 1920s, but just as it was becoming a mass movement it was deflected by war preparations in the early 1930s. In both phases, it was largely ameliorative in focus.

During the 1870s substantial discussion and debate over the role of women in a modernizing Japan was conducted, primarily by male officials and intellectuals. The government, however, was not inclined to permit any changes in the traditional female role (Sievers 1983: chap. 2). A spate of books were published in the late 1870s and 1880s concerned especially with the issue of educational opportunities for women (Robins-Mowry 1983:42). By then, women had begun to participate in the discussion of their future role (Sievers 1983: chap. 3). Feminist intellectuals, calling themselves Bluestockings after their Western counterparts, published copiously all the way up until World War I, including their own journals (Robins-Mowry 1983:60).

In the 1880s the most outspoken advocate of women's rights was a woman named Kishida. Political opposition parties, such as the Popular Rights Movement and the Liberal Party, which women had begun to join, started to advocate her ideas concerning the educational and economic needs of women (Sievers 1983:33). Her agenda was "similar to that raised by women in the United States and Europe" and included equal education, an end to the sexual double standard and concubinage, and reform in property and civil law. In 1883 she was instrumental in organizing the Kyoto Women's Lecture Society, which attracted 2000 women to its first meeting (1983:36–38) and also the Society for the Liberation of Women (Robins-Mowry 1983:63). In the first few years of the 1880s there was "a very high level of political activity among women, who organized associations, lecture and study groups, 'freedom houses' and cooperative societies 'to promote women,' " (Sievers, 1983:42) in seven cities. They set up schools for girls and petitioned the government for educational opportunity for females. However, government repression of political opposition parties, with which the feminists were allied, and the arrest of Kishida, resulted in the virtual collapse of the women's movement by 1884. Feminist writers continued to publish, but their audience shrunk and the feminists became increasingly isolated (1983:42–48).

The later half of the 1880s witnessed the arrival of the WCTU in Japan (1886), which immediately became involved in a variety of reform issues, including women's suffrage (Robins-Mowry 1983:52). Middle-class Christian women also organized the Tokyo Women's Reform Society in 1885, dedicated to raising the status of women through increasing their educational and other opportunities, and ending prostitution and concubinage (Sievers 1983:50). At the same time, women silk workers in Kofu organized the first strike in Japanese history. The result of all this activity was that by the end of the decade laws were passed prohibiting women from joining political organizations or from attending political meetings. Thus, the first wave of active organizational effort on behalf of women ended.

As elsewhere, the feminists of the 1880s failed to concern themselves with issues of poverty and exploitation among industrially employed women, and therefore no connections were made between feminists and the working class. Apparently, they also failed to expand from the cities into rural areas. By the 1890s, unable to engage in political activism, middle-class women in large numbers devoted their attention to social reform and philanthropy, as their counterparts were doing in many nations in the West (Sievers 1983: chap. 5). In about 1904 women socialists began to advocate some feminist issues. Males in the party were unsympathetic, leading a small group of women to split from the party. In 1905 they petitioned the government to abolish the law prohibiting women from political involvement, but their petition had only 500 signatures. At any rate, the government repressed the "tiny" Socialist Party in 1905 (1983:120–22).

In 1911 a women's literary journal, *Bluestocking*, was begun, with a circulation only numbering a couple of thousand. It quickly became outspokenly feminist, raising issues pertaining to female sexuality, including advocating abortion. It related issues of sexuality to women's deprived status, and advocated economic, emotional, and psychological independence for women. Banned by the government as disruptive of public morality and the family structure, it became defunct in 1916. Sievers, however, argued that this journal sparked the beginning of a new women's movement (1983:161–88). In 1920 the New Women's Society formed, advocating political power for women. In the same year the *Women's League* was begun, a women's suffrage magazine (1983:187; Robins-Mowry 1983:58–59). The New Women's Association was a federation of local groups which sought sexual equality, "taking into account the functional differences of the sexes and the need for women to develop their own 'innate potentialities' " (Robins-Mowry 1983:65–66). Its membership was somewhat in excess of 200, and in 1922 it garnered only 1500 women's signatures on a petition to end the ban on women's political participation. The organization quickly dissolved, but not before it had established "a somewhat more receptive public mood to the issues of women's rights" (1983:68–69).

In 1921 the first socialist women's organization was founded, the Red Wave Society, comprised mostly of the wives of socialists. Police repression ended its existence by 1925. At any rate, as elsewhere, Japanese socialist women perceived feminism as "bourgeois" and general social revolution as the top priority (Robins-Mowry 1983:69).

In the aftermath of the Great Earthquake of 1923, the Federation of Women's Associations of Tokyo was founded, comprised of 42 organizations, in order to aid in relief and reconstruction. It quickly turned its attention to women's issues, including the end of licensed prostitution, property rights, and economic independence for women, improved working conditions for women, and female suffrage. The WCTU joined the suffrage campaign, and in 1924 the Women's Suffrage League was formed as well. The Suffrage Movement soon attracted others: the All-Kansai Federation, the Osaka Asahi Shimbun Women's Group, and some working-class women as well. By 1930 membership in organizations supporting female suffrage numbered over 3,000,000 (Robins-Mowry 1983:71–80).

After that, Japan began war preparations and a mood of conservative nationalism blanketed the country. By 1937 Japan was at war with China and women's organizations turned their attention to wartime problems and relief. In 1942 the government disbanded all nongovernment-sponsored organizations (Robins-Mowry 1983:80–82). In short, by the early 1930s the women's movement had peaked, and by the late 1930s it was dead.

Clearly, the demands of women throughout the period in question were ameliorative in nature, save for a small number of more truly feminist writers. The first phase of activity in the 1880s probably never went beyond the incipient level, although in the absence of specific quantitative information it is difficult to say. The second wave of activism in the 1920s appears to have approached the mass level briefly. Once again we see the effects of government repression on the ability of women to organize on their own behalf and to expand their following.

INDIA

The status of women in nineteenth-century India was, especially among the nonpoor, at least as suppressed as in China and Japan. *Purdah* (the seclusion of women) was practiced by both the Hindu and Moslim communities. Child-marriage was the norm. Women could not divorce and widows could not remarry among Hindus. *Sati* (widow suicide), although declared illegal by the British colonizers, was still practiced by some wealthy and high-caste Hindus. While most males were illiterate, virtually all females were. Women were also largely deprived of property and inheritance rights.

As in China and Japan, the issue of improving the status of women, and especially education for women, was first raised by a small number of urban, middle-class, Westernized males, who sought modernization for their society. Beginning in the 1880s, they pressured female relatives into adopting a Westernized point of view, gave them a Christian education, and argued against *sati, purdah,* and child-marriage (Desai 1966:274; Everett 1979:48–49). They even began the first women's associations in India in the late nineteenth and first decade of the twentieth centuries (Everett 1979:51, 54). Of these male reformers Mazumdar wrote: "There was no questioning of women's traditional familial roles or dependence on others. Instead, most reformers pleaded that increasing women's efficiency would strengthen the hold of the family and traditions in society" (1979:xi; see also Everett 1979: chap. 4).

By the end of the nineteenth century, a small number of educated, Hindu reformist women organized reform associations in several Indian cities and published their own journal. Their main concern was the abolition of *purdah*, which was necessary in order to educate Indian women. But these organizations were really only segregated " ladies gatherings" attached to larger, male reform groups (Forbes 1982:526–27). Thomas concluded about the nineteenth-century Indian movement on behalf of women, "Right down to the beginning of the twentieth century, men were generally fighting the battle of women and there were not a dozen women in the whole country who could effectively represent the cause of the sex" (1964:357).

The Congress Party was founded in 1885 in Bombay by middle-class, British-oriented Indian men seeking the modernizaton of India. By the turn-of-the-century, a Hindu revival movement was underway which became anti-British and which gradually spread to Congress. Shortly after World War I, Gandhi had become the leader of the Indian Nationalist Movement, rooted in Congress organizationally, and in Hindu revivalism ideologically (Thomas 1964: chap.

11). In the name of uplifting India, reforms in the status of women, especially in the areas of education and child-marriage, were adopted by the nationalists, and women quickly became involved in the struggle. However, the focus remained traditional, inasmuch as the purpose of "women's uplift" was to enhance their ability to function in their separate domain as wife and mother (Everett 1979: chap. 4).

The women's movement in India began in the second decade of the twentieth century with the formation of several organizations by and for women. A short-lived women's organization, *Mahamandal*, was founded in 1910 (Forbes 1982:528). Then, in 1917, the issue of women's suffrage surfaced under the auspices of the newly formed Women's Indian Association (WIA), founded by two British women with strong ties to the suffrage movement in their homeland, and one Indian woman (Everett 1979:70). A suffrage petition in that year gathered 800 signatures (Forbes 1979:6). The WIA was the first national women's organization in India (Thomas 1964:357). By 1922 it had 43 branches and 2300 members, and in 1927, 80 branches with a total of 4000 members. Besides suffrage, it sought educational and social reform, calling for self-development by and for women and the abolition of child marriages (Everett 1979:72). From 1917 until her death in 1933, Annie Besant led the WIA (Forbes 1979:4). In 1924 the National Council of Women in India (NCWI) was founded in Bombay, also by a British woman, and ten years later it numbered 8201 members in 180 groups (Everett 1979:73). In 1927 the All-India Women's Conference was called, again organized in part by British women, and it quickly became an organization (AIWC). It too was concerned with educational and legal reform, suffrage, health, and employment policies relevant to women. By 1945 it consisted of 41 organizations and 25,000 members (1979:73–75). The AIWC spearheaded the suffrage campaign and by the 1930s was the single most important women's organization in India (Desai 1966: chap. 16).

The AIWC was tied very closely to the Nationalist Movement, the Congress Party, and its leadership (Baig 1976:25; Everett 1979:75). During especially the 1930s and 1940s, except for the NCWI which maintained independence from the Nationalist Movement, the other organizations viewed independence as the necessary precondition to solving women's problems. They rejected the label "feminist" because it implied for them that women's rights had priority over the national interest. Not "men" but "custom" was defined as the "enemy." An ongoing debate racked the AIWC on this issue of priorities (Forbes 1982:529).

Together, all three organizations represented several thousand members in a nation of nearly 200,000,000 women. They were in contact "with the majority of India's educated women" (Forbes 1979:3), but evidently no other women. While they claimed to speak for all Indian women (1979:3), in fact the issues with which they were concerned were largely irrelevant to the masses of poor, low caste, rural and working-class Indian women (Everett 1979:80; Mazumdar 1979:xi). Unlike male organizations, however, the women's associations encompassed all of the diverse religious communities in India (Everett 1979:44). However, they remained comprised of urban, educated, middle- and upper-class and caste women, and made no effort to mobilize a mass movement. Not once was a mass demonstration on behalf of women's rights ever held (1979:149). As Everett stated, "the Indian women's movement was small in size and elite in composition with many ties with Indian political leaders" (1979:102).

Ideologically, until about 1931 the main emphasis was on women's uplift. This approach assumed that the sexes were different, and sought reform so that women could better discharge their traditional roles and expand traditional feminine values into the public realm, thus bringing about an age of greatness in India. After 1931, the AIWC in particular began to stress the Western concept of "equal rights." This approach argued that women must be permitted to reach their potential in all areas of life (Everett 1979: chap. 5). The equal rights emphasis was expanded to concern with all deprived groups and thus linked the women's movement yet more closely with the Nationalist Movement and Congress Party (1979:93–94). Nonetheless, the issues stressed continued to be those of political, educational, and legal reform on behalf of women, and no direct challenge to the traditional division of the sexes into separate spheres was mounted. While Congress leaders were very sympathetic to the women's cause, many conservative Hindus, and especially Muslims within the Nationalist Movement fought change in property rights, purdah, and child marriage (Forbes 1982:530). As we have seen in many other contexts, women have had to sacrifice their own issues, or give them low priority, when their movement became intertwined with a male-dominated one, because of the intractability of many rank-and-file male members.

Because of their close ties with Indian political leaders, by 1929 women had been enfranchised in all provinces, on the same limited bases as men. The 1930s witnessed continued work by the various women's organizations for further political rights and various legal reforms. With independence, the primacy of the Congress Party, and a new constitution, women were granted full formal equality (although in practice many of the relevant laws and constitutional provisions are ignored to this day). Mazumdar concluded that equal rights came to Indian women with independence "without much struggle on their part" (1979:xxii). At any rate, after independence the women's movement faded (Forbes 1982:532).

In conclusion, it is clear that from 1917 until about 1950 there existed in India an incipient, ameliorative women's movement. Its political and legal successes were substantially out of proportion to its following, due to its close ties with male political elites, much as in Canada and Norway. As we have seen repeatedly, organizationally independent women's movements in this era tended to be largely middle-class phenomena. In India, the educated middle class constituted a tiny minority of the total population, and thus a mass women's movement was all but impossible. In this, India was similar to some other societies discussed to this point, such as Russia and China.

INDONESIA

Indonesia is a predominantly Muslim society, but one with a long tradition of relatively high status and substantial independence for women. Extreme customs such as *purdah* and veiling, associated with Muslim women in many societies, were never practiced there (Vreede-de Stuers 1960:50 ff.). Nonetheless, in the nineteenth century women were not educated (nor were most men); child marriages, polygamy, and prostitution were practiced; and religious law in terms of marriage and family, which seriously disadvantaged women, was in effect.

In the last two decades of the nineteenth century, a few women, working independently, addressed the issue of education for women. In 1912 the Independent Women Association was founded in Djakarta, with the aid of a men's organization, as a cultural and educational organization of women. It raised the issue of child marriage as well. About the same time an organization called the Improvement of Women founded schools for girls, and soon several other organizations were doing likewise (Vreede-de Stuers 1960:61–63). These groups, all comprised of women "from the leading classes of society, . . . aimed at the improvement of the woman's position by means of education in household practices, . . . courses on child welfare, and so forth" (1960:64).

In the 1920s and 1930s, Indonesia experienced a nationalistic and religious reform movement. It was as an adjunct of this that a women's movement was born, as we have seen in other Asian nations (see Vreede-de Stuers 1960: chap. 3).

The first Indonesian Women's Conference was held in Djakarta in 1928. Nearly 30 women's organizations were represented. The focus was upon issues of education and marriage; political issues were not dealt with. This led to the founding of the Federation of Indonesian Women, which in 1929 became the Federation of Indonesian Women's Associations (PPII). This organization, "leaving all political questions to one side, set out to improve the social position of women and family life as a whole" (Vreede-de Stuers 1960:89). At the same time, female nationalists held a meeting (of about 600–1000 women) to discuss prostitution, polygamy, and education for women (1960:90). A more radical group of women founded an organization called the Alert Woman in 1930. It insisted on the abolition of polygamy, a stance not supported by the PPII. By 1932 the Alert Woman was calling for independence, education for all, and an improvement in working conditions for proletarian women (1960:93). Three feminist journals were also begun during the 1930s (1960:98–99).

The second congress of women in 1935 had a broader agenda than the first. It called for employment opportunities for women, literacy, the improvement of the status of women under Islamic law, and nationalism (Vreede-de Stuers 1960:93). By the third congress in 1938, female suffrage had been added to the agenda. Ironically, while women could not vote, they could be elected to certain local offices at that time (1960:95). However, the movement was split over issues of reform in divorce and polygamy (1960:103).

The Japanese invasion ended the women's movement, just after women received the vote in 1941. Vreede-de Stuers (1960), the only English source on the Indonesian women's movement we could locate, gave no figures that would allow us to estimate the size of the women's movement. The issues raised by it were ameliorative, and most were not very relevant to the needs of lower-class women (1960:98).

PERSIA/IRAN

The position of women in this overwhelmingly Muslim society during the nineteenth century was one of virtually total seclusion and extensive suppression. When women left the home, they went in heavy veils and a "cloak" (*chador*) which covered everything but their eyes. Indeed, Iranian women were more completely covered than their Muslim sisters elsewhere (Nashat 1983:20). There was no education for them. Child marriage and polygamy were widely practiced, including large harems for the wealthy (1983:19–20). In the closing decades of that century, a movement for constitutional government began to grow among Westernized males. They also began to educate their daughters at home, predicated on the assumption that educated women would raise better children (1983:15), a phenomenon we have witnessed in other non-Western societies. A revolution led by reformers in 1905 attracted large groups of women of various social classes to its cause (Bayat-Philipp 1978:298).

A constitutional government was established in 1906, but civil war followed since the new monarch did not accept it. The constitutionalists, heavily comprised of Westernized men already concerned with the degraded status of women, saw the need to mobilize women in their struggle, not unlike China and India (Bámdád 1977:25–26). These men helped a group of women found the Women's Freedom Society in Tehran to discuss the status of Iranian women. Attacked by a mob, it soon disbanded, never having involved more than a "few" people (1977:30). Other groups of women, mostly upper class, organized dozens of secret societies in support of the constitutionalist cause. They also concerned themselves with the issue of women's education (Bayat-Philipp 1978:299). Some women supporters of the revolution protested the fact that the new constitution did not enfranchise women, but other than acquiring one spokesman in Parliament, their campaign failed (1978:300–301). Some women marched through the streets unveiled, proclaiming their freedom, but soon ceased upon receiving adverse public reaction (1978:301–302). But in general, the zeal of most women was reserved for the national cause, not for their own. Bámdád stated that "thousands" (1977:34–35) of women were active in this movement between about 1906 and 1911.

Iran was invaded by several armies during World War I and as a result the women's groups stopped meeting (Nashat 1983:25). Chaos followed the war until the reformist Pahlavi Dynasty was founded in 1925. From then until his abdication in 1941, the Shah decreed a number of changes concerning women, including opening numerous state schools for girls (some private, Muslim schools had been founded previously in 1907–11), a ban on veils (1936), and opening universities to women (1936). A small group of educated, Westernized, middle- and upper-class women supported these changes, but the mass of Iranian women did not. Indeed, upon his abdication, most women began to wear the veil again (1983:27); the activists were alone in seeing the veil as a symbol of women's subjegation (1983:26).

In 1922 the Patriotic Women's League was founded to teach child care, household management, and hygiene to women. It was begun by women with "socialist tendencies" and was affiliated with the Socialist Party (Nashat 1983:28). It stressed schools for girls, literacy for women, hospitals and orphanages for poor females, nationalism, and a respect for Islam. It held adult classes and published a journal (Bámdád 1977:56, 63–64). In 1932 a group of Arab women from abroad asked Iranian women activists to host a Congress of Women of the East, which was held in Tehran. Illiteracy of women was the main focus, and the delegates seemed to share a sense that it was premature to seek other reforms (1977:77).

In 1932 the Shah closed down the Women's Patriotic League and three years later replaced it with the Ladies Center. With his impetus and under his patronage, a group of women teachers met weekly for the stated purpose of "pioneering in social services and activities which would enable Iran's women to escape seclusion and catch up with the rest of the world's women" (Bámdád 1977:92). One of its early goals was also to promote the abandonment of the veil (1977:94).

In 1941 a conservative reaction followed the abdication of the Shah, threatening the gains women had made. In order to prevent such setbacks, urban, educated women organized in the early 1940s: the Women's Party (renamed the Council of Women), the Iranian Women's League (renamed in 1956 the Iranian Women's League of Supporters of the Declaration of Human Rights), and the New Path Society. These three, and three other women's organizations, federated in 1956. Then in 1959 a princess sponsored and helped organize the High Council of Iranian Women's Associations (Bámdád 1977:107–12). These groups called for women's suffrage, but evidently they were quite weak, inasmuch as Nashat talked of "hundreds of women professionals, teachers, and students" (1983:30) as involved.

During the 1940s the Communist Tudeh Party "launched the most consistent campaign advocating women's rights" (Nashat 1983:29). It was able to attract a number of educated women, who thereupon formed the Society for Democratic Women in 1949. This group campaigned for education for women, equal pay, and suffrage. In fact, it collected 100,000 signatures on a 1952 petition for women's suffrage. In 1953 both the party and the women's group were suppressed by the government.

In general, it appears that there wasn't much of an independent women's movement in Iran, at least relative to most societies examined to this point. Variously organized by male reformers, the government, and the Socialist and Communist Parties, only a few independent women's organizations emerged to fight for their own cause. The numbers involved were small and members were largely drawn from the urban educated elite. Besides educational opportunities for girls and literacy for women, few specific reforms were explicitly sought, except possibly suffrage by the 1940s. Even unveiling seems to have emanated more from the government than as a response to demands by women activists. Social service to women, rather than reform in women's rights, seems to have been the major focus of activism. We therefore conclude that Iran experienced an incipient, minimally ameliorative women's movement between about 1906 and the 1950s.

EGYPT

The story of the Egyptian women's movement is by now a familiar one. In this predominantly Muslim society, women, especially those of the upper and middle classes, were secluded, veiled, married young into arranged unions, and often lived in harems. Prior to World War I, the women's issue was raised by some male reformers who were also nationalists seeking Egyptian independence from British colonial rule. The basis of their support for women's rights was to produce women who would make better wives and mothers, thus raising "enlightened" children (Philipp, 1978:277–78; Zwemer and Zwemer 1926:97). Concretely, they supported basic education for women (in domestic science), an end to polygamy, and an increase in age of marriage for females (Philipp 1978:278; Zwemer and Zwemer 1926:98). But neither then nor later did the male reformers have any "intention to lead the woman out of her traditional realm into a more public arena or positions and professions" (Philipp 1978:286).

In 1919 a nationalist revolution occurred in which women, for the first time, took an active public role (Marsot 1978:268–69). However, the new constitution which followed offered no political rights or other reforms for women (Philipp 1978:278).

When the new Parliament opened in 1924, "a few women demonstrated for the right to vote" (Philipp 1978:289). In general, however, suffrage and women's political rights did not emerge as an issue for the small, timid women's movement that emerged in the aftermath of the 1919 Revolution, until the mid-1930s (1978:291). Nor did activist women support professional opportunities for women, except for those who had no husbands (1978:287). In 1923 the Egyptian Feminist Union was founded. It focused its attention on education for women, welfare activities, and reform in laws pertaining to marriage and divorce, including an end to polygamy, arranged, and child marriages (1978:290; Zwemer 1926:99–100). In addition, the early 1920s saw the arrival of the WCTU on the Egyptian scene, and the creation of several other women's rights organizations:

the Women's Educational Union, the Young Womanhood of Young Egypt, the Feminist Movement, and the Egyptian Women's Union (Zwemer and Zwemer 1926:86–87, 106). By and large, however, the focus of women's organizations in the 1920s and 1930s was social service and philanthropy (Marsot 1978:269).

According to Philipp (1978:282), the movement was restricted to educated, middle- and upper-class women, who made no attempt to mobilize mass support or even to address issues of relevance to women in the lower classes. In short, the Egyptian case is yet another example of an incipient, ameliorative women's movement.

CARIBBEAN ISLANDS

We were able to locate some English-language sources that document the existence of ameliorative women's movements during the early decades of the twentieth century in three Caribbean Islands: Puerto Rico, the Dominican Republic, and Cuba. Given the limited amount of information available, what follows is simply a brief description of each.

Puerto Rico

In the later half of the nineteenth century, the issue of women's rights "permeated the educated and liberal sector of Puerto Rican society" (Ferrer: 1979:39). As in so many other cases examined, it was educated males who emphasized the need for women's education.

At the turn of the century, the population of Puerto Rico was just under 1,000,000, yet only 1387 women were literate (Hernández 1979:25). Industrialization was underway, and by the second decade of the new century working-class women began to organize their own unions, in which "they pronounced a total rejection of the ideal women that prevented their full participation and remuneration in industry. They rejected notions of feminine frailty, weakness, social purity, moral superiority, and passivity" (1979:32). The working-class women's movement fought for rights primarily within the labor movement. In 1919 the First Congress of Women Workers of Puerto Rico met and supported universal suffrage and better working conditions for women. They also organized a standing committee to function within the main Puerto Rican labor union, the Free Federation of Labor (Ferrer 1979:41). In the next year, working-class women formed the Popular Feminist Association of Puerto Rico to train women workers in feminism and to fight for civil and political rights for women, as well as better working conditions (1979:41).

Simultaneously, middle-class, educated, professionally employed women began to organize the Puerto Rican Feminist League (1917) and the Puerto Rican Association of Suffragist Women. For this branch of the women's movement, suffrage was evidently the only issue. As we have seen elsewhere, the two branches, representing two different social classes, had no ties to one another (Ferrer 1979:39, 41; Hernández 1979:34). By 1929 women had won limited suffrage, confined to the literate, and the middle-class movement ended (Hernández 1979:25). Universal suffrage was granted in 1936 and even the working-class movement dissolved after that (Ferrer 1979:41).

In the absence of more information, it is impossible to estimate the size of the Puerto Rican women's movement; however, the ideology appears to have been basically ameliorative.

Dominican Republic

A very timid women's movement arose in the 1930s in the Dominican Republic, with the tacit support of the dictator Trujillio (Mota 1976:267). The Accíon Feminista Dominicana was founded in 1931. It permitted as members only literate women of "good conduct" over the age of 18 (at the time, the population was 70 percent illiterate). Its leaders, many of whom were college educated, were primarily teachers. Its program was primarily "moralistic and familistic," focusing on the "lack of education for women, the destruction of the family, prostitution, . . . alcoholism, drugs" (1976:266). Education was seen as needed to improve the home, and to enable women to train for decent jobs "should the need arise" (1976:267). They also called for political rights for women so that they could bring into the political realm home virtues (1976:267). Feminist clubs were also formed in the provinces during the 1930s. A series of reforms, including partial female suffrage in 1934 and full suffrage in 1942, spelled the end of the Accíon Feminista. After 1942, the Trujillista Party formed and controlled a "Feminist Section" (1976:271). The large masses of women remained unaffected by the movement or by the reforms gained. It would appear, then, that the Dominican Republic experienced an ameliorative, incipient women's movement of about a decade's duration during the 1930s.

Cuba

An ameliorative women's movement began in Cuba in the second decade of the twentieth century. By 1914 the National Feminist Party had 10,000 members. Its program stressed reserving a quota of jobs specifically for women, access to teaching jobs, equal wages, access to education at all levels, and legal, civil and political equality. In 1921, eleven women's organizations, representing 9000 women, formed the National Federation of Women's Associations in order to work for educational opportunity and suffrage for women. Two years later, the First National Congress in Havana called for women's suffrage, equal civil rights, and an end to prostitution. By the mid 1920s the women's movement split into revolutionary and reformist branches (all information taken from the Latin American and Caribbean Women's Collective 1977:35). We were able to locate no information concerning the subsequent history of the movement. We conclude, therefore, that Cuba experienced an ameliorative women's movement from about 1914 until about 1927, that was possibly of intermediate size.

MEXICO

The earliest stirrings of a women's movement in Mexico occurred in the later decades of the nineteenth century. As early as 1833, groups of women demanded educational opportunity (Latin American and Caribbean Women's Collective 1977:28). In the 1870s some teachers founded *La Siempreviva* in the Yucatán, which published a newspaper and worked to enhance educational opportunities for women (Macías 1978:287). Also before the turn of the century, working women had become involved in strikes and unions, and formed a group called *Regeneracion et Concordia*, which linked class struggle and women's rights (Latin American and Caribbean Women's Collective 1977:27). However, it was not until after the turn of the century that the women's movement really developed momentum, in the aftermath of the Mexican Revolution.

In 1904 *La Sociedad Protectora de la Mujer* was founded in Mexico City (Macías 1978:295). In that same year, a group called Admirers of Juárez was formed by women "to diffuse ideas about women's rights, but it seems to have aroused more ridicule than support" (Morton 1962:2). Activity picked up in the teens when a feminist magazine, *Mujer Moderna*, was published (1915–19) and an International Congress of Women was held in Merida in the Yucatán (1916). Women at the Congress demanded educational and vocational opportunities and equal legal and political rights (Macías 1978:288). However, the new constitution of 1917 failed to grant women legal equality or political rights.

The early 1920s witnessed the growth of feminist organizations. In Yucatán, with the encouragement of male socialist leaders, feminist leagues began to devote attention to the elimination of drugs, alcohol, and prostitution; literacy for women; birth control; and practical courses in child-care and home economics for poor women (Macías 1978:291). They also asked for land reallocation irrespective of sex (Latin American and Caribbean Women's Collective 1977:30–31). Given a very sympathetic, leftist governor, the Yucatán women's movement was quite successful in its efforts at reform (Latin American and Caribbean Women's Collective 1977:30–31; Macías 1978). In 1923 the Pan American League for the Elevation of Woman met in Mexico City and was attended primarily by Mexican professional women (Macías 1978:294). The more radical delegates from the Yucatán denounced marriage as "legal slavery," advocated birth control, sex education, and some even "free love." These positions were rejected by the Congress, which focused on calling for a single sexual standard of monogamy, and equal political rights for women (1978:295–96).

Yet more activism was apparent in the 1930s. The decade began with a 1931 Congress Against Prostitution, which was legalized and government-controlled at the time (Latin American and Caribbean Women's Collective 1977:31). In that same year, organized labor took up the issue of women's rights and formed the Women's Protective Union to defend the rights of women in industry, commerce, and agriculture (Morton 1962:15). In 1934, the Feminist Revolutionary Party formed to support the Party of the Mexican Revolution (PNR), which was running a male for president who was sympathetic to women's issues. This group soon became incorporated into the PNR (1962:17). By 1935, women from every class, including professionals, peasants, and workers, organized the United Front for Women's Rights. It soon numbered 50,000 members in 800 affiliated organizations (1962:21). Its program stressed women's suffrage and the right to hold office, equality before the law, sexual equality in governmental land grants, work centers for unemployed women, and cultural education programs for women (Morton 1962:18; Latin American and Caribbean Women's Collective 1977:31). Other groups also emerged in the mid and late 1930s: the Mexican Feminine Confederation, the Co-ordinating Committee of Feminine Groups, the Atheneum of Women, and various women's professional groups (1962:29, 36–37). In 1940, with the defeat of women's suffrage when it had appeared likely to pass, and the departure from office of President Cardenas who had supported their cause, the women's movement died (Latin American and Caribbean Women's Collective 1977:31; Morton 1962:37). Full political rights for women had to wait another 13 years.

From at least the mid 1910s until about 1940, Mexico experienced a largely ameliorative women's movement, which included a more radical feminist contingent based in the Yucatán. It appears to have grown to at least intermediate size during the 1930s (the absence of data prevents us from determining if it reached mass proportion), with the support and encouragement, but not control, of left-wing political parties and their male leaders.

ARGENTINA

The origins of a women's movement in Argentina date back earlier than those of most societies discussed to this point, to the 1820s. In 1823 a (male) government minister established the Society of Beneficence, comprised of wealthy women, and designed to establish and run elementary schools for girls. This organization, which lasted over a century until 1948, ultimately expanded to encompass all social services for women and children (Little 1978:236). By mid-century, a newspaper subtitled *Equality between the Sexes* was being published (Latin American and Caribbean Women's Collective 1977:28). In the late nineteenth century male reformers, whose goal was the modernization of Argentina, took up the issue of education for females. As we have so often seen, however, their justification stressed that educated women make better wives and mothers (Little 1978:238). Also in the late nineteenth century, socialist women had begun to try to organize women workers (Latin American and Caribbean Women's Collective 1977:28). From its founding in 1896, the Argentine Socialist party was an outspoken supporter of women's rights, including suffrage and legal equality (Little 1978:243).

Just after the turn of the century, organizations for women began to proliferate. In 1900 a group of wealthy, educated women formed the National Council of Argentinian Women. This group followed in the footsteps of the benevolent society begun eighty years earlier, and was neither a "militant pressure group" nor was it concerned with the issue of political rights for women (Latin American and Caribbean Women's Collective 1977:29). However, five years later the Feminist Center was founded to press for equal rights for women, protective legislation for working women, and day care (Little 1978:243). In 1910 the National Council held a Women's Conference which focused on education, but not on political involvement (1978:244). In that same year the Argentine Association of University Women sponsored the First International Feminist Congress of Buenos Aires, most of whose participants were from that city. It espoused a socialist ideology and concerned itself with the issues of education, suffrage, legal equality, physical fitness for women, and a single standard of sexual morality. It attacked prostitution and called for changes in the divorce law and in property rights (1978:245–46).

From 1910 until World War I, "a number of groups dedicated to suffrage and civil rights for women started up, only to dissolve within a year or two because of discouragement from a lack of widespread support" (Little 1978:247). This period also witnessed the arrival of temperance activism on the Argentine scene (1978:242). Besides a lack of support, the ideological basis of women's groups in this period was very traditional. "Feminists . . . based their actions on a belief in women's moral superiority that would enable them to cleanse the world of war, poverty, and prostitution" (1978:247). As elsewhere, women's activism on behalf of their own cause waned during World War I. However, the end of the war brought with it renewed organizational efforts. In 1918 the National Feminist Union was founded to pursue political and civil equality. Two years later this organization sponsored a mock election, but only 3000 women participated (1978:247). During the 1920s the Women's Rights Association tried to organize women of all religions, classes, and political ideologies to pursue civil rights for women. It grew to 11,000 members. After a new Civil Code was enacted in 1926, which incorporated many of its demands, attention was turned to women's suffrage (1978:247–48).

In point of fact, the Argentinian women's movement was unable to integrate different social classes and thereby remained an essentially middle-class phenomenon which emphasized women's traditional roles. Little concluded that it "did not claim sufficient memberships . . . to sway the mainstream of life" (1978:249).

Later, in the 1940s, under Juan Peron's dictatorship, a Peronist Party-sponsored women's movement reemerged and focused on issues of better pay and women's suffrage. However, as an organization sponsored by the ruling party, this aspect of the struggle for women's rights is outside the scope of this book. In general, we therefore conclude that from shortly after the turn of the century into the 1930s, Argentina experienced an ameliorative, incipient women's movement.

BRAZIL

As in so many other cases we have discussed, the seeds of a twentieth-century women's movement were planted in the late decades of the nineteenth century in Brazil, when a series of feminist journals were published, beginning in the 1870s. "Starting with calls for improved education and additional respect for women, some then supported changes in women's legal position and careers outside the home. Several finally advocated the right to vote" (Hahner 1978:254). While the nineteenth century did witness the slow growth of educational opportunities for Brazilian women, as late as 1873 only about 10 percent of the women were literate (as computed from data provided by Hahner 1978:256), although in urban areas the figure was much higher (e.g., nealy 44 percent in Rio de Janeiro in 1890) (1978:268). Therefore, the potential audience for the nineteenth-century feminist journals was small and almost entirely urban. In addition, even some of the "feminist editors demonstrated ambivalence about the role of women beyond the family . . ." (1978:278).

The 1880s witnessed the rise of women's activism in other social causes, mainly the slave abolitionist movement. They did not speak publicly on the issue, but women did organize their own abolitionist groups to raise funds for the movement (Hahner 1978:271–72). During the same decade, some women's rights advocates demanded the vote for the first time, but they received very little support (1978:273; 1980). After a republic was founded in 1889, support for this issue began to slowly increase. Nonetheless, women's rights advocates remained a "small band of pioneers" in the nineteenth century (1978:277; 1980).

The organized women's movement in Brazil may be said to have begun in about 1920, with the founding of the League for the Intellectual Emancipation of Women (Latin American and Caribbean Women's Collective 1977:34 cited 1919, Blachman 1976:246 claimed 1921 as the founding date). It was the first organization for Brazilian women that was not religiously sponsored (Blachman 1976:246). In 1922 the organization was replaced by the Brazilian Federation for the Advancement of Women. The goals of the Federation included promotion of education for females, protective labor legislation and the improvement of working conditions for women, opening the professions to women, and political rights for women. It placed most of its emphasis on the last of these, and specifically on women's suffrage (Blachman 1976:246–47; Latin American and Caribbean Women's Collective 1977:34; Saffioti 1978: chap. 9). It very quickly developed affiliated leagues in 13 states. However, a 1927 petition garnered only 2000 signatures in a nation comprised of 2.5 million literate women (Blachman 1976:247). As elsewhere, activists in the movement were primarily members of the middle and upper classes, and leadership was provided by professionally employed women (Hahner 1980:95, 100).

In 1932 a new constitution was drafted, which was finally adopted in 1934. During these few years the Federation worked hard, in cooperation with several other women's groups, to ensure that the new constitution would enfranchise women. These other groups included Liga Electoral, the Union of University Women, the Union of Professional Women, and the Union of Public Officials (Blachman 1976:248). Blachman noted that "many" urban, middle- and upper middle-class women were involved, although Hahner (1980:103) suggested that many were not and that lower-class women were totally absent. With success in gaining the vote in 1934, the Federation turned its attention to trying to get women and male supporters of women's rights issues, elected. Along with suffrage, the other issue of central importance to the movement was educational opportunity (1980:102). At any rate, with governmental repression of political parties in 1937 came the death of the women's movement as well (Blachman 1976:248-49).

In general, we conclude that Brazil experienced an ameliorative movement, which probably never surpassed the incipient stage of growth, and which was almost entirely urban and middle class, from about 1920 until 1937.

CHILE, PERU, AND URUGUAY

We were able to locate a small amount of material on women's movements in Chile, Peru, and Uruguay. What follows is a brief description of each.

Chile

The first secular women's group of any kind in Chile was the Women's Reading Circle, founded in 1915. Simultaneously, an upper-class women's organization called Club de Señoras formed. In 1919 the two joined together as the National Council of Women, which became "the principal agitator for the feminist movement during the 1920s" (Chaney 1979:75). Between 1920 and 1940 several other groups formed to work for women's rights, but most had a "limited life." These, as well as the National Council, attracted only the educated and well-to-do; the mass of women remained untouched. In 1944 the First National Congress was held, which was the beginning of a more diversified movement. As an outgrowth of that congress, the Federation of Women's Organizations was formed to embrace women of all political ideologies. With women's suffrage five years later came the end of the women's movement altogether (1979:75).

Peru

Between 1911 and 1925 one woman, Maria Alvarado, almost alone fought for women's suffrage in Peru. She formed the first women's organization in that nation, Feminine Revolution, in 1915, but it remained small. In the early 1920s a few other small women's groups also worked for suffrage (Chaney 1979:69–71). The National Council of Women in Peru was founded in 1924, but members disagreed on the suffrage issue and even over proposed civil code reforms to grant married women equality before the law (1979:72). Alvarado was jailed, then exiled in 1925, spelling the end of women's activism on behalf of their own rights. In general, Chaney concluded that "women never succeeded in building a movement in Peru" so when the vote came in 1955, it "caught most women by surprise; it came as a gift for which they had not expended any large amounts of energy" (1979:73).

Uruguay

During the 1910s, a few women's rights groups formed in Uruguay, beginning in 1916 with the National Council of Uruguayan Women. This group worked for women's suffrage and for the abolition of the white slave trade. Three years later a purely suffrage organization formed called the Uruguayan Alliance of Women's Suffrage. However, women were not enfranchised until 1932 (all information from the Latin American and Caribbean Women's Collective 1977: 32; see also Little 1975).

Apparently, Chile experienced an incipient ameliorative movement from the 1920s through the 1940s. Although information is very scanty, Uruguay probably did so also, between about 1916 and 1932. It is questionable whether Peru even reached the incipient stage of movement development, and activism at any level was confined to the decade 1915–25.

CONCLUSIONS

Table 4.1 presents a summary of the previous case studies in terms of the dependent variables that constitute the focus of this book: scope of ideology and movement size. Several things are immediately apparent when that table is examined. First, women's movements of the nineteenth and first half of the twentieth centuries were overwhelmingly ameliorative in ideology, irrespective of where or exactly when they occurred. Moreover, in the few cases where they existed, ideologically more broadly feminist movements never grew beyond the incipient stage. Indeed, if a society experienced a feminist movement and subsequently the movement developed beyond the incipient stage, the ideology narrowed to the ameliorative level (e.g., the United States and France), or at best the larger, ameliorative movement coexisted with a much smaller, feminist

Table 4.1 Estimates of Relative Size, Ideological Scope, and Approximate Dates of Independent First-Wave Women's Movements

	Years	Size	Ideology
United States	1848–c.1870	incipient	feminist
	c.1870–1920	mass	ameliorative
Great Britain	c.1860–1900	incipient	ameliorative
	c.1900–1918	mass and incipient	ameliorative and feminist
Canada	c.1880–1918	intermediate	ameliorative
Australia	c.1880–1901	incipient or intermediate	ameliorative
New Zealand	1885–1893	incipient or intermediate	ameliorative
Finland	c.1880–1906	incipient	ameliorative
Norway	c.1885–1913	incipient	ameliorative
Sweden	c.1870–c.1910	intermediate to mass	ameliorative
Denmark	c.1870–c.1910	intermediate to mass	ameliorative
Iceland	c.1894–c.1910	intermediate to mass	ameliorative
Holland	1894–c.1913	intermediate	ameliorative
Belgium	No discernible movement		
France	c.1870–1900	incipient	feminist
	c.1900–1914	intermediate	ameliorative
Russia	1905–1918	incipient	ameliorative
Germany	c.1865–1914	incipient	ameliorative
	c.1914–c.1920	intermediate or mass	ameliorative
Italy	c.1867–1914	incipient	possibly feminist
Austro-Hungarian Empire	1893–c.1920	incipient	ameliorative
China	1911–1927	incipient	ameliorative
Japan	1880–1923	incipient	ameliorative
	1923–c.1930	intermediate or mass	ameliorative
India	1917–c.1950	incipient	ameliorative
Indonesia	1928–1942	?	ameliorative
Iran/Persia	1906–c.1950s	incipient	ameliorative
Egypt	1919–c.1935	incipient	ameliorative
Puerto Rico	1917–1936	?	ameliorative
Dominican Republic	1931–1942	incipient	ameliorative
Cuba	c.1914–c.1927	probably intermediate	ameliorative
Mexico	1904–c.1940	intermediate and incipient	ameliorative and feminist

(continued)

Table 4.1   (Continued)

	Years	Size	Ideology
Argentina	c.1900–c.1930s	incipient	ameliorative
Brazil	c.1920;–1937	incipient	ameliorative
Chile	1915–1949	incipient	ameliorative
Peru	c.1915–1925	less than incipient	ameliorative
Uruguay	1916–c.1932	incipient	ameliorative

Note: Relative size refers to the largest size achieved by a movement during the time period in question. A question mark indicates that no size estimate is possible.

branch (e.g., Great Britain and Mexico). We were able to estimate the maximum size of 30 movements. Only two (the United States and Great Britain) were unambiguously mass at some point in their history. Five more may be said to have reached mass proportions (Germany, Sweden, Denmark, Iceland, and Japan), while five were intermediate in size (Canada, France, Holland, Cuba, and Mexico) and two others may also have reached a level in between incipient and mass (Australia and New Zealand). In all, at least sixteen, or over half of the cases for which data are available, never grew beyond the incipient stage; two of the sixteen probably did not even reach an incipient level of development.

There was remarkable similarity in the process of movement development among practically all of the cases studied. The first issue to surface concerning women was almost everywhere that of education. In Europe and North America, where literacy rates were very high, women organized first to fight for higher educational opportunities. In Asia, Latin America, and the Middle East, where few if any women were literate, reform-oriented, Westernized males usually first raised the issue of basic education for women. This issue was then taken up by small groups women, often relatives of the reformers, comprised of those who had been the first to become educated. As a cadre of educated women developed—about a generation later—in all cases examined they organized to fight for basic legal reforms. While there was variation in agenda from society to society, depending on the precise nature of women's disadvantages, there were some striking similarities as well. Almost everywhere women fought the sexual double standard by demanding male monogamy. Where legalized prostitution and/or concubinage existed, they were fought, as was polygamy. Where they did not, other approaches were taken to the informal sexual double standard. Reform in inheritance and property rights and divorce law, as well as employment opportunities for women (especially access to the professions) were part of the agenda for almost all women's movements. Suffrage arose as an issue in every case, eventually. But, typically it arose later than these other issues and often because women came to feel that other reforms could be won only if they were first enfranchised. While female suffrage thus became an issue as a means to other reforms, quite often movements focused so much attention on this issue that the reasons for wanting the vote were obscured. The means often became the de facto end, and with success on that issue, the movement often ended. Also, temperance activity, and specifically the WCTU, played a major role in the pursuit of legal and political reform in a substantial number of societies.

In every case where the movement became mass or intermediate, and almost all incipient movements as well, women's demands were justified on the basis of inherent sexual differences. Repeatedly we saw that most women activists did not challenge the fact that, at least for the vast majority of women, their primary roles were those of wife and mother. In addition, virtually everywhere it was assumed that role differentiation is related to superior morality, compassion, and pacifism among women, including special concern for children and the needy. The various reforms demanded, including temperance and the end of the sexual double standard, as well as political, legal, and educational equality, were predicated on one or both of two goals: women would be better wives and mothers and the family would be strengthened; and national policy would be enriched by the inclusion of women's "special" virtues and concerns. Where demands for employment opportunities were made, it was usually in recognition that some women would never marry and that others would be widowed; such women needed to be able to live independently. Only a few individuals explicitly propounded the views that married women should have careers if they choose, or that women should be free to choose the single life without stigmatization.

Independent women's movements, regardless of size or ideological scope, where overwhelmingly middle-class, urban phenomena (see Evans 1977:31–32). Especially the leaders, but apparently most followers as well, were considerably better educated than the average woman of their society. Many were employed, at least at some point in their lives, as educators, journalists, writers, or in the medical profession. In addition, in most societies, women's rights activists were typically involved in social welfare and philanthropic activities as well.

Where women's movements grew beyond the incipient level, a sizable proportion of the total population was urban, educated, and middle class, as will be demonstrated in chapter 6. In other words, there was an ample pool of women sharing the characteristics which typified women's rights activists from which to recruit. Protestantism tended in general to emphasize education more than did other major religions, including Catholicism. Therefore, it is not surprising that of the fourteen nations which may have experienced women's movements beyond the incipient level, ten were predominantly Protestant (United States, Great Britain, Canada, Australia, New Zealand, Sweden, Denmark, Iceland, Holland, and Germany). Moreover, the only Protestant societies that failed to develop movements larger than incipient in size were Finland and Norway, where women were enfranchised quite early anyway. Of the remaining (Cuba, Mexico, France, and Japan), all but France grew beyond the incipient level only after World War I, and in France the literacy rate was high relative to most other

European Catholic nations in the prewar era, and at any rate activists were disproportionately French Protestants. We do not believe that there is a direct link between religion and women's rights activism. Rather, religion is linked to education, and in turn, to a stress on individual, including minority rights, which are the primary variables that explain the emergence and growth of women's movements. From this perspective, the active and visible role of Quakers in the U.S. movement was not a function of their theology, but of their emphasis on education and individualism for both sexes. Likewise, many of the women's leaders in Asian nations were converts to Christianity, or at least had been educated in Christian schools. We argue that it was the superior education of these women compared to other women in their own societies, not Christianity per se, which explains their activism.

Incipient and some intermediate movements failed to grow for one or more of three reasons. Chief among them was undoubtedly the absence of a large enough pool of women with the appropriate characteristics from which to recruit, an issue to which we will return in chapter 6. In some cases, however, the movements were cut short by the actions of sympathetic and powerful male leaders, who rendered moot some of the issues raised by the movement by passing appropriate legislation relatively quickly (e.g., New Zealand, Australia, Norway, and Finland). These were all nations in which women were enfranchised early (i.e., before World War I). Finally, governmental repression was only too effective in a number of cases (see Evans 1977:91ff). Laws restricting the right of women to join political organizations, attend political meetings or publicly discuss political issues probably retarded movement development in Germany, Russia, China and Japan. Direct government suppression of independent women's organizations occurred at various times in France, Russia, China, Japan, Indonesia, Iran, Brazil and Peru.

The focus of this book is on *independent* women's movements, namely those that are organizationally independent of control by male-dominated parties, movements, and/or governments. As we have seen, such movements were overwhelmingly middle class. We have also seen that working-class women often organized during this period in unions and in socialist parties. By and large, their basic needs for decent pay and working conditions, and for protection from exploitation, led them to place priority on their class rather than on their sexual disadvantages. Where permitted or encouraged, activist working-class women joined male-dominated movements and organizations working on behalf of their class. Many such organizations spawned women's groups, often with feminist goals and leaders. Nevertheless, as stepchildren of another movement, their priorities as women were generally suspect and almost always sacrificed to the "larger" cause. The same was true in the many cases of nationalistic movements.

The middle-class women's movements fought for issues that in most societies were largely perceived as irrelevant by the masses of women. Therefore, where both working-class and middle-class women were organized, they only rarely cooperated, and then not for long. Indeed, the interests of the different classes of women were not infrequently antithetical. Middle-class women often fought for equality in the labor force, meaning for them equal access to prestigious employment. Working-class women usually wanted special protective legislation which, by its very nature, sets them off from men. Sometimes middle-class women fought for women's suffrage limited only to the literate; that is, themselves, in fear of lower-class radicalism. Left-wing and radical women sometimes opposed female enfranchisement, in fear of the proreligious and conservative nature of the masses of women in their society.

By and large, the major ameliorative changes sought by women activists of the nineteenth and first half of the twentieth centuries were in place shortly after the end of World War II, if not decades before, in most countries. Hindsight permits us to understand that legal and political equality do not result in social and economic equality. As vast numbers of contemporary scholars have pointed out, in accepting the traditional division of labor and in failing to challenge traditional gender role definitions, real equality could not emanate from the formal equality sought be "first-wave" women's activists. Social equality is fundamentally rooted in the relative economic resources of the sexes (see Chafetz 1984). It was left to a new generation of women activists, beginning in the 1960s, to discover this fact and to begin anew women's movements around the world. These are the focus of the next chapter.

5 The Second Wave: Women's Movements since the Late 1960s

The issues of women's rights and status did not die after the ameliorative movements collapsed following their success. In some cases, ameliorative movements continued into the post-World War II years before gaining their goals. Where they were successful earlier, organizations and individuals often continued the struggle through the interwar and post-World War II years. What died almost everywhere after 1950, if not sometime in the preceeding thirty years, was publicly visible *movement* activity. Since this is not a social or intellectual history of feminism, we will not discuss the continuities between waves of movement activism. Rather, our focus in this chapter is the reemergence of publicly visible women's movements in several societies in the years after the mid 1960s.

The nineteenth and early twentieth century women's movements were almost all ameliorative, inasmuch as attention was focused on educational opportunities for women, moral reform, a series of legal reforms designed to abolish the formal liabilities under which women—especially married women—lived, and in most cases, women's suffrage. Feminists often raised other issues, but organized, not to mention mass movement activity focused rather narrowly on these issues. They were women's *rights* movements in a substantially literal sense. As numerous analyses have demonstrated, in nation after nation formal political, and even increased legal equality (complete legal equality was not achieved in most places) have nowhere resulted in general equality of status between the sexes. Relative to their male compatriots, females remained substantially disadvantaged in every society discussed in the last chapter.

When movement activity reemerged nearly twenty years ago, the agenda was ideologically quite broad, as it had been for some individuals and groups earlier. This time, however, the conditions in some societies were ripe for feminism to become an intermediate-size or mass movement.

Continuing the emphasis in the last chapter on independent women's movements, we will exclude from consideration in this chapter those cases where totalitarian governments, either directly or through their party machinery, organize and mobilize women. It is not that they lack a commitment to feminist ideology or that they fail to substantially improve the status of women. Some do; some don't. By definition, they are not social movements, however. Therefore, we will not discuss such societies as China, Cuba, East Germany, Vietnam, or the USSR, despite the existence of available literature which documents activism on behalf of women, and often substantial improvement in the relative status of women. We will also continue to deemphasize feminist activism that is organizationally subsumed within an essentially male-dominated party or movement in nontotalitarian societies.

Literature available in the United States which details the organizations, membership, and ideologies of current women's movements is scarce, with the exception of our own movement. Hints that such movements are fairly widespread across the globe, and general (but not nation-specific) discussions of feminist ideology can be found. They are of little help to this project, however. The material called upon in the last chapter was produced mostly by historians, who by now have done a fair job of documenting first-wave women's movements in nations other than their own. However, as a rule, historians do not study the present. Social scientists, and especially sociologists, would be inclined to document contemporary social movements. It is an indication of the ethnocentrism of our discipline that so little cross-national material is available in the United States concerning contemporary women's movements outside the United States. The result, unfortunately, is a relative paucity of materials for this chapter, excepting, of course, the United States.

THE UNITED STATES

In chapter 2 we discussed several aspects of the emergence of a women's movement in the United States, beginning in the late 1960s. Here, we will reiterate some of the points made earlier and add additional information. It is clear that within a very few years after the first publicly visible stirrings of movement activity, a very broad and diverse feminist movement had developed a mass following, organized into a large array of organizations and claiming huge numbers of "fellow travelers" not officially affiliated with movement organizations.

All analyses of the contemporary U.S. women's movement trace its origins to two distinct, and originally completely independent sources. Labeled variously the "older," "liberal," or "women's rights" branch, one began with the founding of the National Organization for Women (NOW) in June 1966, by 28 people, and its subsequent October organizational meeting of 300 women and men. Within a few years, such other organizations as Women's Equity Action League (WEAL, 1968), National Women's Political Caucus (NWPC, 1971), Federally Employed Women (FEW, 1968), Human Rights for Women (1968), Coalition of Labor Union Women (CLUE, 1974), Older Women's Liberation (OWL, 1970), National Black Feminist Organization (NBFO, 1973), and dozens of women's caucuses within professional and other work-oriented organizations, had sprung up. Simultaneously, that branch of the movement variously known as the "younger," "radical," or "women's liberation" component was emerging, based in numerous, small, local groups with no overarching national organization, and in many cases no separate names. As we shall see, by the eary 1970s the two branches were coalescing into one movement, characterized by substantial ideological, tactical, and organizational diversity, but also a set of common themes, concepts, and goals.

The "older" branch of the movement may be dated to the founding of NOW. It quickly became, and has remained, the "largest and most prominant organization" within the movement (Freeman 1975:73). By 1967 NOW numbered 700 members in 14 chapters, growing to 150 chapters and somewhere between 5000 and 10,000 members in 1971, 1000 chapters and 40,000 members in 1974, 60,000 members in 1977, 150,000 in 1981, and 175,000 in 1983 (Bouchier 1983:47; Freeman 1975:87; Deckard 1983:326, 373, 388).The NWPC is the second largest of the national organizations, numbering 30,000–35,000 members in 500–700 local chapters in 1973 (Carden 1974:139) and 50,000 in 1978 (Gelb and Palley 1982:28–29). Gelb and Palley reported that the 5 largest national organizations in the movement had a combined membership of over a quarter of a million in 1978, whereas at the beginning of the decade they numbered only about a quarter of that (1982:50). Not only did membership swell during the 1970s in the organizations representing this branch of the movement, so too did the number of organizations proliferate wildly (see Carden 1974: chap. 10). NOW remained a general purpose organization. A variety of single-purpose groups arose, such as the NWPC and the National Abortion Rights Action League (NARAL) with 90,000 members by late 1970s (Gelb and Palley 1982:35–36). Too, women organized within their professional organizations into caucuses (by 1975 there were over 75 in academic disciplines alone; Freeman 1975:168); union women formed CLUE (16,000 members in 1982); feminist office workers founded Working Women (Deckard 1983:347). Women sharing a minority status beyond sex organized into such groups as OWL and NBFO, which in its first year attracted 2000 members (Freeman 1975:156). Litigation and research organizations emerged in the 1970s as well.

The members and leaders of organizations within this branch of the movement have been overwhelmingly middle class and college educated. Initially, they were mostly employed in relatively high prestige careers, and "older," meaning beyond their 20s. The first board of NOW, comprised of 29 people (4 of whom were male), had 7 professors or university administrators, 4 government officials, 5 labor union officials, and 4 business executives (Carden 1974:104). By the 1970s there were more housewives, more women in their 20s, and more women employed in less prestigious occupations in NOW. In 1974 about 17 percent of NOW members were housewives, 14 percent students, and only about 25 percent were employed professionally. Moreover, half were under age 30 and a third did not have college degrees (Freeman 1975:91). By and large, however, working-class and minority women have been absent from the organizations in this branch of the movement (and the other as well), except, of course, those specifically oriented to their double status, such as CLUE, NBFO, and some Chicana groups which formed especially in California (Deckard 1983:346). In 1975 only 5 percent of NOW members were black (Freeman 1975:91).

The "younger" branch of the movement began independently in several places during the years 1964–68, as women active in New Left groups such as the Students for Democratic Society (SDS) began to meet separately to deal with their own issues—which were ignored or ridiculed by male activists (see Freeman 1975:56ff.). Its symbolic beginning may be traced to the adoption of a Women's Manifesto at a Women's Liberation Workshop held during the 1967 SDS national conference (Yates 1975:7). By 1969 such groups were forming all over the country and probably involved more participants than the "older" branch (Freeman 1975:62). Comprised of about 5–30 women each, the groups were loosely coordinated through personal contacts and feminist publications, and within a city often around a women's center or a coordinating committee (1975:103–4). In 1968 this branch held its first national gathering in Sandy Springs, Maryland, which 22 women from 6 cities attended. Later that year they held a national conference in Chicago, attended by 200 women from 20 states. Their first national newsletter, *Voice of the Women's Liberation Movement*, grew from a circulation of 200 to 2000 in a 16-month period in 1968–69. In 1970 the radical-feminist publication *Notes from the Second Year* sold 40,000 copies (Bouchier 1983:97–98). By 1975 there were over 150 such publications in existence (Freeman 1975:109–11). According to Bouchier (1983:55), by the end of 1969 there were at least 500 women's liberation groups. In late 1970, a directory of such groups listed "several hundred"; three years later, "several thousand" (Freeman 1975:147). Carden (1974:2) estimated combined membership in this branch of the movement at 15,000. Yates (1975:1) cited a range of possible members from 10,000 to 500,000. By 1970, New York had 50 groups, Chicago 30, Boston 25, and San Francisco 35 (1974:64). The individual groups generally had a short-lived existence, on the order of several months. But in the early 1970s new ones were constantly forming, recruiting new members to the movement. Like the other branch, members have been overwhelmingly white, middle class, and college educated. However, since they were mostly in their 20s, they tended to be less frequently married and to have lower status employment than women in the "older" branch (1974:20–21).

Many of the early recruits to the younger branch were socialists. In the early 1970s autonomous socialist-feminist groups arose in "dozens" of cities (Deckard 1983:334). However, most of these women concluded that women's problems would not be solved by socialist revolution and chose to dedicate their energies to feminism. In 1970–71 the Young Socialist Alliance and the Socialist Workers Party attempted to infiltrate and take over this branch of the movement. They failed to do so. Nor were they ever able to develop "a strong separate identity," thus remaining "outside the mainstream" of the women's movement (Bouchier 1983:136,125). A 1975 National Socialist Feminist Conference drew over 2000 women, however (Deckard 1983:335). Ideologically, socialist-feminism constitutes a third branch, albeit small, of the movement and a third ideology (see Yates 1975).

Combining both major branches of the women's movement, it is unlikely that even as many as 500,000 women have belonged to an explicitly feminist organi-

zation or group. Bouchier claimed that about 1 in 300 women has been attached
to a feminist group of some kind (1983:181). What has made this a mass movement are two additional phenomena. First, an array of "traditional" and long-
standing organizations, ranging from the YWCA to the Federation of Business
and Professional Women's Clubs, the League of Women Voters, various wom-
en's church groups, labor unions, the American Civil Liberties Union, and the
American Association of University Women, which collectively represent several million members, have, since about 1970, supported a variety of the specific
reforms and laws proposed by the movement (see Banks 1981:247; Carden
1974:3, 144ff., Freeman 1975:214ff.; Gelb and Palley 1982:14, 27). Many of these
reforms have been sufficiently radical to warrant the conclusion that traditional
groups are supporting feminist, not merely ameliorative demands. These groups
regularly form coalitions with various specifically feminist organizations around
specific issues (Gelb and Palley 1982:37). A 1981 poll showed that 4 percent of
American women were "either members of or contributors to an organization
promoting women's rights," which translates to about 3,000,000 women. An additional 500,000 men were also involved in such groups (Bouchier 1983:180).

Second, the early and mid-1970s witnessed a substantial alteration in public
opinion, and millions of people, including over half of all women, came to support many of the principles and specific demands made by movement organizations and activists (Chafe 1977:139). Despite such disclaimers as "I'm not a wom-
en's libber," these issue supporters may appropriately be considered fellow travelers. For instance, in 1972 47 percent of women polled said that women should
have an equal role, and 29 percent said their place was in the home. Eight years
later, the respective percentages were 58:20 (Deckard 1983:396). Among women,
40 percent favored the effort to strengthen women's status in 1970, 64 percent in
1980, while opposition to that assertion dwindled from 42 percent to 24 percent
(1983:397). A 1975 Harris Poll saw an increase in support for legalized abortion
from 46 to 54 percent in four years, and an increase from 56 to 67 percent in support of more child care centers (Bouchier 1983:123). A 1972–73 poll showed 55
percent of adults either "completely for" or "more for than against" the women's
movement, an increase of 6 percent in one year (Whitehurst 1977:149). By 1981,
63 percent of Americans favored passage of the ERA (Deckard 1983:447).

Another indication of widespread support for feminism may be gleaned from
the success of publications directed to feminist audiences. The first issue of Ms., a
glossy, somewhat moderate feminist monthly magazine, appeared in 1972, and
within 8 days sold out its run of 300,000 copies (Deckard 1983:355; Yates
1975:127). Moreover, Freeman (1975:36) noted that about 80 percent of Ms. sub-
scribers are not members of any movement organization. By 1982 its circulation
was 500,000. In 1983 about 30 national feminist news and opinion magazines existed, along with an additional 20 academic journals dealing with feminism,
women's studies, and/or women's issues (Bouchier 1983:104–5).

Discussions concerning the contemporary U.S. women's movement all concur in pointing to extensive ideological diversity, rooted in the diverse origins of

the two major branches of the movement. At least as far as the first few years of the movement's history, there is little doubt that the older branch was ideologically less radical or more conservative than the younger. Therefore, if an examination of this branch shows it to be fully feminist and not simply ameliorative in its goals, then it is safe to conclude that the entire movement may be so designated, without much exploration of the other strands of movement ideology (i.e., "radical" and "socialist"; see Yates 1975).

The original "Bill of Rights" demanded by NOW contained eight demands, only two of which were not consensually agreed upon. The six agreed upon were enforcement of antiemployment discrimination laws, maternity leave rights, tax deduction for child care expenses of working parents, child care centers, equal and unsegregated education, and equal job training and allowances for low-income women. Disagreement came from those with a union affiliation who opposed the ERA and left the organization, and from some who objected to legalized abortion, which was included in a demand for the right of women to control their own reproductive lives. These women too, left, and soon formed WEAL (Deckard 1983:325). While many of these demands were indeed ameliorative, they also represented a challenge to the gender role system, by denying that it is women's obligation to forego a career to raise children. Indeed, NOW's founding statement stressed that "it is no longer . . . necessary or possible for women to devote the greater part of their lives to child-rearing; yet childbearing and rearing . . . still is used to justify barring women from equal professional and economic participation and advance" (Freeman 1975:74). That statement went on to propose "a different concept of marriage, an equitable sharing of the responsibilities of home and children and of the economic burdens of their support." And, finally, to state that

> we are . . . opposed to all policies and practices—in church, state, college, factory, or office—which, in the guise of protectiveness, not only deny opportunities but also foster in women self-denigration, dependence, and evasion of responsibility, undermine their confidence in their own abilities and foster contempt for women [Freeman 1975:74].

NOW then established seven task forces, including one concerned with discrimination in religion, one with women's image in the mass media, and one concerned with the problems of poor women (Freeman 1975:75). It is interesting to note that by 1972 three quarters of NOW's original Bill of Rights had been at least partially enacted (Bouchier 1983:123).

In 1969 a Congress to Unite Women was held which involved 500 women from both branches of the movement. They were able to agree upon a 10-point program, including abortion prohibition repeal, 24-hour child care, an end to sex role socialization of children, and passage of the ERA (Deckard 1983:335). Further cooperation between the two branches occurred the next year when NOW organized a Women's Strike for Equality to commemorate the fiftieth anniversary of the Nineteenth Amendment. Three demands were voiced: abortion, 24-hour child care, and equal education and employment opportunity. Women "by the thousands" turned out in cities across the nation; "the sheer numbers shocked everyone" (Freeman 1975:84). It was the largest women's demonstration in history. In New York City alone 50,000 women marched (Bouchier 1983:96). The immediate impact was a 50–70 percent growth of NOW chapters, with the new members including many low-level white-collar workers and housewives. Less knowledgeable about feminism than the original members, NOW adopted the technique of consciousness-raising (C-R) groups from the younger branch of the movement in order to better incorporate this flood of new recruits. Many see this as the start of the "radicalization" of the older branch of the movement (see Banks 1981:235; Mandle 1978:171). It became increasingly concerned with the plight of poor and nonwhite women; by 1973 it was pushing to decriminalize prostitution; after 1971 it became committed to supporting the rights of lesbians. Gradually, it turned its attention to such issues as rape, sexual harassment at work and at school, and the role of women in sport (see Freeman 1975:97–100).

As the 1970s progressed, younger women were increasingly attracted to NOW and to other groups from that branch of the movement. The younger branch emphasized C-R and structurelessness. It had no real mechanism to turn consciousness into action, however. Many of these women, although remaining feminist, drifted away from movement activism after a year or two of C-R; some sought action-oriented groups. Carden (1974:73) estimated that between 5 and 15 percent went on to become involved in social action projects. A plethora of such groups developed at the local level, oriented primarily to providing services and/or referral for women, for instance, feminist bookstores, abortion counseling, day care, health centers, battered women's shelters, and rape crisis centers. But many chose NOW and other nationally organized groups as a vehicle for action projects. In general, these young women served to radicalize the older branch, both in ideology and in organizational structure. But it was the older branch that led the fight for institutional change. By the mid 1970s, the two streams had coalesced (Bouchier 1978:137; Carden 1974:118). Meanwhile, it was spreading rapidly into suburbs and small towns, in areas where movement activism did not exist before the mid-1970s (Cassell 1977:181). Unlike the earlier movement which grew more conservative and ameliorative as it became mass in size, the growth of the contemporary movement went hand-in-hand with an expansion of feminist issues within the major, national women's organization. Originally structured around 7 task forces, by 1973 NOW had 30 such issue-area task forces (Carden 1974:115). As Freeman put it: "The existence of a diverse movement spanning a wide spectrum of feminist attitudes pushed the leaders of the more respectable women's organizations to more strongly feminist positions" (1975:235).

The International Women's Year, 1975, witnessed the establishment of the Women's Action Alliance. It coordinated over 100 women's groups to create a

U.S. National Women's Agenda, supported by 90 of the groups, representing more than 30,000,000 women. Its program included fair representation in the political process, equal education and training, equal access to economic power, child care for all children, and fair treatment by, and access to, the media (Deckard 1983:369). Two years later, the 1977 Houston Women's Conference demonstrated that "the movement had truly come of age. The meeting showed that women of all ages, races, and economic conditions were concerned with feminist issues and that, despite their diversity, they could work together" (1983:374). Over 130,000 women attended state and territorial meetings to develop resolutions and to choose delegates. Virtually the entire 25-point program developed by the feminists passed (1983:375–76). Bouchier claimed that this conference "marked the full incorporation into mainstream politics of feminist demands which had *seemed* revolutionary nine years earlier" (1983:140). The next year 100,000 people participated in a march in Washington to demand ratification of the ERA (Mandle 1978:180).

In general, the contemporary women's movement in the United States has been comprised of an enormous array of groups, many if not most of which concentrate on a small number or one issue, and most of which are local or decentralized and have firm grass roots. Movement activists have recognized "the pitfalls of thinking there was any single answer to inequality or sex role stereotyping. The result was a plethora of related but separate activities. . ." (Chafe 1977:130). Underlying all is consensus that "individuals should be free . . . to determine their own life-style, sexual preference, occupation, and personal values" (1977:133); that social institutions, not biology, restrict people on the basis of their sex (Carden 1974:11); and that the role of both sexes must change. The diverse activities of the movement "represent a scrutiny and criticism of and, often an attack on all institutions—prisons, welfare systems, churches, the law, industry, . . . governments, schools, colleges, unions, and the mass media" (1974:10). In her book on the various ideologies of the movement, Yates stressed that what all activists were calling for was "a complete transformation of American society" (1975:2), that they were challenging the basic role assignments of the sexes, not merely demanding equal rights (1975:13–14). Mandle expressed the ideological core as a shared desire for "the destruction of traditional ideas of female inferiority, passivity, and domesticity" (1978:185). Whitehurst defined the core ideology as "the belief in the existence of sexism and in the importance of freedom from oppression through structural and personal change" (1977:146–47). Besides legal equality, an end to discrimination, control over their own bodies, and political power, the diverse members and groups in the women's movement have shared a desire to eliminate sex stereotypes, to enable women "to pursue alternatives without stigma," to develop a "sense of history, solidarity and sisterhood," and to improve women's self-image and opinions of other women (1977:147). Virtually all agree on the fundamental need to restructure the family (Yates 1975:chap. 4).

These descriptions fit our own definition of a fully feminist movement which challenges all aspects of the sex stratification and gender role definition systems by addressing all major social institutions. It is safe to conclude that since about 1970, the United States has experienced a mass feminist movement.

GREAT BRITAIN

Strongly affected by the ideas being developed across the Atlantic, by 1970 Great Britain had a publicly visable, fully feminist movement underway. Unlike its U.S. counterpart, however, it has not grown to a mass level. It has also never developed any general, national movement organization, rather remaining a loose collection of local groups and single-purpose national committees.

Bouchier (1978:108–9; 1983:57) dated the beginning of the movement in Britain to 1968. While no single incident may be said to have signaled its start, several things occurred that year. In Hull, a group of fishermen's wives, joined by a number of middle-class women, organized to protest safety conditions on their husbands' ships. Out of this emerged the primarily middle-class Equal Rights Association. Women workers at Ford struck for equal pay, and London bus conductresses struck for the right to become drivers, in that same year. Out of these came the union-sponsored National Joint Action Committee for Women's Equal Rights. Also in 1968, women in the International Marxist Group began to discuss feminist ideas, and in 1969 they split off to form their own group. Women in other socialist/communist organizations quickly followed. Most of these groups maintained "close ties with male-dominated organizations" and stressed not so much issues of sexism and male power as the "exploitation of women by capitalist bosses and government" (1983:57). They specifically sought equal pay, unionization of women, free nurseries, price and rent controls, and better welfare benefits (1983:57). At the same time, independent women's groups were springing up across England, and by 1969 had spread to Wales and Scotland (1983:59). The women in these groups, too, were sympathetic to socialism, although their groups were independent and they tended to be suspicious of male organizations (1978:109). In 1969 the London Women's Liberation Workshop was founded to coordinate the various local groups, regardless of political persuasion. In 1970 it numbered 50 affiliated groups, by 1971, 70. It emphasized issues of equal pay, the media image of women, sex role socialization, and legal inequities (1983:58–59; 1978:109).

For Rowbotham (1983:39; see also Currell 1974:115) the beginning of the movement dates to 1970, when a conference attended by 500 people (Bouchier 1978:110 claimed 600) was held at Oxford. In the aftermath of the conference, there was a rapid growth of feminist groups. Bouchier described this conference as "the public and political baptism of the women's liberation movement in Britain" (1983:60). Out of it came the Women's National Coordinating Committee, a very loosely structured, temporary (one year) mechanism to disseminate information among the various local groups. Later, in 1975, by a narrow margin the annual conference defeated a proposal to establish a national organization. In that same year the Women's Informational and Referral Service was begun as a central clearinghouse and information center for the movement in England (1983:102).

The 1970 conference developed four demands: equal pay, equal educational opportunity, 24-hour nurseries, and free contraception and abortion on demand. These, along with three additional demands developed during later annual conferences, have constituted the only unified statement of goals of the movement. In 1971 a London demonstration on behalf of these demands was attended by "several hundred" (Bouchier 1983:94). At the conference in 1974, financial and legal independence for women and the right to self-defined sexuality were added. Finally, amid much controversy, 1978 saw the addition of a seventh demand: freedom from violence, threats, and aggression from males (1983:132).

For all intents and purposes, the British movement has been comprised of a myriad of local groups, each numbering about a dozen members, typically middle-class women in their 20s or 30s (Bouchier 1983:95; Rowbotham 1983:40). There have been many local, but few large national demonstrations. Like the United States, but fewer in number, local groups have founded women's centers; published newsletters; run shelters for battered women; conducted health clinics and rape crisis and day-care centers (1983:89). Their publications are, with a few exceptions, circulated to only a couple of thousand readers. *Shrew*, the journal of the London Women's Liberation Workshop, had a circulation of 5000 by 1975. *Socialist Women* has a national circulation of about 5000, while the one widely circulated national journal, *Spare Rib*, sold out 20,000 copies of its first issue in 1972, and reached a high point with 32,000 readers. While socialist in orientation, this journal is less sectarian than any other (1983:100–1). Some academic journals, women's presses, and women's libraries have also been founded. But very little of any of this feminist material is readily available to the mass public (1983:103).

Nationally, several single-issue "campaigns" have been organized, each as an independent organization. They have mostly been organized by socialist feminists (Bouchier 1983:82). The Campaign for Financial and Legal Independence began in 1974, concerned with a variety of concrete issues such as pensions, insurance, various legal reforms, mortgages, loans, and student grants. A Campaign for Wages for Housework began in about 1975 (opposed by many feminists, especially socialists), while a Campaign for Free Abortion on Demand also emerged (only 18 percent of the public endorsed abortion on demand in a 1975 poll) (1983:109–13). This campaign became, in 1975, the National Abortion Campaign and was supported by unions and the National Council for Civil Liberties, which also supported other women's rights issues (1983:109, 117). In 1976 Women Against Rape was formed, while at about the same time the National Women's Aid Federation grew up to deal with the issue of battered women. In 1981, 800 women participated in a conference run by Women Against Violence Against Women. In 1980 the "300 Group" was formed to organize and train women for political candidacy. It has about 1,500 members and appears to be similar to the NWPC in the United States, albeit much smaller (1983:196).

Besides the socialists, there has been a second major branch of the British women's movement: the radical feminists. This branch is the direct counterpart of the younger branch of the U.S. movement. It has defined sexism and males — not capitalism — as the primary problem and, as the 1970s progressed, it increasingly propounded separatism from males and male institutions as its fundamental goal (see Bouchier 1983:130ff.). There has been substantial and increasing conflict between the two branches, and unlike the United States, women sympathizing with neither have had no real place in the movement (1983:159). Indeed, since 1978 there has not even been a national conference, as the differences between the branches have intensified (1983:222). Since "many, if not most women found aspects of socialist and radical feminist programmes morally or personally repugnant" (1983:158–59) they have had to align themselves with the Labour Party and trade unions which have supported many of the more concrete demands made by movement activists.

Bouchier (1983:177–78) concluded that Britain has not had a mass feminist movement. He used words such as "small and fragile," "tiny," and "fragmented" to describe it. Currell estimated the size of the movement in the mid 1970s at 4000–5000 (1974:115). According to Bouchier (1983:179) there are about 2000 core activists in each branch; a total of about 10,000 women are regularly involved and 20,000 marginally active in movement groups and activities. About 1 in 1000 adult females are involved. However, for single issues, the numbers are more substantial. For instance, one abortion demonstration drew 60,000 women participants. Activists are "heavily concentrated in large urban areas," especially London, Bristol, Leeds, Nottingham, and Sheffield. Though small, the movement is nationwide in scope. Over 40 cities have women's centers, which have served to attract increasing numbers of working-class women to the movement. Bouchier (1983:179) described the "typical provincial city" as having one or more C-R groups, a women's center, a shelter for battered women, a rape crisis center, a branch of the National Abortion Campaign, a lesbian group, a nursery campaign or co-op, a health group, some art or writing groups, some socialist and revolutionary feminist groups, a bookstore, and one or more newsletters.

Because of the central importance of socialist doctrine to most feminist activists, the British movement has developed an ideology that is more focused on economic phenomena than has the United States (Bouchier 1978:133). It has made greater efforts, and probably has been somewhat more successful than the U.S. movement, to involve working-class women and to work actively on issues of central importance to them (Curell 1974:116). In terms of general politics, the British movement has been more radical than its U.S. counterpart. However, like the U.S. movement, feminist activists in Britain have questioned every social institution and demanded reforms in every area of social life, the personal and interpersonal, as well as the legal, economic, educational, and political aspects. This is scarcely surprising since the English language books and publications written on one side of the Atlantic have routinely found their way to the opposite shores. We therefore conclude that Great Britain has experienced an intermediate-sized feminist movement since about 1970, comprised of a relatively small number of activists split into two branches, plus support for many specific demands from unions, moderate single-purpose organizations, the Labour Party, and numerous small parties of the far left.

CANADA

In Canada, a feminist movement arose during the late 1960s which was heavily influenced by, and similar to, the U.S. movement, while also sharing many features of the British movement. Apparently, it has reached at least an intermediate size, although we have no concrete numbers of organizational members upon which to rely for an estimate.

Teather (1976:316) spoke of three branches of the movement, all of which existed by 1969: the women's rights, women's liberation, and radical feminist. The women's rights branch may be dated to the 1966 founding of the Committee for Equality of Women. It produced a brief which was endorsed by 32 women's organizations representing 2,000,000 women (in a nation with a total population of only 23,000,000) (1976:317). As a result of pressure by this group, the following year the government established the Royal Commission on the Status of Women, which was similar to the commission established a few years earlier by President Kennedy in the United States. The National Action Committee on the Status of Women, which demanded equal pay, child care, birth control and abortion, and reforms in family property laws, was soon launched. At the same time, the Fédération des Femmes du Quebec, an umbrella group for 36 women's organizations, called for equal pay, greater representation of women in politics, and reforms concerning matrimonial property. Traditional women's organizations, such as the YWCA, the Canadian Federation of University Women, the National Council of Women, and the National Council of Jewish Women in Canada, also came out in support of these basic demands (1976:318–19). Also, women working within the major political parties, especially the New Democratic and Liberal Parties, organized and began to pressure their parties to support many of these demands. Similar to the NWPC in the United States, in 1972 Women for Political Action was formed to support the election of women, to act as a pressure group, and to increase the participation of women in the political process (1976:334). The women's rights branch of the movement has been comprised primarily of married, middle-class women who are at least middle aged (1976:317).

The women's liberation branch, like its counterpart in the United States, sprang from the New Left Movement in the final years of the 1960s. Comprised of young, middle-class, college-educated women, most members of this branch have been socialist in sympathy, as in Great Britain. They have divided over the issue of whether socialist revolution or sexism is the first priority, however, often resulting in severe conflict (Teather 1976:321). As in the United States, male-dominated socialist organizations such as the League for Socialist Action and the Young Socialist Alliance, tried but failed to infiltrate and take over this branch around 1969–70 (1976:325–26). The women's liberation branch, as its British counterpart, has been strongly oriented toward mobilizing working women, supporting their strikes and issues (1976:227–28). Another major concern of theirs has been abortion. The beginning of this branch may be dated to the 1967 emergence of a group in Toronto, followed in the next four years by rapid growth in larger cities throughout Canada (1976:323–24). In 1969 the first of several conferences was held in Sudbury, followed by one in Vancouver which resulted in Women's Liberation in the West (1976:324).

The third branch, the radical feminists, has been heavily oriented to C-R and to the development of feminist theory or ideology. They too work on issues of abortion and equal access to jobs and education, but are especially concerned with sex role socialization and family roles. They emerged first in Toronto with the 1969 founding of the New Feminists. Teather noted, however, that this branch is gradually disbanding, as it did in the United States, as talking gives way to a desire for concrete action (1976:329).

As in the United States and especially Great Britain, for the most part the movement is comprised of "a . . . mosaic of groups, councils, centers, committees" (Teather 1976:302) primarily functioning at the local level, and spread across the entire nation. However, some areas, such as the Maritime Provinces, have been slow to develop movement activity, while others, such as British Columbia, have women's centers in almost every city and town (1976:336). The movement has been decentralized and characterized by constant turnover, as groups come and go (1976:320–23). The same wide range of local activities described for Great Britain has characterized the Canadian movement (1976:333). As in the United States and Britain, there has been substantial proliferation of single-purpose and single-constituency women's organizations, such as the Women and Film Project, the Ontario Native Women's Association, the Native Women's Association of Canada, the Black Women's Congress (1976:337–40), and various lesbian feminist groups (Wall 1982:22–23).

Despite the diversity and locally based nature of the movement, as well as ongoing conflict between socialist and radical feminists, Teather noted that in the mid 1970s there was a growing tendency toward unification at the provincial level, through the establishment of federations and information exchange organizations. In fact, a national women's news service was formed in 1975. However, that same year, at a conference at Thunder Bay attended by representatives from a variety of women's groups and centers, the idea of a unified, national organization was rejected (1976:343–44).

Combining the three branches and the support of traditional women's groups for many specific issues, we conclude that, at a minimum, Canada has experienced an intermediate-size movement since about 1970, and possibly one that has reached mass proportions. The range of issues and concerns is very similar to the United States and Great Britain, and at least among the younger two branches of the movement, include an attack on the gender role system and virtually all social institutions (see also Wall 1982). The demand for child-care and abortion by the older branch suggests a rejection of traditional role definitions as well. In sum, Canada's women's movement is feminist in ideology.

NORWAY AND FINLAND

Women have virtually complete formal, legal equality in Scandanavia. As elsewhere, however, formal equality has not automatically produced real equality between the sexes. The scanty information available to us shows that at least Norway and Finland have experienced feminist movements since the early 1970s.

Norway

In Norway the 1970s witnessed both the birth of several new feminist organizations and the revival of feminist activity within several traditional ones. The new organizations include the New Feminists, the Women's Front, Bread-and-Roses, and the Lesbian Movement. The older, reactivated ones include the Association of Women's Rights, the National Council of Women, various female trade unions, and the female sections of various political parties. Two branches, liberal and socialist, are to be found within the movement, with some cooperation between them, especially around the issue of increasing the proportion of female elected officials. Other issues of concern to the movement include greater economic equality, parental rather than simply maternal work leaves, and equal participation in household work by husbands (all information taken from Blom 1982:571-73). Despite the array of groups involved, Blom noted that the numbers of people are not very substantial and that only "a minority of Norwegian women" (1982:571-72) support feminist organizations. However, the Labour government does support movement demands. We suggest, therefore, that the movement might appropriately be considered intermediate in size, and given its emphasis on equality within both the household and the economy, feminist in ideology.

Finland

In Finland, a short-lived group comprised of both sexes, called Group 9, began in 1969, oriented to the discussion of sex roles. The feminist movement dates to a few years later, with the formation of new groups, a change in orientation among some older ones, and the emergence of two feminist magazines. However, until about 1978 the movement was confined to two cities, Helsinki and Turku. Since then, it has spread to towns throughout at least the southern half of Finland. As elsewhere, the impetus for the movement came both from a Council of Equality established by the government in 1972, and from the New Left Movement of that era. However, many women who were not previously politically active also quickly joined its ranks.

The Feminists, an organization comprised of small groups consisting of 5–10 members, was founded in 1975. They are apparently chiefly consciousness-raising (C-R) groups oriented to raising women's self-esteem and concentrating on issues of the general role of women, marriage, sexuality, and abortion. The older Women's Union was effectively taken over by younger women and became a feminist organization during this time. Neither of these organizations is aligned with any political party or stance. The Women's League (in Turku) is a left-wing group comprised of women who felt that left-wing parties were unwilling to deal with feminist concerns. All of these organizations are structured around small, democratically run groups. A major issue shared by all is pacifism. Also, their emphasis is not on formal equality, which has already been achieved, but on attitude and value change. An indication of the range of feminist concerns in Finland comes from the series of demands formally stated by the Women's Union, which includes women's studies in every university, reform in the state-controlled mass media depiction of women, an increase in the number of women in all decision-making roles, equal pay for equal work, child care, parental leave for both sexes rather than just women, nonsexist child socialization and education, free contraception and the right to abortion, the destruction of the myth of motherhood, and stronger legislation concerning violence against women (all information on Finland taken from Juusola-Halonen 1981).

In light of the spread of movement groups since 1978, we estimate that the Finnish movement might be considered intermediate in size. It is unlikely that it is any larger, given Juusola-Halonen's statement that "attitudes toward a feminist movement are . . . changing slowly" (1981:460). Ideologically, it is clearly feminist in scope.

WEST GERMANY

As elsewhere in the industrialized West, the late 1960s were a time of radical student protest, heavily socialist in orientation, in the Federal Republic of Germany. And also as elsewhere, many women active in the leftist movement became disillusioned by the treatment they received at the hands of their male comrades. From this emerged an autonomous women's movement beginning in 1968–69, which possibly grew to intermediate size, and which was fully feminist in its ideology.

The first signs of the new women's movement came in 1968 with the formation of the Action Council for Women's Liberation in West Berlin. This group, which initially attempted to combat male dominance within the German SDS (Students for Democratic Society), also organized day-care centers and tried to combat sexism within education. However, by 1969 it returned to the SDS fold and essentially abandoned its feminist commitment (Altbach 1984:454–55; see also Schlaeger 1978:62–63). Also in 1968, a short-lived Women's Committee was founded in Frankfurt, which ironically fell apart just one year later because it became too large for the leaderless, structureless type of organization to which it was ideologically committed (Kawan and Weber 1981:427). In 1970 this group was reconstituted as a study group comprised primarily of students with a strong leftist orientation, and calling itself the Socialist Women of Frankfurt (1981:427–28). Despite the strong socialist base of the original feminist groups, the movement rather rapidly became "de-politicized," and by the mid 1970s had come to regard socialism with "mistrust or even enmity" (Schlaeger 1978:63–64). Altbach even argued that the "alienation of feminists from the Left seems more complete in the Federal Republic than in the U.S." (1984:461).

In 1970–71 a politically more broad-based women's movement was emerging, beginning with a campaign to abolish the abortion law. Groups focused on this issue arose in Frankfurt, Munich, and Berlin (Kawan and Weber 1981:428). Delegates from seven towns met at Düsseldorf in 1971 to organize the abortion law repeal campaign (1981:429). The first national women's conference was held in Frankfurt in 1971, which Kawan and Weber claimed "really marked the birth of the new German women's movement" (1981:429). It adopted exclusion of males from movement organizations as a fundamental principle, after which the split with socialism was readily apparent.

By the next year the first women's centers and homes for battered women were opening, "even in smaller towns" (Altbach 1984:455, Kawan and Weber 1981:432). C-R groups were forming, lesbians were beginning to organize publicly, and abortion groups were "growing up everywhere" (Kawan and Weber 1981:429). The first women's center, begun in Berlin with 50 members in 1973, numbered 300 a year later (1981:429). The first women's self-defense conference was held in 1974, while a women's health movement got under way in 1974–75. By the mid-1970s feminist publications, films, bookstores, cafés, art galleries, theaters, and other cultural institutions had sprung up, centered in Berlin (Altbach 1984:476). In 1976 a campaign for wages for housework was begun (Kawan and Weber 1981:430). It attracted substantial credibility, and reflected the fact that "more than most women's movements, except perhaps the Italian, the new German movement has attempted to make the needs of mothers and the issue of housework the basis of theoretical and practical work" (Altbach 1984:465; see also Gerhard 1982:566). Toward the end of the decade movement activists also became involved in issues of antiterrorism, ecology, and the antinuclear movement. Initially heavy supporters of the peace-ecology political party, Greens, party refusal to support abortion rights in 1980 has driven many feminists from it (Altbach 1984:467). In 1979 a Women's Party was formed, but as the eighth one since 1951, it did not appear likely to survive and grow, according to Altbach (1984:457).

The German movement has been completely decentralized. No counterpart to NOW exists; indeed, there is no nationwide feminist organization of any kind (Altbach 1984:476; Schlaeger 1978:59). In general, the German movement has been far less involved than its U.S. counterpart in activities such as lobbying, lawsuits, and attempts to influence formal institutions (Altbach 1984:468). In fact, until the late 1970s it explicitly rejected the idea of working through existing, established institutions, focusing on theory and literature rather than on practical politics (Gerhard 1982:566; Schlaeger 1978:59, 66). Comprised of young, middle-class women, "Female blue-collar and white-collar workers, housewives and mothers with children, women of the lower classes or racial minorities find no access to the movement" (Schlaeger 1978:66). Descriptions of the movement use terms such as "fragile" (Altbach 1984:468) and "weak . . . compared to . . . other countries" (Jacobs 1978:173). There is some evidence, however, to suggest that the movement may be somewhat larger than incipient. Jacobs (1978:173) argued that because of it, women in Germany are becoming more aware of their "oppression." More telling, in the absence of any other numbers, are media circulation rates. In 1976 a feminist magazine reflecting a socialist orientation was founded in Berlin, called *Courage*. The next year *Emma* was begun in Cologne as a general feminist magazine, much on the order of *Ms.* in the United States. Both are available on newstands throughout the country. With an initial run of 5000, by 1978 *Courage* had a circulation of 65,000. The 1978 circulation of *Emma* was 300,000 (Frank 1978:181). Scores of other feminist periodicals are published, but only a few have circulations of at least a few thousand (see Frank 1978). A 1977 feminist calendar-datebook sold 60,000 copies (1978:190). Also by 1978, eleven cities had feminist bookstores (1978:181).

We conclude from this that the core activists in Germany are probably relatively few in number, but enough fellow travelers exist to possibly allow us to define the movement as intermediate in size. Ideologically it appears little different from the other movements described up to this point, questioning and attacking a rather full range of social institutions and thus qualifying as a fully feminist movement.

NETHERLANDS

Like the other societies examined, a women's movement in the Netherlands surfaced in the late 1960s, partially as an outgrowth of New Left activism, partly as an outgrowth of a rather uniquely Dutch public discussion of sexuality, homosexuality, love, and marriage earlier in the decade (De Vries 1981:391). It quickly developed into a mass feminist movement.

In the late 1960s an organization began, comprised of professional women and men who advocated equal rights and opportunities, called the Man-Woman-Society. About the same time a radical, leftist feminist group began, called Mad Mina, which also included men among its membership. It raised the issue of free abortion and contraception, and "in a short time attracted thousands of women from many different places and backgrounds" (De Vries 1981:392). While both organizations continue today, neither is very influential. Very quickly after their founding, women began to break away to form C-R groups, which multiplied rapidly (1981:394-95). By the late 1970s lesbian, black, working-class, and migrant women were forming their own organizations.

The bulk of movement activists have been socialist-feminists. At one extreme are those whose first commitment is to socialism; they have continued their allegiance to male-dominated parties and unions. At the other extreme stand the radical feminists, who often advocate separatism from males. In between stand those who combine socialism and feminism, some of whom are directly aligned with political parties and unions, others of whom are independent (De Vries 1981:396). Within the parties and unions feminists have their own caucuses and organizations. Unlike some other societies, little conflict exists between the various branches, and groups representing them often work together (1981:396-97).

As elsewhere, a number of autonomous local projects have been developed, including shelters for battered women, rape crisis centers, C-R groups, and feminist adult education groups. Political activity has centered on abortion; medical and psychiatric care; family, divorce, and labor law; opposition to cuts in social services; and day care. Feminist cultural activities, including theater groups, bookstores, publishers, cafés, film projects, and art showings have also developed (De Vries 1981:399-400). De Vries claimed that "feminism has spread all over the country . . . even very small towns often have a women's center, a women's cafe or a local group of otherwise active feminists" (1981:389). Moreover, in terms of its sociocultural activities, "what feminism offers daily is 'consumed' by a broad layer of women who have organized themselves around women's issues and problems but who do not call themselves feminist" (1981:401). In a nation with a total population of only 14,000,000, a 1981 feminist publication sold 60,000 copies (1981:389).

We conclude that Dutch feminism is mass in appeal. Moreover, ideologically it differs little from the cases already examined and thus is fully feminist.

FRANCE

The decade of the 1960s was "a period of steady reformist feminist activity" (Marks and Courtivron 1980:28-29), including a number of publications concerning the status and roles of women in France. However, scholars concerned with the contemporary French women's movement concur in dating it to the spring 1968 student and worker general strike (Kaufmann-McCall 1983:282; Marks and Courtivron 1980:29; Sauter-Bailliet 1981:410). As we have seen elsewhere, the behavior of their left-wing male comrades led many French women to split off and form their own feminist groups.

The first organizational signs of the new women's movement came in 1967 when a group of Marxist women formed the Feminist-Marxist Action (Sauter-Bailliet 1981:410). More leftist women began to do likewise in the aftermath of the 1968 strikes, in Paris, Lyon, and Toulouse. In 1970 the press labeled these diverse groups the Mouvement de Libération des Femmes (MFL) (Marks and Courtivron 1980:30; Sauter-Bailliet 1981:410). This occurred in response to a public demonstration at the Tomb of the Unknown Soldier, at which feminists laid a wreath inscribed "to the unknown wife of the unknown soldier" (Marks and Courtivron 1980:31). This is usually seen as the public "birth" of the movement.

The early years of the 1970s witnessed the rapid growth of an array of organizations, publications, and demonstrations. In 1970 a women's march for contraception and free abortion on demand occurred in Paris. That same year witnessed the beginning of the Féministes Revolutionnaires, a group of radical feminists devoted to the "total destruction of the patriarchal order," and dedicated to C-R and separatism from males. Choisir, an abortion rights organization, was begun in 1971. Spirale, a group founded to study women's culture, Ecologie-Féminisme, devoted to halting male exploitation and waste of the earth, and Cercle Dimitriev, which attempted to organize small neighborhood committees, all emerged in 1972, along with the Movement for Freedom of Abortion and Contraception, and an organization of feminist actresses and filmmakers called Musidora. The mid-1970s witnessed the founding of the League of Women's Rights, the first president of which was Simone de Beauvoir. It established refuges for female victims of male violence, denounced sexism, and worked for new rights for women (all information taken from Marks and Courtivron 1980:26–35).

Sauter-Bailliet described four branches of the French movement after 1970. The first is the Féministes Revolutionnaires, who perceived patriarchy, not class, as the root of women's "oppression" (1981:411). They have advocated liberalized abortion, support for unwed mothers, and allied themselves with the League of Women's Rights and SOS Femmes Alternative to combat rape, wife battering, and the general victimization of women. The second branch is centered around a group, founded in Paris in 1968, called Politique and Psychanalyse, or Psych et Po, which has tried to integrate Marxian, Freudian, and feminist thought. It has been "the cultural and intellectual center" of the MLF, and has run a very large feminist publishing house and bookstores in Paris, Marseilles, and Lyon. It is an "avant-garde intellectual" group devoted to subverting the entire belief and language structures. It publishes a weekly entitled *Des femmes en mouvements hebdo*, which has a circulation of 150,000 (Kaufmann-McCall 1983:287; Marks and Courtivron 1980:31–32). This group has stimulated C-R within the movement and also has been in the forefront of raising issues pertaining to lesbianism. The third branch is represented by the Cercle Dimitriev and has remained faithful to the political left. Finally, the fourth branch is organized as Les Pétroleuses and it has placed first priority on class struggle.

All four branches are decentralized and opposed to structure and hierarchy. They are centered primarily in Paris (Kaufmann-McCall 1983:283). According to Sauter-Bailliet (1981:412), the entire MLF numbered only about 4000 in 1972. By 1980 there were a total of 60 groups, and demonstrations that year and the next drew "thousands" of women. Choisir, which was originally an abortion rights organization (the abortion law was changed in 1975), became oriented to political activism in the late 1970s. It ran candidates for the 1978 election of French representatives to the European Parliament, but garnered only 1.5 percent of the vote (1981:413–14).

Marks and Courtivron concluded that "in general, French feminists, whether radical or reformist, attack male systems, male values, the pervasiveness of misogyny, more vigorously than do American feminists" (1980:35–37). However, to date French feminism has had less impact on French women than its American counterpart. We conclude that the French movement is feminist in ideology, but at most intermediate in size.

ITALY

Observers of the contemporary Italian women's movement date its appearance to 1970–71, and see it as at least a partial outgrowth of the leftist student movement of the late 1960s (Colombo 1981:461; Pitch 1979:2). Unlike the other nations examined so far in this chapter, in Italy a large feminist organization has existed since 1944, the Union of Italian Women (UDI), comprised of socialists and especially communists, and associated with the Communist Party. Ironically, this organization came to comprise the "reform" wing of the Italian women's movement, and is often denied the label "feminist" by more radically feminist groups. Between the end of World War II and the present, it has worked quite successfully for passage of a series of reforms of concern to women including equal pay, pensions for housewives, day care, divorce law reform, and maternity leave (Colombo 1981:467; Dodds 1982:149; Pitch 1979:2).

In the early years of the 1970s, several women's groups emerged from the left, the two major ones being the Women's Liberation Movement (MLD) and the Roman Feminist Movement (Colombo 1981:461). Groups demonstrating in Rome, Trento, and Milan were met with violence by males and even by the police (1981:462). By 1972 the movement was growing "very rapidly," centered around issues of abortion and contraception (the most potent issue in the early 1970s), wages for housework (an organization devoted to this one issue flourished in northern Italy, the Feminist Struggle), divorce, and the demand for nonsexist education (1981:462). Several leftist groups tried to maintain priority commitment to the class struggle, but "most of these women finally left the extreme left groups" (Colombo 1981:462) in pursuit of feminism. The movement was comprised mostly of small collectives which were leaderless and structureless, and sprang up in schools, in neighborhoods, and within political parties and trade unions (Colombo 1981:462; Pitch 1979:1). C-R was adopted by many groups and the issue of separatism from males divided various organizations, as it did elsewhere. (Dodds 1982:151).

More so than most cases described to this point, the Italian women's movement attracted adherents from diverse socioeconomic circumstances. By the mid-1970s union women had organized in Torino, Milan, Genoa, and Rome, and women workers "all over the country" were affected. By 1977 "almost every large office or factory" (Colombo 1981:415) had a feminist group. A feminist publishing house, libraries, theaters, and film groups emerged in 1976–77. One feminist TV program reached an audience of 8,000,000. Women's centers opened in a number of cities, including a very large one in Rome (1981:466), which has been the center of the Italian movement (Dodds 1982:148). By 1978 the Rome women's center, sponsored by the MLD, represented 80 different groups (1982:152). Colombo wrote that "in every small city at some point there was a feminist group" (1981:465). In 1978 a daily feminist newspaper was begun.

It appears that the Italian movement reached intermediate to mass proportions by about 1977. *Effe*, a feminist journal begun in 1973, reached a circulation of 50,000. National rallies almost "always gathered more than 50,000 women" (Colombo 1981:465). A bill concerning violence against women was initiated by a petition signed by 250,000 people (1981:461, although Dodds 1982:158 claimed 350,000). The UDI alone has 150,000 members in 55 branches (Dodds 1982:151, although Colombo 1981:467 claimed twice that number). On the other hand, Dodds claimed that "the attitudes of both women and men have not changed nearly as rapidly as the laws" (1982:158) leaving some question as to whether the movement should be considered mass. Clearly, the same range of activities and ideological positions have characterized this movement as others discussed, marking it as fully feminist.

SPAIN AND PORTUGAL

Even under Franco's dictatorship a feminist movement began to emerge in Spain after 1970. At that time, the Women's Democratic Movement arose out of the Communist Party, and soon left the party to pursue feminism. Simultaneously, a second branch of the women's movement arose, oriented to C-R and involving progressive Catholics (Rague-Arias 1981:471–72). The older Association of University Women of Barcelona became involved in this branch.

After the United Nations International Women's Year in 1975, many new feminist groups arose, often out of traditional women's organizations. Feminist collectives began in Barcelona and Madrid (Rague-Arias 1981:472). The next year, at a meeting in Barcelona, feminists called for legal equality; an end to discrimination in the work-place, in education, and in leisure; equal parental authority; legal abortion and contraception; equal rights for unmarried mothers and their children; and homosexual rights (1981:473). Abortion and contraception were the central issues for the entire movement. Out of this meeting came the Barcelona Women's Coordinating Committee and the apolitical Catalonian Association of Women, whose priorities were nurseries, legal aid, and family planning. An anarchist group, Free Women; a Marxist one, People's Organization of Women; a socialist organization, Women's Liberation Front; and radical feminist groups with names such as the Witches and the Magicians, emerged at the same time. By 1977 neighborhood-level self-help, health groups had formed. Divorced and separated women founded their own organizations as well.

In short, organizations grew up, split, and dissolved with great frequency during the latter half of the 1970s (Rague-Arias 1981:475). As elsewhere, some have been chiefly oriented to C-R, some to separatism, some to working with existing political parties on concrete demands. The movement has been largely confined to Madrid and Barcelona and, although we have no concrete numbers, almost certainly has not attained a mass level, and probably only incipient. The array of issues raised is essentially the same as elsewhere in Europe and North America, and thus clearly the movement has been feminist ideologically.

A small, minimally focused women's movement has developed in Portugal since 1974. In that year the trial of three feminist writers, the Three Marias, sparked the formation in Lisbon of a Women's Liberation Movement. Although a "small group," it was far more heterogeneous than most described to this point, comprised of housewives, students, workers, prostitutes, and academics (Barbosa 1981:478). Women's groups also developed within two political parties, but they had little autonomy (1981:480). In addition, a few independent groups emerged in the urban areas of Lisbon, Porto, and Coimbra. A feminist publishing house exists in Lisbon, but a lack of funding restricts its activities. Perhaps the largest part of the movement is the National Abortion and Contraception Campaign, supported by both the various women's liberation groups and by leftist political parties (1981:480). Before the new, 1976 Constitution and Family Code granted equal rights to both sexes, this constituted a demand made by women activists. They have also opposed stereotyped conceptions of women. But in general, they have not yet worked out an agenda of demands (1981:478). We conclude from this that the movement is incipient in size. Inasmuch as so few concrete issues apparently have been raised, it is difficult to characterize its ideology. However, it is at least minimally feminist, given opposition to sex stereotypes and its campaign for reproductive freedom.

JAPAN

The contemporary women's movement in Japan was begun in 1970, when the feminist poet and philosopher Tanaka Mitsu called a meeting of 27 women. The next year a feminist conference was held in Tokyo, attended by 1000 women, followed by workshops in Nogana and Hokkaidō in 1971–72 (Robins-Mowry 1983:134). As elsewhere, movement activists often emerged out of the radical student and peace movements, where they had become disillusioned with the treatment accorded them by male comrades (1983:133–34). Within a few years, a women's center was founded in Tokyo, which served as a communications link for the entire movement. Newsletters proliferated, along with the founding of new groups: two concerned with "middle-age women's lib"; "PTA libbers"; "womanpower rally," an organization devoted to encouraging women to improve their labor market skills and to gaining equality in the work force; groups working for reform in the laws pertaining to abortion and contraception, which were joined by the Planned Parenthood Association of Japan; the Japan Women's Party, begun in 1977 but receiving little support; and the All Japan Feminist Association, also founded in 1977 (1983:135–36). C-R has been an important component of many of these groups (1983:135). General goals have stressed economic independence for women and the substitution of "vertical" for "horizontal" (or hierarchical) relationships in Japan (1983:134). Despite the proliferation of groups, Robins-Mowry described the movement as consisting of "only a handful" (1983:133) and estimated membership at 2000–3000. While we have only sketchy information at hand, apparently the movement is ideologically sufficiently broad to term it feminist, but it is only incipient in size — if even that.

INDIA

Since about 1973 India has experienced an incipient feminist movement, largely confined to a few cities and towns (Omvedt 1980:156), especially in the State of Maharashtra (the largest city of which is Bombay), plus Delhi. While Everett spoke of four "strands" (1983) to the movement, we may simplify this to two, which have been connected to one another only very loosely (see also Omvedt 1980, esp. the afterword). On the one hand, there is middle-class feminism, comprised of urban, well-educated, mostly young women with leftist leanings, who want to support their less fortunate lower-class sisters. On the other hand are organizations comprised of lower-class women, including tribal, working class, and union women, and self-help associations of women in the "informal sector" of the economy (e.g., trading, petty production, contract labor, and service activities) (Everett 1983:18).

In 1971 the government created a Commission on the Status of Women, which reported in 1975 on the deterioration of women's status in health, education and employment (Everett 1983:20). This gave impetus to the fledgling middle-class feminist movement, which, during the remainder of the 1970s, formed a series of short-lived groups in many of the larger cities of India, and helped to organize a series of marches, demonstrations, and conferences. The primary concerns of this branch have been violence against women, including rape and dowry murder-suicide (murders of new brides by in-laws, made to look like suicides, over what they defined as inadequate dowries), the practice of dowry itself (outlawed in 1961 but still widespread and rapidly escalating in cost), and the exploitation of female labor. By the 1980s issues of health and medical practice concerning women had also become central (1983:21). Members have been primarily professionals, students, and homemakers. In 1979 they began publication in Delhi of *Manushi* (Woman), a feminist magazine with a circulation of 11,000 in India (1983:20). This, along with some conferences and newsletters, plus personal contacts, constitute the communications network of the movement. According to Everett, middle-class feminism is characterized by "fluidity," organizations typically developing around one issue, broadening, then lapsing. Very recently several "resource centers," which collect information concerning women's issues, and "support and referral centers" (1983:21) have grown up in cities like Bombay, Delhi, and Kanpur. Also, chiefly as an outgrowth of the research activities of the Commission on the Status of Women, feminist scholars have been developing women's studies centers. While issues of economic inequality and the effects of modernization on lower-class women are the primary foci of their research, they also study housework, legal change, health and family planning, and violence against women (1983:22).

Lower-class women's activism also emerged in the mid-1970s, triggered in large measure by tribal women in Sahada, Maharashtra, who agitated during a famine, including a march by 20,000 women. Subsequently, they organized to fight rape, wife-beating, sexual harassment, and economic exploitation (Everett 1983:19, 22). Their leaders came from the Socialist and Communist parties (1983:19). At about the same time, the Women's Anti-Price Rise Front mobilized "thousands" of middle- and working-class women in Bombay into a consumer movement. Meanwhile, a group of women tobacco workers formed their own union and struck (unsuccessfully). They then united with a group of prostitutes (whose work is rooted in temple prostitution which, though illegal, has flourished) to call for the end of prostitution (1983:23). Also in the mid-1970s, the Self-Employed Women's Association formed in Ahmedabad. It was the first of several self-help groups to form among lower-class women in the informal economy. By 1982 it numbered 5000 members. It concentrated on the issue of credit accessibility for women, and by 1982 had a union seeking better wages and working conditions and providing health and welfare services, a cooperative bank providing low interest credit, training programs, marketing assistance, and other kinds of cooperatives (1983:24).

Despite the fact that lower-class women took the initiative to organize on several fronts, they lacked "the numerical strength and resources to make inroads in organizing the broad mass of women workers." As a result, they, unlike their middle-class sisters, have turned to left-wing parties and unions for support, and in doing so, largely lost their autonomy (see Everett 1983:23; Omvedt 1980: afterword). Independent groups remain "fragile" (Omvedt 1980:161) and unable to build enduring contacts with the masses of women. The result has been that, despite the upsurge of feminist activism during the past decade, little has been accomplished except to awaken "a fair amount of awareness of women's issues." Only a "small minority of women" have been "touched by women's activism" (Everett 1983:24). As Omvedt concluded:

> There is a significant spread of consciousness about the oppression of women. There is a fair amount of activity continuing in the form of marches, demonstrations, sit-ins, new magazines, conferences, programes. Middle-class women, students and young employees, come together on a spontaneous basis to fight various forms of oppression, but their organizations remain in flux, hampered by . . . lack of solidarity and the absence of a common perspective. Working-class and rural women respond enthusiastically to calls to fight oppression but remain unable to organize . . . on their own; instead they are . . . mobilized through parties and unions. [1980:163].

Clearly, the contemporary Indian women's movement is incipient in size. Movement issues already mentioned include all forms of violence against women, economic exploitation and disadvantage of women, health care delivery, and sexual exploitation and harassment. In addition, at least some movement group(s) have also included issues of enforcement of laws pertaining to dowry, equal pay and work, maternity leaves and child care centers, the inequities of the traditional division of household labor, and cultural ideologies supportive of gender stereotypes (see Omvedt 1980:169–73). We therefore conclude that the movement is fully feminist ideologically.

ISRAEL

The Jews who settled in Israel (then Palestine) during the early decades of this century were primarily socialists with an ideological commitment to sexual equality. As we saw in chapter I, however, this commitment was quickly sacrificed. In fact, Izraeli (1981) documented a women's movement within the Jewish Palestinian community and its institutional structures, from about 1910 through the 1920s, that emerged as a response to the unanticipated sexual inequities which women were experiencing. This movement focused primarily on employment opportunities for women in agriculture, construction, and other manual trades, and on collective child care. Despite this tradition, today Israel has a cadre of feminists which may be too small to even be termed an incipient movement. Hazelton estimated that there were 200–500 women in the "small, new movement" (1977:188). Furthermore, she wrote that feminism "is absolutely unacceptable to the Israeli public, women and men" (1977:188). This handful of feminists constitutes an "enclave of well-educated upper-middle class . . . women talking more to each other than to other women" (1977:189). They are ideological purists, involved extensively in C-R, who in some cases have refused to pursue political reforms because they define the system as irrelevant. However, a group of feminists did found a Women's Party for the 1977 elections, stressing issues concerning women's sexuality, recognition of housewives as professional workers, rape, prostitution, health care for women, and equality of education and work. They received one half of one percent of the vote (1977:189–90).

In 1976, partially in response to feminist demands, the government established a Commission on the Status of Women, which "brought most of Israel's leading women academicians, politicians, and administrators into a joint working framework for the first time." Many "went through a gradual process of . . . consciousness-raising. . . ." While most do not define themselves as feminists, they are now "talking feminism" (Hazelton 1977:196–98). At the same time, some traditional women's magazines and organizations are also beginning to take more actively feminist stances (1977:198–200).

Hazelton argued that Israeli women have retreated into the home and now glorify the feminine mystique. Many politicians and parties which ostensibly support women's equality, along with most of the public, place national unity above all else. This means not alienating the religious right, upon which coalition governments depend, and whose views are antithetical to sexual equality. Given this national orientation, the tiny feminist movement, including its fellow travelers, is not likely to grow substantially in the near future. We conclude that Israel has a truly feminist, but minimally incipient women's movement.

BRAZIL

With the gradual political liberalization of Brazil after the mid 1970s, came the emergence of organized feminist groups, comprised of middle-class women but committed to working for the needs of lower-class women, as well as for other feminist goals (Schmink 1981:117). These groups have been able to work cooperatively with independent working-class women's organizations in pursuit of several common goals, but not without conflict over priorities (1981). Movement organization and activism is confined, however, to three cities: Rio de Janeiro, São Paulo, and Belo Horizonte.

The United Nations International Women's Year (1975) stimulated the emergence of organized feminism (Latin American and Caribbean Women's Collective 1977:40). In that year, the United Nations and the Brazilian Press Association sponsored a meeting in Rio de Janeiro to discuss the status of women in Brazil. In its aftermath, a group of professional women formed the Brazilian Women's Center (CMB). Issues of concern to this group have included reproductive rights, educational and job opportunity, day care, reform of the Civil Code, the end of protective labor legislation, and recognition of women's contributions to art and culture (Latin American and Caribbean Women's Collective 1977:41; Schmink 1981:117). In that same year, representatives of 38 union, political party, church and women's groups in São Paulo formed the Center for the Development of the Brazilian Woman (CDMB). Their efforts have been directed at researching issues of maternal health, education, day care, political participation by women, and women's working conditions (Schmink 1981:118). Two feminist newspapers also emerged in the mid-1970s. By 1979 there were at least 8 "solid women's groups" (1981:118).

As elsewhere, feminist groups have expanded, proliferated, and splintered rapidly. Most are comprised of 20–30 middle-class, professionally employed women. While these women have also typically been involved in the political movement working for the democratization of Brazil, and are often leftist in their politics, they have been committed to maintaining the autonomy of their feminist organizations from male-dominated parties (Schmink 1981:119). They became especially active during the 1978 local elections. The CMB worked for candidates who supported its stance on such issues as day care, equal pay for equal work, family planning, an end to the use of females as sex objects in advertisements, educational equality, and access to political posts. Other groups added the right to abortion and equal responsibility of both sexes for household work to the list of demands (1981:118).

Beginning in São Paulo in the 1960s, and spreading to Rio de Janeiro and Belo Horizonte, working-class women have been organizing themselves in neighborhood groups. The initial issue of concern was child care, but their interests soon broadened to a host of working-class needs, most not specific to women (Schmink 1981:120). Especially since the mid-1970s, however, they have become more independent of male influence and stressed raising the consciousness of working-class women to recognize the value of their work within the home, to consider the effects of their double work load, and to appreciate their own capabilities (1981:121). Nonetheless, they resist not only the demands made by more radical feminists, but the label "feminist" as well (1981:122). Where middle-class feminists attack the family as "patriarchal" and "oppressive," working-class women are inclined to view it as the instrument of survival (1981:132). In a separate effort, small numbers of working-class women have also been working (unsuccessfully) to get their unions to pay attention to such specifically female issues as equal pay for equal work, access to training courses, and day care (1981:123).

Basically, the various women's groups are small and powerless. This has led to attempts to unite, which have been effective only in São Paulo. Class antagonisms have rendered this difficult and conflictual in that city, and impossible in Rio and Belo Horizonte (Schmink 1981:124). The first move toward unification in São Paulo occurred in 1978, when nine organizations representative of both classes cooperated on an International Women's Day commemoration. They agreed to stress the issue that domestic work and children's education are the responsibility of both sexes. The next year these same groups cooperatively planned the First Congress of São Paulo Women, attended by 800. There, they agreed that child care was the top priority, and as a result, they jointly established an organization called the Movement of Struggle for Day Care. Also, the Congress expanded the coordinating structure and it grew to encompass 50 different entities (mostly neighborhood and union, not feminist groups) working on behalf of women (1981:125, 128). By the Second Congress 4000 women participated, including professionals, students, homemakers and working-class women. However, conflicts over priorities became so intense that it was forced to end early (1981:126–27).

We conclude from this that Brazil has experienced, since the mid-1970s, an ideologically feminist movement of very small size, supported on some issues by a larger constituency of working-class women. Nonetheless, confined to three cities, it would be difficult to define it as more than an incipient feminist movement.

PUERTO RICO

With only very scanty information at our disposal, it appears that Puerto Rico has developed, since the mid-1970s, an incipient feminist movement, based largely in two organizations. In 1972 the Mujer Intégrate Ahora (MIA) was founded, with its main objective being "to help achieve a complete realization of the woman as a self-directed individual . . . with full equality of rights in all spheres of life" (Ferrer 1979:46). Specifically, it sought greater political representation of women, an end to sexist education, and the development of consciousness among women. It grew out of public hearings held by the Civil Rights Commission on the issue of sex discrimination. Comprised of mostly students and young professionals, with frequent changes in members and goals, the organization is apparently quite small (ibid.). The other major group is the Federacíon de Mujeres Puertorriqueñas (FMP), founded in 1975. It is a more broad-based organization, comprised of workers, students, homemakers, and professionals, representing all social, religious, and political sectors of the society. Its chief priority is C-R (ibid.; Latin American and Caribbean Women's Collective 1977:42–43). The FMP has close ties to the leftist Progressive Labor Movement. The various political parties in Puerto Rico have established women's bureaus in recent years, chiefly designed to mobilize their support for the party. However, these women's bureaus have, in some instances, been moderately effective in raising issues of specific concern to women, and among the leftist parties, there is substantial support for feminist demands. Nonetheless, as we have so often seen, women's issues are low priority, and many feminists have departed left-wing parties as a result (1979:46–47). On the basis of this scanty evidence, we conclude that there is probably an incipient feminist movement in Puerto Rico.

ENDNOTE ON LATIN AMERICA

During the past decade, few Latin American societies appear to have developed even the modest level of feminist activity we call incipient. Chaney explicitly stated that Chile and Peru showed "few signs" of such a movement, then generalized to all of Latin America, predicting that "feminist movements probably will not develop for many years." She further stated that "small pockets of feminist activity exist today in almost every large Latin American city, but that the activists are isolated and beleaguered" (1979:76–81). The Latin American and Caribbean Women's Collective presented information that suggests that there is one organization in Columbia which deals with women's issues, but is more broadly committed to agrarian issues (1977:39); a couple of autonomous women's groups exist in Venezuela, along with a government Women's Commission and a women's movement within the Socialist Party (1977:39–39); and, since the early 1970s, several C-R and feminist study groups have emerged in Mexico City, along with organized feminist activity within leftist parties and unions, all united chiefly around the issue of abortion (1977:41–42).

In attempting to explain the paucity of feminist activism, especially in Chile and Peru, Chaney made an argument that is especially interesting in light of the theory presented in chapter 3. She pointed out that middle- and upper middle-class women in the work force are overwhelmingly employed in a totally female context, where no males are present even in supervisory positions. Furthermore, their education, including college, is likewise completely sex segregated. As a result, women "do not develop 'colleague relationships' with men, nor do they have much opportunity for regular collaboration with them in their work" (1979:77). In terms of our theory, such women have no opportunity to use males as a comparative reference group.

CONCLUSIONS

As we noted at the outset of this chapter, there is little available literature on contemporary women's movements outside of the United States. Apparently, feminism today, as expressed through social movement activity (and all contemporary movements examined are more or less feminist in ideological scope), is a phenomenon of primarily Western industrial societies. In addition, few such movements (at a maximum nine) appear to have grown beyond the incipient level, and only four may have reached mass proportions. Table 5.1 summarizes our conclusions in terms of the size and ideological scope of contemporary women's movements. The literature concerning women in Muslim societies (e.g., Bámdád 1977; Beck and Keddie 1978; Mernissi 1975; Nashat 1983) suggests that independent women's movements are totally absent in that part of the world today. Nor did we find any evidence of such movements in Asia, outside of Japan, and little in Latin America as well.

Table 5.1   Estimates of Relative Size and Ideological Scope of Independent Second-Wave Women's Movements

	Size	Ideological Scope
United States	mass	feminist
Great Britain	intermediate	feminist
Canada	intermediate to mass	feminist
Norway	probably intermediate	feminist
Finland	probably intermediate	feminist
West Germany	incipient to intermediate	feminist
Holland	mass	feminist
France	incipient to intermediate	feminist
Italy	intermediate to mass	feminist
Spain	probably incipient	feminist
Portugal	incipient	feminist
Japan	incipient	feminist
India	incipient	feminist
Israel	incipient	feminist
Brazil	incipient	feminist
Puerto Rico	incipient	feminist

One reason for such an apparent paucity of contemporary independent women's movements is probably the large number of repressive political regimes in existence today. The so-called Communist countries often sponsor "women's movements," but they are scarcely independent movements as conceptualized in this book. In Latin America, dictatorships are widespread and independent social movements all but impossible (e.g., Bolivia, Chile, and Uruguay). In some of these countries, middle- and upper middle-class women, who might provide leadership for a women's movement, have been co-opted into the ruling party and/or governmental positions, often women's commissions or bureaus. Some repressive regimes (e.g., Iran and Chile) have actually reversed socioeconomic and legal gains made by women in recent decades, and would certainly not permit the emergence of grass-roots movements opposed to governmental policy. The technology of governmental repression is much more efficient today than 50–100 years ago, rendering even more problematic women's ability to organize themselves under nondemocratic regimes than was the case during the earlier wave of activism.

Where contemporary women's movements have emerged, they have been very similar to one another. Like their earlier predecessors, they have been generally middle class in composition, including especially well-educated and professionally employed women. In most societies, a substantial proportion of movement activists have also been young and leftist in political orientation. Except where they reach substantial size, feminist movements are concentrated almost exclusively in large urban areas, as were earlier women's movements.

Ideologically, there are several recurrent themes cross-nationally. Equity issues such as equal employment and educational opportunity, equal pay for equal work, complete legal equality (if there remain legal inequities), and/or the en-forcement of existing legislation granting equality, are universal in this wave of movement activism. Unlike the earlier wave, however, which raised similar is-sues in many societies, there is no suggestion that employment opportunity is only an issue for unmarried women; that the sexes by and large inhabit different spheres, with women's normally being confined to the domestic. While several different ideologies of feminism coexist in most societies examined, all appear to agree on the need to end gender stereotyping, and with that, the straitjacket of predefined gender roles and spheres. In this connection, almost everywhere re-productive freedom (i.e., easy, legal access to contraception and abortion) is sought (India is an exception due to the fact that such policies already exist and are not under challenge). Government-funded child care is also a recurrent de-mand. These two issues together further buttress the contemporary feminist de-mand that women be freed from confinement to the domestic sphere. Other is-sues raised frequently by contemporary women's movements include the nature of health care provided to women, all forms of violence and sexual harassment by men against women, lesbian rights, the status and rights of homemakers, and greater political power for women.

Organizationally, the current wave of women's movements is mostly charac-terized by large numbers of small, local, short-lived groups, rather than by a few large, national organizations (the United States is a partial exception to this). Feminists have everywhere manifested substantial antipathy to authoritatively structured organizations, which has probably often rendered their movements less successful than might otherwise be the case. Outside the United States, and partially within as well, movement activism has been expressed chiefly through small C-R groups; health, crisis intervention, research, art, literary, and film col-lectives; women's centers and shelters; research and/or publishing groups; and single-issue organizations. Temporary coalition formation around concrete de-mands and/or for specific demonstrations, conferences, projects are the com-mon form of larger-scale organization. Communications between groups is achieved through such coalitions and also through the plethora of newsletters and other publications spawned by the myriad of groups.

The general image that emerges from this description of contemporary wom-en's movements is that because of the realization (largely through C-R) of the im-mense scope and magnitude of problems confronting women, no one or two is-sues have usurped center stage; there has been no issue to parallel the role played by the demand for suffrage in the first-wave movements. Rather, small groups of women typically devote their energies to one or a few issues within their own backyards, so to speak. Collectively, however, such groups question and chal-lenge virtually every aspect of the status quo. In this way, second-wave women's movements represent the most total form of self-conscious female revolt in history.

6 Structural Influences on the Size and Ideological Scope of Women's Movements: Testing the Theory

The two previous chapters provided a series of case studies from which we were able to assess the size and ideological scope of a sample of first- and second-wave women's movements. In this, the final chapter of the book, we shall offer a systematic statistical test of some of the components of the theory we delineated in chapter 3. It should be recalled that in the third chapter we specified a series of ten hypotheses which could be tested across societies and time periods using census data. The hypotheses collectively test some aspects of our theory about the size and ideology of women's movements. However, as we stated in the third chapter, a full test of the theory is not possible, given the absence of social psychological indexes.

When one works with census data from around the world, enumerated as early as the 1840s and as late as 1970, one quickly learns to make compromises in the selection of variables. Even censuses collected by the most industrialized and best-educated nations are characterized by computational errors. Censuses in many nations are actually political acts, conducted to justify the privileged positions of those in power. In some countries men were asked to answer questions about women; in others, minority populations were either never enumerated, or were only partly counted; and in still others, the kinds of questions which needed to be asked to provide an adequate test for our theory were never asked. Frequently, a work activity, especially engaged in by women (or by peasants or minorities), in one time and place is redefined in another. National boundaries also changed over time, making direct population comparisons all the more difficult. Even in the United States, the concept of labor force participation changed between the nineteenth and twentieth centuries; while in Mexico, the employment status of peasants was often not enumerated. A host of nations in all parts of the world failed to report the sex of primary school students. Countries like India utilized different census techniques for regions under British colonial authority and for those that were under the rule of local maharajas.

Some nations collect vast quantities of information on their populace and report it in an accessible form. To develop coding categories and operationalizations of constructs based upon the richest of data sources is to preclude reporting on nations with scantier sets of information. Thus, we have had to operationalize our variables in terms of data collectible from most, if not all of the national censuses, with the result that our measures are often quite simple. Nonetheless, the findings are highly suggestive of the utility of our theory.

The data utilized to test the theory on first-wave movements are from the census nearest the end point of the movement for each nation, except in those few cases where such an end point was also the beginning point of a more massive movement and/or a major ideological shift. In the cases of the United States, Great Britain, France, Germany, and Japan, we selected a point in time approximately midway between the emergence and the end of the movement to demarcate the first phase of each movement, while retaining the end point for the later phase. For the second-wave movements, we relied upon censuses in or near 1970 for each nation, since most emerged within a few years of that date.

Readers may realize that the selection of an end point for the measurement of the independent variables in the case of the first wave seems to run counter to our theory pertaining to the emergence of women's movements. The problem is that even when a beginning date is known, that date often reflects a time at which the movement was less than even incipient—a time in which the structural variables were operative on only a few of the earliest leaders. From the data we gleaned from historical writings presented in chapters 4 and 5, we know principally the size and ideological scope of movements at their peak. Additionally, selection of the earliest date would mean reliance upon censuses which, for some of the early movements, would provide us with almost no usable data with which to test the theory, as such data were not enumerated at all, or not enumerated on women until their levels became more salient. Obviously, we also report data only on countries which had discernible movements. If movements occurred in other nations, but were not reported in a literature which was at our disposal, we could not possibly include that nation in our sample. One consequence of this is that we cannot test the general theory concerning the emergence of women's movements. It is possible that some countries met the necessary structural conditions but did not develop movements.

The theory developed in chapter 3 contains several social-psychological variables that obviously occur at the individual level. The data we present in this chapter are aggregate, referring to total societies. The question may arise as to whether we are committing an ecological fallacy; that is, assuming that findings found for an aggregate also apply to the individuals who make up the aggregate. It is not our contention that all, or even most women affected by urbanization, industrialization, role expansions, and the other structural forces will join such movements. Rather, we maintain that an increase in the magnitude of each of the structural factors enlarges the *pool* of women likely to become involved in women's movements. In turn, an enlarged pool is likely to produce an enlarged movement. Thus, we seek to explain rates of structural variables. There is therefore an isomorphism in the levels of measurement of independent and dependent variables. The need for such isomorphism has recently been suggested by Almquist, Rossman, and Darville (1980), who criticized Snyder and Tilly (1972) for testing a theory of relative deprivation and collective violence through the use of aggregate economic data (standard of living, wage levels, availability of manufactured goods, etc.). Almquist and her colleagues correctly maintained that the use of aggregate measures to assess individual decisions constitutes the commission of an ecological fallacy. To avoid such a fallacy data must be measured for the same unit of analysis. In the present research we utilize rates of the independent variables (urbanization, industrialization, size of the middle class, role expansion, etc.) and rates of movement activity. We argue that an increase in activism is due to changes in the pool of available movement participants — not that all or even most individuals who fit the demographic profile will become activists.

TESTING THE THEORY

We begin with a discussion of our operationalizations of the structural variables which constitute the independent variables in our theory. Censuses have provided the data for most of these variables, with the exception of the assessment of political cooptation and/or repression, which comes from an analysis of case studies, presented in chapter 4. Measurement of the dependent variables — movement size and ideological scope — is drawn from tabular materials presented in chapters 4 and 5. In order to insure comparability, we generally utilize a single, widely available, consistently measurable, variable to operationalize each construct in the theory.

Industrialization. The form of industrialization has varied across time and space, with few nations exactly duplicating the conditions present in Great Britain and in the United States. Thus, to rely upon coal or steel production, or to examine exports and imports, would provide for noncomparable data. However, one obvious and readily accessible indicator of the level of industrialization has been a diminished percentage of the population engaged in the primary economic sector (agriculture, forestry, mining, and related extractive industries). We therefore measured the level of industrialization as the percentage of the total labor force that was engaged in the nonprimary sectors, including manufacturing, construction, transportation, and the white-collar and service sectors.

Urbanization. Nations have rarely been consistent in their measures of urban areas. Some define as urban any location with a population of 2,000 or more, others set limits closer to 50,000, and still others have not developed such indexes. Some nations, such as the United States, speak of SMSAs (standard metropolitan statistical areas), while others define the political boundaries of a province as their metropolitan area, even if several large cities are within the area, or if some regions of the province have no communication link with the large cities. We therefore elected to count the population of the largest cities (those with populations of 100,000 or more) and divide that figure by the total national population. The resulting figure represents the proportion of the population in large cities. Considerable evidence, including that previously presented in earlier chapters, suggests that it is in the largest cities that the movements first take hold.

Size of the middle class. Statistics on the distribution of wealth are often unavailable, especially for the nineteenth century and for several of the developing nations. However, it has long been argued that in the absence of traditional claims to authority, the middle class tends to rely upon meritocratic criteria, of which educational attainment is the most universal (see Durkheim 1953; Williams 1960). Thus, we assess the size of the middle class by the proportion of the school-aged population (i.e., children aged 5–19) actually enrolled in school (elementary and secondary school). Since social movements are not mounted by children, we have used the percentage two decades prior to the year we have selected to assess the level of urbanization and industrialization—that is, 20 years prior to the end point of the movement, or a census as close to that date as possible. Of course, for more developed nations with more universal public education, this figure will overestimate the actual size of the middle class. However, our concern is for a consistent measure of the relative, not absolute, size of the middle class.

Role expansion. This is a construct which is operationalized differently for first- and second-wave movements. Role expansion involves participation in public sphere roles which previously were the domain of males. In explaining first-wave movements, which did not challenge the gender role system, our emphasis is upon public roles exclusive of paid employment. For second-wave movements, paid employment represents one of the paramount forms of role expansion for women.

In testing our theory on first-wave movements role expansion is operationalized two ways. From the census data we extracted information on the level of schooling achieved by women. Like the measurement of the size of the middle class, role expansion examines the percentage of women between the ages of 5 and 19 who were in school (elementary and secondary) 20 years prior to the peak year of the first-wave movement. While this measure should bear a high correlation with our operationalization of the size of the middle class (also based on school enrollment), it is not expected to be isomorphic. In many societies public education, especially in the nineteenth and early twentieth centuries, meant male education. We argue that as long as females were denied an education, they were unlikely to mount a social movement in their own behalf. For first-wave movements we did not measure only secondary or college education. For many of the countries which had first-wave movements college, and even high school education was such a rarity that the amount of variance in the percentage of the population with such training would be minimal. Combining the primary and secondary education data is also necessary because several of the societies did not report grade level or sex by grade level comparisons.

An additional index of role expansion in societies where first-wave movements occurred involves public sphere roles in philanthropic and welfare societies;

moral reform organizations; nationalistic, revolutionary, and political reform movements; and political parties. All such voluntary association participation took women out of traditional roles in the home and placed them in public roles, thereby facilitating the development of new reference group comparisons. Obviously, in order to avoid a tautology, such roles could not include participation in women's movements. It is also important to recognize that such expanded roles are principally the activities of middle-class women. We exclude labor force participation because prior to the post-World War II era, such participation was overwhelmingly the activity of working-class and peasant women, or the temporary activity of young, unmarried, middle-class women prior to their assumption of the wife/mother roles. There are no census data on the level or rate of such public sphere participation. However, in all but seven of the societies discussed in chapter 4, there was an indication that middle-class women were engaged in such expanded roles. The seven cases where there is no indication of such participation (Iceland, Holland, Italy, Puerto Rico, Cuba, Chile, and Uruguay) were all described briefly because of the paucity of available data. It is therefore possible, indeed likely, that in these cases as well, women's public roles had expanded by the time they mounted their own movement.

For the measurement of role expansion in second-wave movements, the central indicator should be employment of middle-class, married women, who heretofore were largely absent from the paid labor force. It is unfortunate, however, that only a few of the 16 nations which had a women's movements in the 1970s reported simultaneously marital status and educational level for women in the labor force. As a consequence, we must ignore a pivotal aspect of our employment argument, relying instead on the measurement of level of employment of all women, regardless of social class or marital status. We do so using three separate variables. The first is the percentage of women over 19 years of age who are in the nonprimary sector of the labor force. We omit the percentage of women in the primary sector both because the conditions necessary for coalitions (Dahrendorf 1959) are largely absent there and because of cross-national variation in whether farmers' wives are considered as participants in the labor force. The second measure is the percentage of women over 19 years of age who are in the tertiary sector of the labor force (white-collar and service occupations). A plethora of studies, including the work of Oppenheimer (1970), Snyder, Hayward, and Hudis (1978), and Bridges (1980, 1982) have demonstrated that it is in this sector that the greatest number of jobs for women have been created in recent decades. It is in such jobs that most married middle-class women are likely to be found.

It is necessary to introduce a caveat with regard to the measurement of the tertiary sector. The sector is intended to encompass white-collar and professional occupations. However, it was not until 1943 that a coding scheme (the Edwards Scale) was developed to accomplish such a task (see Edwards 1943). Prior to that time nations categorized workers by the general industries in which they worked (e.g., agriculture, extracting, manufacturing, banking, and finance). Many nations still use this system of categorization. Thus, the lawyer or the secretary employed by a coal mine and the actual miners are both coded mining workers. By contrast, the Edwards categorizes occupations as professional; technical; managerial; official; clerical; sales; skilled, semiskilled, and unskilled labor; service and so forth, regardless of industry. Whenever possible, the Edwards Scale has been used to assess the tertiary occupations for the second wave. However, when we compare first- and second-wave tertiary, we must rely upon the general industry codes, looking specifically at the percentages employed in commercial, banking, finance, and retail trades.

A final pair of indicators of role expansion are the percentage of females aged 5–19 in school 20 years earlier (the first-wave indicator of role expansion) and the percentage of women aged 15–24 enrolled in colleges and universities a decade prior to the peak year of the movement. Education, and especially college, provides the necessary credentials for higher-status employment, and hence, a more legitimate claim to challenging systems of sex stratification and gender roles. It is also true that some women's organizations developed on, or gained recruits from, college campuses. Both educational measures are used because, while college is a prerequisite for high-status jobs and much of a movement's leadership will come from among the college educated, many tertiary sector jobs and much of the rank and file of a movement have only a secondary education, especially outside of the United States.

Role/status dilemmas.   Like the assessment of role expansion, role/status dilemmas are operationalized differently for first- and second-wave movements. Role/status dilemmas refer to the structurally induced contradictions between the socially defined traditional roles performed by members of an ascribed status (i.e., women) and the emerging roles performed by members of that status. The more members of a lower-status group perform roles normally monopolized by those of a higher-status group, without an accompanying change in the former's status, the greater will be the role/status dilemmas. Thus, at the time of the first-wave movements women were increasing their participation in the educational roles which men had monopolized. To the extent that such role performances were defined as the domain of males, as the percentage of females and males approached educational parity, the role/status dilemmas increased. At the time of second-wave movements, as women increasingly took over work roles which were the exclusive domain of men, role/status dilemmas increased, provided that the gender role definitions which gave males a monopoly over such work roles did not change.

The measurement of role/status dilemmas for societies having first-wave movements is based upon the percentage of females aged 5–19 in school two decades prior to the peak year of the movement, divided by the percentage of males aged 5–19 in school at that time. As before, we pool elementary and secondary school enrollments. The first measure for role/status dilemmas for societies experiencing second-wave movements is the percentage of women over 19 years of age in the nonprimary sector divided by the percentage of males over 19 years of age employed in the nonprimary sector. The second measure is the percentage of females over 19 employed in the tertiary sector divided by the percentage of males over 19 employed in the tertiary sector. The final two measures of role/status dilemmas for societies with second-wave movements are indicators of educational parity. The first is the percentage of females aged 5–19 in school twenty years before the peak year of the movement, divided by the percentage of males aged 5–19 in school at the same time (the first-wave measure of role/status dilemmas). The second is the percentage of females aged 15–24 in college ten years before the peak year of the movement, divided by the percentage of males aged 15–24 in college at that time.

Labor force statistics continue to create problems in the assessment of status/role dilemmas, and caution should be noted in their use. Numerous investigations, including those by Bridges (1980, 1982), Cohn (1985), and Lorence (forthcoming) point to the fact that even reliance upon occupation does not correct for differences in gender labor markets. Simply stated, there is male work and female work within such a global sector as the tertiary. Thus, among the professions there are doctors and nurses; among clerical staff there are clerks and secretaries; even within the public schools the modal form is for teachers to be female and for principals and other administrators to be male. Such job segregation within census categories attenuates the explanatory power of our employment measures. Nonetheless, for many of the nations in our sample, they are the only indexes available.

The logic of our explanation of the size of women's movements predicts that the magnitude of the movements varies directly with the magnitude of the independent variables. However, the logic of our explanation of movement ideology is different. Feminist movements challenge the entire structure of sex stratification and gender role differentiation. Ameliorative movements do not. It is our contention that a change in degree of certain role expansion and role/status dilemma variables produce a difference in kind of ideology. Specifically, we have argued in the third chapter that as long as women's participation in the labor force was low and hence, likely limited to working-class and young, unmarried, middle-class women, women's movements would be all but exclusively ameliorative. As women's labor force participation expanded such that middle-class, married women were heavily involved in the labor force, feminist movements were likely. We therefore expect a substantial increase in the economic role expansion of women between the first-wave ameliorative and second-wave feminist movements, as well as a substantial increase in the role/status dilemmas involved. We test our explanation of ideological scope by comparing first- and second-wave movements, using the definitions of role expansion and role/status dilemmas which we use to test the explanation of the size of feminist movements (women in the nonprimary sector, in the tertiary, and in college, and the ratios of females to males in each).

Explaining the Size of First-wave Movements

Presented in Table 6.1 are the demographic data on the independent variables used to test that part of the theory which explains the size of first-wave movements. At least some data were available for a total of 28 different nations, plus data relevant to two movement phases in five nations (France, Germany, Great Britain, Japan, and the United States). However, for some countries, like China and Peru, only the level of urbanization is included, due to inadequacies in the census data or the absence of a census on or near the terminal date of their movements. Likewise, countries such as Argentina and Brazil had no census on or near the peak movement years, but some figures have been estimated by the United Nations (see the appropriate Statistical Yearbooks of the League of Nations and the United Nations, listed in the appendix). We are able, therefore, to test our theory on 33 first-wave movements, spanning the years 1860–1950.

Upon careful inspection of Table 6.1, one is struck by the amount of general consistency across countries in the magnitude of the independent variables. There seem to be critical levels of urbanization, industrialization, size of the middle class, and female role expansion and role/status dilemmas in order for a movement to grow larger than incipient. This point can be demonstrated more dramatically in Table 6.2. Here we have cross-classified the independent variables, one at a time, by the dependent variable. We use the median of the ranked distribution of countries on each independent variable as the cutting point to determine high or low levels of that independent variable. Countries which cluster within a percentage point or two have been grouped together, even if such a grouping crosses the median value, provided that there is a clear percentage separation between those countries and ones either higher or lower. We dichotomize the dependent variable by whether the movement was incipient or larger.

As Tables 6.1 and 6.2 illustrate, no movement was larger than incipient unless the percentage of the population living in cities of 100,000 people or more exceeded 10 percent (the median of the distribution). However, 6 countries (Argentina, Brazil, Chile, Egypt, Great Britain 1, and Japan 1) exceeded the minimum urbanization level, but still had incipient movements. Once we examine the four independent variables, we shall offer an explanation for some of these nonfitting cases.

With the exception of Mexico, one never gets a movement that is larger than incipient unless at least 50 percent (the median) of the labor force is not in the primary sector. However, Chile, Great Britain 1, New Zealand, and Norway exceeded that prerequisite and still did not have movements that were larger than incipient. In Mexico's case, except for a radical, incipient feminist branch in the Yucatán, movement activism was confined to industrialized cities, while the movement was co-opted in New Zealand and Norway. Finally, although the levels of industrialization and urbanization were sufficiently high in Great Britain 1, the crucial middle class was quite small.

	Movement Date	Movement Size	Urb.	Indust.	M.C.	Role Expansion 1	Role/Status Dilemmas
Argentina	1930	Inc.	27.1	N/A	37.4	36.4	97.1
Australia	1900	Inc./Inter.	34.0	63.5	76.3	N/A	N/A
Austro-Hungary	1920	Inc.	4.7	40.5	41.9	N/A	N/A
Brazil	1930	Inc.	11.4	N/A	N/A	N/A	N/A
Canada	1920	Inter.	18.9	85.6	61.8	61.0	98.0
Chile	1950	Inc.	34.8	63.6	36.7	39.0	95.4
China	1920	Inc.	2.2	N/A	N/A	N/A	N/A
Cuba	1920	Inter.	22.5	51.2	10.3	9.4	96.3
Denmark	1910	Inter./Mass	20.0	58.3	50.7	N/A	N/A
Dominican Republic	1940	Inc.	4.7	39.7	31.6	28.5	105.0
Egypt	1930	Inc.	12.7	39.3	11.7	N/A	N/A
Finland	1900	Inc.	5.5	30.8	6.0	N/A	N/A
France 1	1890	Inc.	8.4	44.9	48.6	N/A	N/A
France 2	1910	Inter.	11.0	58.5	56.7	55.2	96.6
Germany 1	1890	Inc.	7.3	42.5	52.1	N/A	N/A
Germany 2	1925	Inter./Mass	16.3	65.6	55.9	N/A	N/A
Great Britain 1	1880	Inc.	27.3	82.0	12.5	N/A	N/A

	Year	Indust.	Urb.	M.C.	R. Exp. 1		
Great Britain 2	1920	Mass	28.6	85.6	47.9	47.2	97.8
Holland	1910	Inter.	14.4	69.6	45.9	N/A	N/A
Iceland	1910	Inter./Mass	29.4	N/A	N/A	N/A	N/A
India	1950	Inc.	4.9	25.9	10.3	N/A	N/A
Iran/Persia	1950	Inc.	6.8	43.3	13.0	N/A	N/A
Italy	1910	Inc.	7.0	43.9	27.1	25.5	90.2
Japan 1	1910	Inc.	11.3	35.7	N/A	N/A	N/A
Japan 2	1930	Inter./Mass	19.0	50.1	50.1	N/A	N/A
Mexico	1940	Inter.	12.3	34.6	N/A	N/A	N/A
New Zealand	1890	Inc.	7.7	64.0	59.2	N/A	N/A
Norway	1910	Inc.	9.6	58.9	48.2	N/A	N/A
Peru	1930	Inc.	3.7	N/A	N/A	N/A	N/A
Russia	1910	Inc.	7.2	40.8	7.2	3.4	47.2
Sweden	1910	Inter./Mass	10.3	60.0	48.8	N/A	N/A
U.S. 1	1860	Inc.	5.5	47.6	47.2	N/A	N/A
U.S. 2	1920	Mass	24.4	71.1	68.8	67.0	90.3

Measurement: Urbanization (Urb.) = Percentage of the population in cities of 100,000 or more.
Industrialization (Indust.) = Percentage of labor force in nonprimary sector.
Size of the Middle Class (M.C.) = Percentage of children aged 5–19 in school 20 years earlier.
Role Expansion 1 (R. Exp. 1) = Percentage of girls aged 5–19 in school 20 years earlier.
Role/Status Dilemmas = Ratio of girls aged 5–19 in school to boys aged 5–19 in school, both 20 years earlier.

Table 6.2 Cross-Classification of First-Wave Movement Size by Urbanization, Industrialization, Size of the Middle Class, Role Expansion, and Role/Status Dilemmas

Urbanization

	Incip. Movement	Inter./Mass Movement
Low Urban	14	0
High Urban	6	13

Chi-Square 14.98   p. = .0001   Q = 1.00

Industrialization

	Incip. Movement	Inter./Mass Movement
Low Indust.	12	1
High Indust.	4	11

Chi-Square 12.72   p. = .002   Q = .94

Size of the Middle Class

	Incip. Movement	Inter./Mass Movement
Small M.C.	9	1
Large M.C.	5	10

Chi-Square 5.69   p. = .02   Q = .90

Role Expansion: Females in School

	Incip. Movement	Inter./Mass Movement
Small R.E.	5	1
Large R.E.	0	4

Chi-Square Fisher's Exact =   p. = .02   Q = 1.00

Role/Status Dilemma

	Incip. Movement	Inter./Mass Movement
Small R/S D.	3	1
Large R/S D.	2	4

Chi-Square Fisher's Exact =   p. = .26   Q = .71

(Not Significant)

Cuba was the only country not to have a large enough middle class and still have a movement that was larger than incipient. In all other instances, unless at least 45 percent (the median) of children aged 5–19 were in school twenty years prior to the peak of the movement, that movement never was larger than incipient. In the instance of Cuba, the movement occurred primarily in Havana, where the 1899 census (two decades prior to the movement's peak year) reported that approximately 70 percent of the children were in school—well over the minimal level. Five countries, Austro-Hungary, France 1, Germany 1, Norway, and the United States 1 met the minimal percentage of middle class, but only had incipient movements.

Unfortunately, for only ten movements is there a measure of role expansion, operationalized in terms of the percentage of girls in school twenty years prior to the peak year of the movement. However, in all cases except Cuba, unless the percentage met or exceeded the median value of 40 percent, no movement attained a size larger than incipient. As in the assessment of the size of the middle class, Cuba far exceeded the minimal value in the city of Havana, where the movement was centered. There, over 60 percent of the girls were in school twenty years prior to the movement's peak year.

Likewise plagued by the absence of many cases, the role/status dilemma measure, the ratio of the percentage of girls in school to boys in school two decades earlier, could not be adequately examined. For the cases presented in Table 6.2, nonfitters accounted for 30 percent of the cases (as such, the number of fitting cases could be explained by chance alone). Additionally, the measure is flawed by the fact that, with the sole exception of Russia, all the cases approached educational parity for females and males. Finally, it is our suspicion that the measure cannot be assessed in isolation. For 60 percent of the cases parity is attained in societies where a majority of neither sex attended school—in societies which failed to attain the minimal middle-class level as operationalized previously. When education is likely to be restricted to the elites among a population, regardless of sex, can one expect it to have the same implications and outcomes as it might when education crosses class lines? We think not. Nevertheless, given our data, we must conclude that our measure of the magnitude of role/status dilemmas does not differentiate movement size during the first wave.

Summarizing our data on urbanization, industrialization, and the size of the middle class, the three variables for which we have measurements for most cases, in only two cases (Cuba and Mexico) is a movement larger than incipient found when any one independent variable predicted a smaller movement. Since the three measures do not precisely covary, clearly if a society is below the median on one or two and above the median on other(s), it must logically be a nonfitter on at least one variable. Where all three variables predict a movement of a given size (incipient or larger), it is always found to be that size. Where two of three variables predict a movement of a given size, it is found to be that size in all but three cases, Great Britain 1, Chile, and Norway, and in one of these cases political conditions obstructed movement development. This leaves no cases that are completely nonfitters, using the three predictive variables.

A more appropriate test of our theory involves a series of zero-order correlation coefficients (Pearson product-moment correlation coefficients) between each independent variable and movement size, along with a linear regression combining the independent variables to examine the extent to which they collectively explain the dependent variable. Table 6.3 displays the zero-order correlation coefficients. Presented also are the levels of statistical significance attained by each association. As can be seen in the table each of the posited relationships are supported, except that concerning role/status dilemmas. Thus, the greater the level of urbanization, industrialization, size of the middle class, and educational role expansion for women, the larger the size of the first-wave women's movements. Recall also that we found additional support for the female role expansion argument based upon material presented in chapter 4. As mentioned earlier, in the overwhelming majority of the nations first-wave movement activity was preceded by evidence that middle-class women were increasingly involved in public sphere activities such as voluntary associations, not directly aimed at upgrading women's status.

One association posited by our model failed to attain statistical significance. We operationalized role/status dilemmas in terms of a ratio of female education to male education. The obtained r value of .036 was not significant. There is no association between first-wave movement size and the ratio of girls to boys in school two decades prior to the peak year of the movement. Perhaps a better indicator should have been selected, or at least one with many more cases where data were available.

Since theories link groups of constructs, even a partial test of the theory necessitates more than the testing of the individual relationships just reported. A test of our theory, or at least the structural linkages in it, requires the use of a multivariate measure such as linear regression. Here one regresses the dependent variable of movement size on a group of independent variables to determine the

Table 6.3   Zero-Order Correlation Coefficients between First-Wave Movement Size and the Independent Variables

Independent Variable	Correlation Coefficient	Sample size	p. =
Urbanization	.411	34	.008
Industrialization	.526	29	.002
Size of middle class	.441	25	.014
Role expansion	.596	10	.033
Role/status dilemmas	.036	10	N.S.

Table 6.4   Revised Model of the Regression of First-Wave Movement Size on the Independent Variables

Variable	Covar. r	b (se)	Beta	t =
Urbanization	.411	.102 (.177)	.144	N.S.
Industrialization	.526	.113 (.104)	.300	N.S.
Size of middle class	.441	.100 (.074)	.257	N.S.
Intercept = 6.10				
R = .574	R² = .330	F = 3.44	p. = .035	

Single Predictor: Industrialization

	Covar. r	b (se)	Beta	t =
	.526	.198 (.062)	.526	3.21
Intercept = 8.60				
R = .526	R² = .276	F = 10.32	p. = .003	

total amount of variance in size explained by the aggregation of independent variables, as well as each independent variable's capacity to explain the dependent variable, once overlaps between independent variables have been eliminated.

Presented in Table 6.4 are the results of a revised regression analysis. Initially, regressing movement size on 4 independent variables (urbanization, industrialization, size of the middle class, and educational role expansion for women) yielded an R of .706 and an R^2 of .499. However, the inclusion of women's education, based upon only 11 of the 36 movements reported during the first wave, makes the regression nonsignificant, in part due to the small sample size. Deletion of the women's educational variable yields an R of .574 and an accompanying R^2 of .330. The associated F-test value for this regression is 3.44, which is statistically significant ($p = .035$). Thus, one third of the total variance in the size of the first-wave movements can be explained by our 3 rather crude measures of urbanization, industrialization, and the size of the middle class. Unfortunately, however, when the 3 independent variables are combined to explain movement size, the significance test (t-value) for each drops below the acceptable criterion. What this means is that each of the independent variables is an equally good predictor of movement size, but each is more highly correlated with one another than with movement size (a condition known as multicollinearity). In essence, in their attempt uniquely to explain the size of women's ameliorative movements, each of the independent variables obliterates one another. Urbanization, industrialization, and the size of the middle class are so intertwined and causally dependent upon one another in nineteenth- and twentieth-century societies, that their independent influence on movement size cannot be isolated. Alternatively, it could be stated that one ought to choose among the predictors, using only the single strongest one. In that case, industrialization would be selected. Its R is .526, with an R^2 of .276 (the regression model using only industrialization has an F-value of 10.32, which is significant at the .003 level).

Explaining the Size of Second-wave Movements

Second-wave movements were all found to be feminist. Feminist movements are totalistic; they challenge the basic sex stratification and gender role definition systems. As such, it is our conviction that they need a substantially different female populace—one which has the potential for, or has begun to attain a substantial degree of economic equality—from first-wave ameliorative movements. Therefore, we emphasize labor force variables in our explanation of the size of second-wave movements.

Table 6.5 presents the relevant population statistics on the 16 nations which we were able to determine experienced second-wave movements. The peak year chosen was 1970. We were able to ascertain that 13 of these nations also had prior first-wave movements. There was no evidence for an earlier movement in Portugal or Spain, and Israel did not yet exist as a state when Jewish Palestine experienced such a movement.

By contrast with Table 6.1, which displayed the population variables for the first wave, Table 6.5 for the second wave depicts greater levels of urbanization, industrialization, a larger middle class, as well as more women in school. These are the natural outcomes of the passage of time and modernization (and especially, the transition into a postindustrial economy). By dichotomizing the distributions of each of the independent variables at their medians, and cross-classifying that dichotomy by whether the country had an incipient movement or one that was larger, it is again possible to detect which countries are nonfitters. This is presented in Table 6.6. In contrast with its role in the first wave, the level of urbanization does not differentiate incipient movements from larger ones. However, the size of the middle class and the original role expansion measure (girls in school twenty years prior to the peak year of the movement) do continue to work. As might be expected, the medians are much higher than in the first wave (both at 55 percent). Using that median for each measure, two anomalies emerge in each: Japan was above the median on each but had only an incipient movement, and Italy was below the median on each but had an intermediate to mass movement. The percentage of the college age population attending college did not play a role in differentiating the magnitude of second-wave movements, with some countries having smaller percentages of the college aged population in college than their movement size would predict, and others having larger percentages than would be expected from the size of the movement.

Industrialization continues to play some role. However, there are nonfitting nations. Japan and Israel, with only incipient movements, were as industrialized as countries with larger movements (the median differentiating high from low levels of industrialization was 76.0 percent). Women in college a decade prior to the peak year of the movement was also a weak measure, just failing to attain statistical significance. There are 4 anomalies out of 16 nations on this measure (the median here was 1.5 percent). Norway and West Germany each had a smaller

Table 6.5   Assessment of the Structural Variables Associated with the Size of Second-Wave Women's Movements Across Societies, 1970

	Movement Size	Urb.	Indust.	M. C.	Col.	R. Exp.1	R. Exp.2	R. Exp.3	R. Exp.4	R/S Dilemma 1	R/S Dilemma 2	R/S Dilemma 3	R/S Dilemma 4
Brazil	Inc.	13.6	55.8	42.2	0.8	21.4	0.4	21.8	17.3	93.4	34.6	40.3	81.0
Canada	Inter./Mass	26.7	91.7	69.0	4.4	68.0	2.1	42.8	30.1	97.2	32.5	54.5	83.9
Finland	Inter.	20.3	76.2	57.4	3.5	58.0	3.2	45.8	23.4	101.8	88.9	73.6	136.8
France	Inc./Inter.	30.7	76.2	60.0	4.3	60.8	3.3	31.9	22.1	102.4	61.9	50.9	79.5
Great Britain	Inter.	64.3	95.9	69.2	2.4	68.0	1.6	46.3	33.7	96.7	50.3	55.3	112.9
Holland	Mass	41.0	93.5	59.0	6.1	57.9	3.2	25.2	17.3	96.1	36.7	35.2	62.0
India	Inc.	10.4	27.4	19.3	0.9	10.2	0.3	4.1	2.6	36.3	20.4	12.9	11.7
Israel	Inc.	33.2	91.1	N/A	4.6	N/A	4.0	31.7	24.7	N/A	74.7	43.0	73.4
Italy	Inter./Mass	29.2	80.6	42.7	2.6	40.2	1.5	19.7	11.3	89.3	41.3	32.5	43.9
Japan	Inc.	51.5	81.1	66.3	3.4	65.2	0.9	42.8	25.7	96.8	15.4	54.8	77.1
Norway	Inter.	24.3	87.8	55.5	2.0	55.3	0.8	27.8	17.1	99.3	27.8	39.5	73.6
Portugal	Inc.	12.8	69.3	28.3	1.8	25.8	1.0	22.1	11.4	84.0	40.5	33.5	41.0
Puerto Rico	Inc.	46.2	69.9	47.7	5.3	46.5	4.8	24.0	18.0	95.4	83.1	41.3	69.2
Spain	Inc.	21.6	74.1	29.8	1.9	29.2	0.8	17.7	10.6	96.4	27.4	27.1	44.7
United States	Mass	31.5	87.9	78.2	13.3	77.6	9.1	42.5	26.2	98.6	52.0	56.8	80.9
West Germany	Inc./Inter.	32.6	90.3	61.3	2.6	60.5	1.1	36.5	20.1	97.7	29.0	46.2	79.5

Measurement: Urbanization (Urb.) = Percentage of the population in cities of 100,000 or more.
Industrialization (Indust.) = Percentage of labor force in nonprimary sector.
Size of the Middle Class (M.C.) = Percentage of children age 5–19 in school 20 years earlier.
College Enrollment (Col.) = Percentage of 15–24 year olds in college 10 years earlier.
Role Expansion 1 (R. Exp.1) = Percentage of girls aged 5–19 in school 20 years earlier.
Role Expansion 2 (R. Exp.2) = Percentage of women aged 15–24 in college 10 years earlier.
Role Expansion 3 (R. Exp.3) = Percentage of women over 19 in the nonprimary labor sector.
Role Expansion 4 (R. Exp.4) = Percentage of women over 19 in the tertiary labor sector.
Role/Status Dilemma 1 = Ratio of girls aged 5–19 in school to boys aged 5–19 in school 20 years earlier.
Role/Status Dilemma 2 = Ratio of women aged 15–24 in college to men aged 15–24 in college 10 years earlier.
Role/Status Dilemma 3 = Ratio of women over 19 in the nonprimary labor sector.
Role/Status Dilemma 4 = Ratio of women of 19 in the tertiary labor sector to men over 19 in the tertiary labor sector.

Table 6.6 Cross-Classification of Second-Wave Movement Size by Urbanization, Industrialization, Size of the Middle Class, Role Expansion, and Role/Status Dilemmas

Urbanization

	Incip. Movement	Inter./Mass Movement
Low Urban with	4	3
High Urban with	3	6

Chi-Square
Fisher's Exact = p. = .329 Q = .455
(Not Significant)

Industrialization

	Incip. Movement	Inter./Mass Movement
Low Indust. with	5	0
High Indust. with	2	4

Chi-Square
Fisher's Exact = p. = .004 Q = 1.00

Size of the Middle Class

	Incip. Movement	Inter./Mass Movement
Low M.C. with	5	1
High M.C. with	1	8

Chi-Square
Fisher's Exact = p. = .001 Q = .95

Role Expansion: Women in the Nonprimary Sector

	Incip. Movement	Inter./Mass Movement
Low N.P.L. with	5	2
High N.P.L. with	2	7

Chi-Square
Fisher's Exact = p. = .071 Q = .08
(Not Signicant)

Role Expansion: Women in the Tertiary Sector

	Incip. Movement	Inter./Mass Movement
Low Tert. with	5	2
High Tert. with	3	6

Chi-Square
Fisher's Exact = p. = .151 Q = .33
(Not Significant)

	Low with Incip. Movement	Low with Inter./Mass Movement	High with Incip. Movement	High with Inter./Mass Movement	Statistics
College	Low College with Incip. Movement 5	Low College with Inter./Mass Movement 2	High College with Incip. Movement 2	High College with Inter./Mass Movement 7	Chi-Square Fisher's Exact = $p. = .071$ $Q = .80$ (Not Significant)

Role Expansion: Females in School

	Low with incip. Movement	Low with Inter./Mass Movement	High with Incip. Movement	High with Inter./Mass Movement	Statistics
School	Low School with incip. Movement 5	Low School with Inter./Mass Movement 1	High School with Incip. Movement 1	High School with Inter./Mass Movement 8	Chi-Square Fisher's Exact = $p. = .011$ $Q = .95$

Role/Status Dilemma: Nonprimary Sector

	Low R/S D. with Incip. Movement	Low R/S D. with Inter./Mass Movement	High R/S D. with Incip. Movement	High R/S D. with Inter./Mass Movement	Statistics
	Low R/S D. with Incip. Movement 5	Low R/S D. with Inter./Mass Movement 2	High R/S D. with Incip. Movement 3	High R/S D. with Inter./Mass Movement 6	Chi-Square Fisher's Exact = $p. = .157$ $Q = .67$ (Not Significant)

Role/Status Dilemma: Tertiary

	Low R/S D. with Incip. Movement	Low R/S D. with Inter./Mass Movement	High R/S D. with Incip. Movement	High R/S D. with Inter./Mass Movement	Statistics
	Low R/S D. with Incip. Movement 4	Low R/S D. with Inter./Mass Movement 2	High R/S D. with Incip. Movement 3	High R/S D. with Inter./Mass Movement 7	Chi-Square Fisher's Exact = $p. = .182$ $Q = .65$ (Not Significant)

Role/Status Dilemma: School

	Low R/S D. with Incip. Movement	Low R/S D. with Inter./Mass Movement	High R/S D. with Incip. Movement	High R/S D. with Inter./Mass Movement	Statistics
	Low R/S D. with Incip. Movement 4	Low R/S D. with Inter./Mass Movement 1	High R/S D. with Incip. Movement 2	High R/S D. with Inter./Mass Movement 8	Chi-Square Fisher's Exact = $p. = .047$ $Q = .88$

Role/Status Dilemma:College

	Low R/S D. with Incip. Movement	Low R/S D. with Inter./Mass Movement	High R/S D. with Incip. Movement	High R/S D. with Inter./Mass Movement	Statistics
	Low R/S D. with Incip. Movement 5	Low R/S D. with Inter./Mass Movement 2	High R/S D. with Incip. Movement 2	High R/S D. with Inter./Mass Movement 7	Chi-Square Fisher's Eact = $p. = .072$ $Q = .80$ (Not Significant)

Table 6.7   Zero-Order Correlation Coefficients between Second-Wave Movement Size and the Independent Variables

Independent variable	Correlation coefficient	Sample size	p. =
Urbanization	.165	16	N.S.
Industrialization	489	16	.027
Size of middle class	.605	15	.008
Role expansion: Nonprimary	.430	16	.048
Role expansion: Tertiary	.421	16	.049
Role expansion: School	.616	15	.007
Role expansion: College	.466	16	.034
Role/status dilemma: Nonprimary	.151	16	N.S.
Role/status dilemma: Tertiary	.285	15	N.S.
Role/status dilemma: School	.318	15	N.S.
Role/status dilemma: College	.050	16	N.S.

percentage of women in universities than did the other nations which had intermediate movements or larger, while Israel and Puerto Rico had a larger percentage than might be expected for countries with only incipient movements. However, the countries clustered so much together that, with the exception of the United States, a difference of one percentage point separated high from low levels of female college attendance. Nonetheless, the college variable will play a role in explaining an anomaly later on.

There are distinctive patterns to the anomalies for the variables of women in the nonprimary labor force and women in the tertiary labor force. In each instance, Japan and Israel had smaller movements than the size of women's economic participation would predict, and Holland and Italy had larger movements than the economic variables would predict. Furthermore, Norway had a larger movement than the female tertiary might predict. However, Norway satisfied the criterion for women in the nonprimary sector, while Holland and Italy had a large enough percentage of women in college – a prerequisite for future middle-class employment. Japan did meet the economic conditions for a larger movement, but did not satisfy the college prerequisite. Israel, however, did satisfy the college variable, but still had only an incipient movement in the presence of sufficient economic role expansion. It remains the only unexplained anomaly, although one might point to the fact that the country was at war during part of the time period and has been in the state of war preparedness throughout the period.

Although we offered no explicit argument linking movement size to role/status dilemmas, the logic is the same as that employed for the first wave. Therefore, we examined these variables. The measures include the ratio of females in school to males in school two decades earlier, the ratio of females in college to males in college two decades earlier, the ratio of females to males in the nonprimary labor force sector, and the ratio of females to males in the tertiary labor force sector. None of these measures attained statistical significance.

Table 6.8   Revised Regression Model of the Second-Wave Movement Size on the Independent Variables

Variable	Covar. r	b (se)	Beta	t =
Female tertiary	.421	.714 (.360)	.761	2.05
Role expansion: School	.616	.479 (.147)	1.271	3.25
Intercept = 5.566				
R = .727 R² = .528 F = 6.71 p. = .01				

Japan and Spain had attained elementary and secondary school parity twenty years prior to the peak year of the movement, but the movement was only incipient; Italy, by comparison, did not reach parity but had a large movement. On the other three measures of role/status dilemmas, there were even larger numbers of anomalies.

As in our examination of the first wave, we can directly test the relationships posited by using zero-order correlation coefficients and regression analysis. These data are presented in Tables 6.7 and 6.8. As in the first wave, significant associations are found between the size of feminist movements and the amount of industrialization, size of the middle class, and the percentage of girls in school two decades earlier. In addition, several statistically significant associations of relevance to the second wave were found, including the percentage of the population between ages 15 and 24 in college ten years prior to the peak year of the movement, the percentage of 15.24-year-old women in college at that same time period, the percentage of women in the nonprimary sector of the labor force, and the percentage of women in the tertiary sector. The size of second-wave movements, however, does not vary with the level of urbanization. Most of the nations had sufficiently high levels of urbanization (well over the critical level needed for mass first-wave movements) that it ceased to be a discriminating variable. Finally, although no explicit arguments were offered regarding the association between role/status dilemmas and second-wave movement size, we did compute the correlation coefficients for these indexes. None was statistically significant. The size of second-wave movements is unrelated to the ratios of males to females in any of the expanded educational or work roles, as we were able to measure them.

As before, a test of the model necessitates a multivariate approach. The linear regression which included all of the univariate measures produced a model which was not statistically significant because of a problem of over-specification. That is, we have too many highly intercorrelated independent variables such that each can do a nearly adequate job in explaining the same part of the dependent variable. Variables were deleted and another regression was run. That multiple regression on the size of feminist movements included the following independent variables: the percentage of women in the tertiary, the percentage of women in the nonprimary, the percentage of girls in school two decades earlier, and the size of the middle class. The obtained multiple R is .794, with an R^2 of .631 ($F = 4.277$, $p = .03$). These four variables can thus explain 63.1 percent of the variance in the size of second-wave movements. However, at that point, the individual variables cease to be statistically significant. A revised model, presented in Table 6.8, reduces the number of predictors to 2, and yields a multiple R of .727, with an R^2 of .528 ($F = 6.71$, $p = .01$). Hence, employment in the tertiary sector and a heightening of educational attainment for women adequately account for more than half of the variance in the size of second-wave movements.

Before leaving this section, the reader might well ask whether the size of movements could actually be explained simply by the size of nations, rather than by the variables we have examined. Could it be that nations with large populations have large movements and nations with small populations have small movements? To allay such fears we correlated population size with movement size for the two waves. The obtained correlation coefficient is –.220, which, in addition to being in the opposite direction from the rival hypothesis, is not statistically significant. There is no evidence that the size of movements varies with the size of national populations.

Explaining the Ideology of Women's Movements

In this section we test the explanation developed in chapter 3 to account for different movement ideologies. Ideology, expressed as ameliorative versus feminist movements, has been operationalized as a dichotomous variable, and as such the concept of variance within it is meaningless, and ordinary least squares regression analysis is inappropriate. One appropriate way of testing our arguments is to run statistical tests of significance between the distribution of percentages on a variable in the first wave versus the distribution on that variable in the second wave. If there is a statistically significant change (we proposed an increase) in the percentage, then our argument is supported. If there is no statistically significant change, or if the change goes in the opposite direction, then we have to reject our argument.

Presented in Table 6.9 are the tests of the significance of difference between the means of each of the independent variables between the ameliorative and feminist waves. In instances where a country had two phases of their ameliorative wave, the test is run on the difference between the second, later phase, and the feminist movement.

The first argument proposed that an increase in the percentage of married women in the labor force would lead to a shift from an ameliorative to a feminist movement. We have noted earlier that no data on the labor force participation of married women were available for the majority of nations. We have had to use as stand-ins several other labor force participation measures. As is evident from the table, there is partial support for our argument. Between the ameliorative and feminist waves there has been an average 11-percent increase in the percent-

Table 6.9 Significance of Difference between First- and Second-Wave Independent Variables

Variable	1st Wave Mean	1st Wave S.D.	2nd Wave Mean	2nd Wave S.D.	t =	p. =
Urbanization	14.59	9.77	30.21	14.80	−3.86	.001
Industrialization	51.50	18.48	77.07	16.93	−4.72	.000
Size of middle class	40.75	19.55	52.39	16.09	−2.05	.050
Role exp.: School	35.17	21.18	49.64	19.91	−1.77	.092
Role exp.: College	0.51	0.86	2.40	2.25	−3.02	.007
Role exp.: Nonprimary	20.16	9.25	27.12	11.10	−2.12	.043
Role exp.: Tertiary	3.70	2.46	10.02	4.76	−4.22	.001
Role/status dilemma: School	95.24	4.78	92.10	16.10	0.71	.485
Role/status dilemma: College	129.86	265.88	72.70	11.17	0.53	.621
Role/status dilemma: Nonprimary	41.54	18.11	53.00	43.70	−1.04	.313
Role/status dilemma: Tertiary	34.90	20.73	73.34	40.84	−2.91	.010

age of women in the nonprimary sector, a difference which is not, however, statistically significant. One reason, soon to be seen in an inspection of the table, is that the percentage of women staying in elementary and secondary school and entering college increased dramatically, thus decreasing the proportion of young women in the labor force. However, we had noted that most prior research has placed the growth of women's employment in the tertiary sector. Here participation during the time of feminist movements was more than 270 percent of what it had been in the era of ameliorative movements. On the basis of this findng we can assert that our argument linking women's employment status to ideology is supported.

In the absence of data on specific occupations in most of the censuses, we cannot adequately test our arguments that participation in male-dominated occupations, or in high-status occupations, is associated with feminist ideology. We can examine the relative proportions of women and men in occupational sectors, recognizing that even within these sectors there is male work and female work, as noted earlier in the chapter. The ratio of women to men in the nonprimary increased, but not significantly, between waves. By contrast, the ratio of women to men in the tertiary increased more than twofold, from an average of 34.9 to 73.3 percent between the two waves. Relying upon this crude measure we can accept, with considerable caution, our arguments linking movement ideology with the influx of women into traditionally male occupations.

Our last argument maintains that feminist movements depend upon educational parity between men and women. An optimal measure would have been educational attainment of adults. However, these data were lacking for most of the first-wave nations and for many of the second-wave nations. What was available were percentages of children in school two decades prior to the peak years and percentages of men and women aged 15–24 in colleges and universities a decade prior to the peak year of the movement. These were the measures we utilized. Although there was more than a 33-percent increase in the percentage of girls attending elementary and secondary school between the two movement waves, the difference was not statistically significant. However, for a comparison of college attendance the percentages increased nearly fivefold, and were statistically significant. The percentage of women of college age attending college was significantly greater during the feminist wave than during the ameliorative wave. Unfortunately, the ratios showed no significant increases, and thus, we must reject our final argument.

Although no specific arguments were offered for differences between waves on these measures, statistically significant differences were also found for urbanization, level of industrialization, size of the middle class, and percentage of the college-aged population in college between the first and second waves. In contrast with ameliorative movements, feminist movements occur in settings where there is a higher percentage of the populace living in big cities; where more of the labor force is not in the primary sector; where the middle class is larger (as measured in terms of school-aged children attending school); and where a larger percentage of individuals between the ages of 15 and 24 attend colleges and universities.

Since we offer a theory of the ideological scope of women's movement, it is again appropriate to utilize a multivariate technique. Presented in Table 6.10 are the results of a discriminant function analysis (a form of multivariate analysis used when the dependent variable is a dichotomy). The canonical correlation coefficient (to be interpreted something like an R) is .850, with the percentage of women in the nonprimary and the tertiary, the percentage of women in college, the level of urbanization, and the size of the middle class having significant effects upon the relationship. The labor force variables had the greatest effect. The discriminant function correctly grouped 94.4 percent of the cases. The exception is the second-wave movement in India, which we characterize as feminist, but which possesses the demographic characteristics of an ameliorative movement.

The portrait consistently depicted by the analysis of the factors which produce feminist movements is that it is actual occupational and preparatory educational gains made by women which are crucial, rather than gains made relative to men. Consequently, as measured in this study, the input of role/status dilemmas pale into nonsignificance when role expansion variables are introduced into the analysis. It may be that the absence of occupational and college academic major data free of sex segregation are needed to provide an adequate estimation of the effect of role/status dilemmas. Stated otherwise, our measures of this variable may simply be too crude to pick up any effects.

Summary of Findings

Recall that we listed a series of ten specific hypotheses in the conclusion of chapter 3. In the preceding discussion we have presented data relevant to each. The

Table 6.10   Discriminant Function Analysis of Ideological Scope: First- versus Second-Wave Movements

Variable	Unstandardized Canonical Discriminant Function Coefficient		Standardized Canonical Discriminant Function Coefficient
Urbanization	.049		.698
Size of middle class	− .031		− .562
Females in college	.309		.671
Females in nonprimary sector	− .103		− 1.516
Females in tertiary sector	.363		1.561

Canonical Correlation	F	d.f.	p. =
.850	4.98	5	.01

Vector:
$V = -.543 + .049X_1 - .031X_2 + .309X_3 - .103X_4 + .363X_5$
(Intercept) (Urb.) (M.C.) (F. Col.) (F. N.P.) (F. Ter.)

following is an assessment of the extent to which each hypothesis has been supported.

We examine first the hypotheses related to movement size.

1. The greater the level of urbanization, the larger the size of the women's movement. This received substantial support for first- but not second-wave movements.

2. The greater the level of industrialization, the larger the size of the women's movement. This hypothesis was supported for both waves.

3. The higher the average educational level of women, the larger the size of the women's movement. For both waves we found that this hypothesis was tenable.

4. The greater the proportion of the population which is middle class, the larger the size of the women's movement. Again, substantial support was garnered in our examination of both waves.

5. The more women who participate in roles monopolized by men in the recent past (i.e., the greater the role expansion), the larger the size of the women's movement. Although we did not directly test this hypothesis, supporting evidence was found in the case of the educational variable for the first wave, and both this and labor force variables for the second wave.

6. The size of a women's movement is related to governmental response in a curvilinear fashion, such that both high levels of repression and co-optation of movement goals by male authorities result in relatively small movement sizes. This hypothesis was tenable only for the first wave, where support was found both in our discussions of case studies and in accounting for anomalies in the statistical data. We could not test it in the second wave, as we found no evidence of co-optation or repression.

We turn now to the ideological scope hypotheses.

7. The greater the proportion of married women in the labor force, the more likely a women's movement will develop a feminist ideology. While there was no direct test of this hypothesis, labor force data did lend it credibility.

8. The greater the proportion of women labor force participants working in male-dominated occupations, the more likely a women's movement will develop a feminist ideology.

9. The greater the proportion of women labor force participants working in high-status occupations (i.e., those most conducive to role/status dilemmas), the more likely a women's movement will develop a feminist ideology. In the absence of usable cross-national labor force data, these two hypotheses could not be tested. The data measuring role/status dilemmas did not support the logic of these hypotheses, but our measurements may have been too crude.

10. The more similar the educational achievements of the two sexes, the more likely a women's movement will develop a feminist ideology. The data did not support this hypothesis.

Finally, in chapter 3 we also predicted interaction effects. Our description of large (intermediate or mass) compared with small (incipient) ameliorative movements was quite accurate. For feminist movements, except for issues of parity, our descriptions of the modal characteristics of large compared to small movements was accurate.

ADDITIONAL CONSIDERATIONS

With the exception of a brief mention in the third chapter, one topic specifically ignored, and obviously not measured, in testing the theory has been communication and cooperation between women's movements in various societies. It has not only been extensive during both waves, it has also been manifest in a large number of international women's conferences and organizations. While clearly the ideologies, tactics, and strategies developed in some countries (especially in the United States and European nations) have influenced women's movements in other societies, we have ignored this variable because it does not contribute directly to an understanding of why, in a given society, a women's movement achieves the specific size and ideology it does. Ideas may be available, yet fall upon deaf ears. Conversely, when conditions are ripe, such ideas are quickly picked up and spread to large numbers of people. It could be that some of the anomalies we reported in which the demographics of a society were too small for the size of the movement obtained could be explained by intersocietal communication, especially in contiguous societies. However, unless the social conditions were present in sufficient magnitude to create a pool of available participants, we contend that communication and cooperation among women's groups cannot produce movements in societies which do not meet the structural conditions. Whether or not a women's movement emerges, how large it becomes, and the nature of its ideology are nearly exclusive functions of the conditions within each specific nation. These issues have, of course, constituted the focus of this work.

It should now be clear to the reader that we tested only a portion of the theory presented in chapter 3. However, one can easily make the case that we have tested more than simply a few structural linkages. In essence, in testing our theory we have logically subsumed a series of social psychological processes into the test. The following is a diagram of the process of analysis:

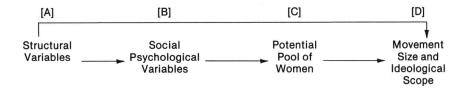

[A]	[B]	[C]	[D]
Structural Variables	Social Psychological Variables	Potential Pool of Women	Movement Size and Ideological Scope

Using census data, we were able to examine the linkage between the structural variables and the size and ideological scope of the women's movements (linking A to D), but had to infer the linkages of A to B, B to C, and C to D. We have argued that the structure facilitates the consciousness of women and enhances the pool of potential participants. That pool serves as the source of members for the movement, obviously affecting its size, but also its ideological scope. A completely thorough test of the theory presented in chapter 3 is an impossibility. Four necessary conditions would have to be met, especially given the historical nature of much of the research. First, attitude surveys of the population pool and behavioral indexes of participants would have needed to have been collected to determine whether the rhetoric of the leadership was falling on deaf ears. However, no such attitudinal surveys are known to have ever been collected, especially during the era of the first-wave movements. Second, we need to improve the nature of the census data collected by nations, including the collection of better educational and labor force data on women. Only with a time machine could we go back to the nineteenth and early twentieth centuries and redo the many censuses. Third, we would need information on countries which had no known movements to ascertain whether, in the absence of the needed levels of structural variables, movements did not emerge. At first glance this seems like an easy task. However, merely because a movement was not written about does not prove that it did not exist. Finally, we would need to collect data on movements which did occur, but about which nothing has been written, either because of poor record-keeping, or because of outright suppression. In the less than perfect world of historical data and cross-national censuses, we have attempted to do our best to test our theory.

CONCLUSIONS

The general theme of this book may be summarized as follows. The intertwined processes of industrialization and urbanization rather rapidly result in increased education for women and their role expansion in the public sphere. In turn, role expansion helps to enhance the formation and spread of gender consciousness and the amassing of personal and collective resources necessary for women to mount a movement on their own behalf. The higher the levels of the independent variables (industrialization, urbanization, size of the middle class, female education, and role expansion), the larger the pool of women potentially available for mobilization, hence the larger the women's movement, in the absence of political obstacles. These hypotheses were tested for a sample of first-wave movements and substantial support was found for them.

However, middle-class women especially, also remained substantially encapsulated in traditional wife/mother roles during the early stages of industrialization. There was relatively little opportunity for such women to participate in the paid labor force, and as a result, married middle-class women rarely did so. The fact that they experienced only partial role expansion resulted in only a partial movement ideology, one which we have called ameliorative. Such an ideology failed to challenge the basic gender role system, rather accepting traditional notions of sexually separate spheres and the primacy of women's domestic and maternal roles.

An ideology of "separate but equal" has rarely resulted in de facto equality. Moreover, women have never attained equality with men when confined primarily to the domestic sphere of activity (Chafetz 1984). The ameliorative, first-wave movements were relatively successful in achieving their stated goals, at least by the 1950s, if not decades earlier. Nonetheless, women remained socially, politically, and economically unequal to men in virtually every nation. The revolution remained clearly "unfinished."

Beginning in the 1950s, in the industrially most advanced nations of the world women once again have experienced role expansion. In such societies, the tertiary sector of the economy has expanded substantially, providing large numbers of new jobs in precisely those occupations long dominated by unmarried women. The result has been a steady, often dramatic increase in the proportion of all women, including married middle-class women, in the labor force.

Increasing numbers of women have come to define paid employment as a relatively permanent commitment. No longer is the world perceived as divided into two totally distinct spheres of activity, one for each sex. In turn, women are increasingly likely to utilize male comparative reference groups, and the same processes of consciousness development and resource mobilization has occurred as did during the earlier phase of role expansion, resulting in second-wave movements. Unlike the earlier wave, many women's roles have finally expanded to encompass the full range of potential social roles by including paid labor force positions along with all other public and domestic roles. In this sense, in contemporary, highly industrialized nations, for sizable numbers of women their roles have expanded to the logical maximal limit. With total role expansion has come an essentially total ideology, which we have called feminist. The size of such movements is a direct function of the proportion of women in the labor force.

In short, the economic structure of a nation is the root explanation of both the size and ideological scope of women's movements. Political conditions of repression or co-optation can retard movement development, but with this exception, our cases are well accounted for by a set of variables which are inexorably linked with the process of industrialization.

This book has focused on independent women's movements. We have also had ample opportunity to note the contemporaneous and/or slightly prior existence of a variety of other social movements during both waves of female activism. We believe that the theory developed in chapter 3, with some modification, can serve to explain why movements on behalf of disadvantaged groups tend to cluster historically. The very socioeconomic changes which have set in motion the processes which produce women's movements undoubtedly affect other minorities in similar ways, producing analogous movements. Root causes, not movement "contagion" are responsible for the phenomenon so often noted and so poorly analyzed.

We have documented in this book forms of female revolt dating back as far as the classical Greco-Roman era and spanning the globe. We have observed that the self-conscious, collective form of such revolt termed *women's movements*, is only a little more than a century old. Finally, the most complete, radical form of such revolt, feminist movements, have been few in number, and for the most part, a scant twenty years old. In historical terms, feminist movements are still in their infancy. It remains to be seen if global economic forces will produce maturity or infant death.

APPENDIX

The following are the resource materials used to generate the census data analyzed in this chapter.

Administración de Reconstrucción de Puerto Rico. 1938. *Censo de Puerto Rico: 1935.* Washington, D.C.: U.S. Government Printing Office.

Allub, Leopoldo. 1974. *Estado y Sociedad Civil: Patrón de Emergencia y Desarrollo del Estado Argentino: 1810–1930.* Mexico City: El Colegio de Mexico.

Broom, Leonard, and F. Lancaster Jones. 1977. *Opportunity and Attainment in Australia.* Stanford, Calif.: Stanford University Press.

Bureau of the Census. 1961. *Historical Statistics of the United States: Colonial Times to 1957.* Washington, D.C.: U.S. Government Printing Office.

———. 1971. *Statistical Abstract of the United States.* Washington, D.C.: Department of Commerce.

Canada Year Book. 1977. *Canada Year Book: 1976–1977 (special edition).* Ottawa: Minister of Supply and Services.

Central Bureau of Statistics. 1972. *Statistical Abstract of Israel: 1972.* Jerusalem: Sivan Press, Ltd.

Central Bureau of Statistics of Norway. 1978. *Historical Statistics: 1978.* Oslo: Central Bureau of Statistics.

Central Statistical Office (Finland). 1972. *Statistical Yearbook of Finland.* Helsinki: Central Statistical Offices.

Central Statistical Organisation (India). 1973. *Statistical Abstract of India: 1972.* New Delhi: Ministry of Printing.

Conselho Nacional de Estatística. 1959. *Anuário Estatístico do Brazil.* IBGE.

Department of Commerce. 1921. *Statistical Abstract of the United States.* Washington, D.C.: U.S. Government Printing Office.

Department of Commerce and Labor. 1912. *Statistical Abstract of the United States: 1911.* Washington, D.C.: U.S. Government Printing Office.

Direccion General de Estadistica. 1945. *Población de la República Dominicana.* Ciudad Trujillo: Seccion de Publicaciones.

———. 1958. *Tercer Censo Nacional de Población: 1950.* Cuidad Trujillo.

Dominion Bureau of Statistics. 1930. *The Canada Yearbook.* Ottawa: F. A. Acland.

Douglas, Sir Arthur P. 1909. *The Domination of New Zealand.* Boston: Little, Brown and Company.

Instituto Nacional de Estatistica (Portugal). 1975. *Anuário Estatístico: 1971.* Lisbon: Instituto Nacional de Estatistica.

League of Nations and United Nations. *Statistical Yearbooks* and *Demographic Yearbooks.* (selected years and publishers).

Mamalakis, Markos J. 1980. *Historical Statistics of Chile: Demography and Labor Force. vol. 2.* Westport, Conn.: Greenwood Press, Inc.

Ministry of Foreign Affairs. 1961. *Statistical Handbook of Japan.* Tokyo: Shinjusha Printing Co.

Mitchell, B. R. 1975. *European Historical Statistics: 1750–1970.* London: Hazell, Watson, and Viney.

———. 1981. *European Historical Statistics: 1750–1975.* 2nd ed. London: Macmillan & Company Ltd.

———. 1982. *International Historical Statistics: Africa and Asia.* New York: New York University Press.

———. 1983. *International Historical Statistics: The Americas and Australasia.* Detroit: Gale Research Company.

Mulhall, Michael G. 1899. *The Dictionary of Statistics.* London: George Routledge.

Oficino de Censo. 1908. *Censo de la República de Cuba.* Washington, D.C.: Office of the Census.

Oliver, W. H., and B. R. Williams. 1981. *The Oxford History of New Zealand.* Wellington, New Zealand: Oxford University Press.

Scobie, James R. 1971. *Argentina: A City and a Nation.* 2nd ed. New York: Oxford University Press, Inc.

Seccion de Publicaciones. 1953. *Tercer Censo Nacional de Población.* Cuidad Trujillo.

Secretaria de Economia. 1948. *Anuario Estadistico de los Estados Unidos Mexicanos.* Mexico, D.F.: Dirección General de Estadístia.

Secreatria de la Economia Nacional. 1941. *Anuario Estadistico de los Estados Unidos Mexicanos: 1939.* Mexico, D.F.: Dirección General de Estadística.

Secretarios de Estado de los Interior y Policia. 1920. *Censo de la República Dominicana.* Santo Domingo.

UNESCO. 1964. *Statistical Yearbook: 1963.* Mayenne, France: Joseph Floch.

United States Department of Commerce. 1943. *Censo Decimosexto de Los Estados Unidos: 1940 (Poblacíon de Puerto Rico).* Washington, D.C.: U.S. Government Printing Office.

United States House of Representatives. 1901. *Statistical Abstract of the United States.* Washington, D.C.: U.S. Government Printing Office.

Urquhart, M. C., and K. A. H. Buckley. 1965. *Historical Statistics of Canada.* Cambridge, England: Cambridge University Press.

War Department. 1900. *Report of the Census of Cuba.* Washington, D.C.: U.S. Government Printing Office.

Ward, Russel. 1977. *The History of Australia.* New York: Harper & Row, Publishers.

Wilkie, James, ed. 1974. *Statistical Abstract of Latin America (Supplement No. 3).* Los Angeles: UCLA Latin American Center.

_____. 1978. *Statistical Abstract of Latin America.* vol. 19. Los Angeles: UCLA Latin American Center.

_____. 1891. *Annuaire Statistique de la France.* Quatorzieme Année.

_____. 1901. *Statistique Générale de la France.* Annuaire Statistique.

_____. 1919. *Census of the Republic of Cuba.* Havana: Maza, Arroyo, y Caso.

_____. 1916. *Statistical Abstract for the United Kingdom. No. 631 (1901–1915).*

_____. 1916. *Tercer Censo Nacional.* Buenos Aires.

Bibliography

Abeles, Ronald P. 1976. "Relative deprivation, rising expectations, and black militancy." *Journal of Social Issues* 32:119–37.

Abramowitz, S. I. 1973. "The comparative competence-adjustment of student left social-political activists." *Journal of Personality* 41:244–60.

Allen, Robert L., with Pamela P. Allen. 1974. *Reluctant Reformers: Racism and Social Reform Movements in the United States*. Washington, D. C.: Howard University Press.

Allport, Gordon W. 1954. *The Nature of Prejudice*. Cambridge, Mass.: Addison-Wesley.

Allport, Gordon W. and Leo Postman. 1947. *The Psychology of Rumor*. New York: Holt, Rinehart and Winston.

Almquist, Elizabeth. 1977. "Women in the labor force." *Signs* 2:843–53.

Almquist, Elizabeth, Edwin Rossman, and Roy Darville. 1980. "Mobilizing feminist organizations: A structural analysis." Paper presented at the 1980 meetings of the Southwestern Sociological Association, Houston, Tex.

Altbach, Edith Hoshino. 1984. "The new German women's movement." *Signs* 9(3):454–69.

Anderson, Nels. 1966. *Desert Saints: The Mormon Frontier in Utah*. Chicago: University of Chicago Press.

Andors, Phyllis. 1983. *The Unfinished Liberation of Chinese Women, 1949–1980*. Bloomington: Indiana University Press.

Andreas, Carol. 1971. *Sex and Caste in America*. Englewood Cliffs, N.J.: Prentice-Hall.

Arizpe, Lourdes. 1977. "Women in the informal labor sector: The case of Mexico City." *Signs* 3:25–37.

Armor, David J. 1980. "White flight and the future of school desegregation." Pp. 187–230 in Walter G. Stephan and Joe R. Feagin, eds., *School Desegregation: Past, Present, and Future*. New York: Plenum Press.

Arrow, Kenneth J. 1973. "The theory of discrimination." Pp. 3–33 in Orley Ashenfelter and Albert Rees, eds., *Discrimination in Labor Markets*. Princeton, N.J.: Princeton University Press.

Bacchi, Carol L. 1982. "First wave feminism in Canada: The ideas of the English-Canadian suffragists, 1877–1918." *Women's Studies International Forum* 5(6):575–83.

———. 1983. *Liberation Deferred? The Ideas of the English-Canadian Suffragists, 1877–1918*. Toronto: University of Toronto Press.

Baig, Tara Ali. 1976. *India's Woman Power*. New Delhi, India: S. Chand & Co.

Bainbridge, William Sims. 1982. "Shaker demographics 1840–1900: An example of the use of U.S. census enumeration schedules." *Journal for the Scientific Study of Religion* 21(4):352–65.

Bámdád, Badr ol-Moluk. 1977. *From Darkness into Light: Women's Emancipation in Iran*, ed. and trans. F. R. C. Bagley. Hicksville, N.Y.: Exposition Press.

Banks, J. A., and Olive Banks. 1964. *Feminism and Family Planning in Victorian England*. New York: Schocken Books.

Banks, Olive. 1981. *Faces of Feminism: A Study of Feminism as a Social Movement*. New York: St. Martin's Press.

Barbosa, Madelena. 1981. "Women in Portugal." *Women's Studies International Quarterly* 4:477–80.

Barrett, Nancy Smith. 1976. "Women in industrial society: An international perspective." Pp. 77–111 in Jane Chapman, ed., *Economic Independence for Women*. Beverly Hills, Calif.: Sage Publications.

Bayat-Philipp, Mangol. 1978. "Women and revolution in Iran, 1905–1911" Pp. 295–308 in L. Beck and N. Keddie, eds., *Women in the Muslim World*. Cambridge: Harvard University Press.

Beck, Lois, and Nikki Keddie, eds. 1978. *Women in the Muslim World*. Cambridge: Harvard University Press.

Becker, Gary S. 1971. *The Economics of Discrimination*. 2nd ed. Chicago: University of Chicago Press.

———. 1975. *Human Capital*. New York: National Bureau of Economic Research.

———. 1976. *The Economic Approach to Human Behavior*. Chicago: University of Chicago Press.

Becker, Howard S. 1963. *Outsiders: Studies in the Sociology of Deviance*. New York: The Free Press of Glencoe.

Benoit-Smullyan, E. 1944. "Status, status types, and status interrelations." *American Sociological Review* 9:151–61.

Benson, J. Kenneth. 1971. "Militant ideologies and organizational context: The war on poverty and the ideology of 'black power.' " *The Sociological Quarterly* 12:328–39.

Berg, Barbara J. 1978. *The Remembered Gate: Origins of American Feminism*. New York: Oxford University Press.

Bettelheim, Bruno. 1943. "Individuals and mass behavior in extreme situations." *Journal of Abnormal and Social Psychology* 38:417–52.

Billington, Rosamund. 1982. "Ideology and feminism: Why the suffragettes were 'wild women'." *Women's Studies International Forum* 5(6):663–74.

Bird, Phyllis. 1973. "Images of women in the Old Testament." in R. Ruether, ed., *Religion and Sexism*. New York: Simon & Schuster.

Blachman, Morris. 1976. "Selective omission and theoretical distortion in studying the political activity of women in Brazil." Pp. 245–64 in J. Nash and H. Safa, eds., *Sex and Class in Latin America*. New York: Praeger Publishers.

Blackburn, Helen. 1971. *Women's Suffrage: A Record of the Women's Suffrage Movement in the British Isles*. New York: Kraus Reprint Co. (orig. pub. 1902).

Blair, Karen J. 1980. *The Clubwoman as Feminist: True Womanhood Redefined, 1868–1914*. New York: Holmes & Meier.

Blalock, H. M. 1967. "Status inconsistency and interaction: Some alternative models." *American Journal of Sociology* 63:305–15.

Blauner, Robert. 1972. *Racial Oppression in America*. New York: Harper & Row.

Blom, Ida. 1982. "A century of organized feminism in Norway." *Women's Studies International Forum* 5(6):569–74.

Blumberg, Rae Lesser. 1978. *Stratification: Socioeconomic and Sexual Inequality*. Dubuque, Iowa: William C. Brown Co.

Blumer, Herbert. 1978. "Social unrest and collective protest." *Studies in Symbolic Interaction* 1:1–54.

Bohachevsky-Chomiak, Martha. 1980. "Socialism and feminism: The first stages of women's organizations in the eastern part of the Austrian Empire." Pp. 44–64 in T. Yedlin, ed., *Women in Eastern Europe and the Soviet Union*. New York: Praeger Publishers.

Bonacich, Edna. 1972. "A theory of ethnic antagonism: The split labor market." *American Sociological Review* 37:547–59.

Bordin, Ruth. 1981. *Women and Temperance: The Quest for Power and Liberty, 1873–1900*. Philadelphia, Pa.: Temple University Press.

Bouchier, David. 1978. *Idealism and Revolution: New Ideologies of Liberation in Britain and the United States*. London: Edward Arnold Publishers.

_____. 1983. *The Feminist Challenge: The Movement for Women's Liberation in Britain and the USA*. New York: Schocken Books.

Boulding, Elise. 1976. "The historical roots of occupational segregation." *Signs* 1:94–117.

Bowles, Samuel, and Herbert Gintis. 1976. *Schooling in Capitalist America*. New York: Basic Books.

Boxer, Marilyn J. 1978. "Socialism faces feminism: The failure of synthesis in France, 1879–1914." Pp. 75–111 in M. Boxer and J. Quataert, eds., *Socialist Women: European Socialist Feminism in the Nineteenth and Early Twentieth Centuries*. New York: Elsevier North-Holland.

_____. 1982. " 'First Wave' feminism in nineteenth-century France: Class, family and religion." *Women's Studies International Forum* 5(6):551–59.

Boxer, Marilyn, and Jean Quataert. 1978. *Socialist Women: European Socialist Feminism in the Nineteenth and Early Twentieth Centuries*. New York: Elsevier North-Holland.

Bridges, William. 1980. "Industry marginality and female employment: a new appraisal." *American Sociological Review* 45:58–75.

_____. 1982. "Sexual segregation of occupations: Theories of labor stratification in industry." *American Journal of Sociology* 88:270–95.

Briffault, Robert. 1963. *The Mothers*. New York: Grosset & Dunlop. abridged (Orig. pub. 1927).

Brink, William, and Louis Harris. 1963. *The Negro Revolution in America*. New York: Clarion Books.

_____. 1966. *Black and White: A Study of Racial Attitudes Today*. New York: Clarion Books.

Brooks, Virginia. 1981. *Minority Stress and Lesbian Women*. Lexington, Mass.: D. C. Heath.

Broom, Leonard. 1959. "Social differentiation and stratification." Pp. 429–41 in Robert K. Merton, Leonard Broom, and Leonard S. Cottrell, Jr., eds., *Sociology Today: Problems and Prospects*. New York City: Basic Books.

Broom, Leonard, and Norval Glenn. 1965. *Transformation of the Negro American*. New York: Harper & Row.

Broverman, Inge, D. M. Broverman, F. E. Clarkson, P. S. Rosenkrantz, and S. R. Vogel. 1970. "Sex-role stereotypes and clinical judgments of mental health." *Journal of Consulting and Clinical Psychology* 34:1–7.

_____. 1972. "Sex role stereotypes: A current appraisal." *Journal of Social Issues* 28:59–78.

Brozek, J. 1953. "Semi-starvation and nutritional rehabilitation." *Journal of Clinical Nutrition* 1:107–18.

Bunch, Charlotte. 1975. "Lesbians in revolt." In N. Myron and C. Bunch, eds., *Lesbianism and the Women's Movement*. Baltimore, Md: Diana Press.

Burke, Mary P. 1980. *Reaching for Justice: The Women's Movement*. Washington, D.C.: Center of Concern.

Caine, Barbara. 1982. "Feminism, suffrage and the nineteenth-century English women's movement." *Women's Studies International Forum* 5(6):537–50.

Caplan, Nathan S. 1970. "The new ghetto man: A review of recent empirical studies." *Journal of Social Issues* 26:59–73.

Caplan, Nathan S., and Jeffrey M. Paige. 1968. "A study of ghetto rioters." *Scientific American* 219(2):15–21.

Carden, Maren Lockwood. 1974. *The New Feminist Movement*. New York: Russell Sage Foundation.

Carmody, Denise Lardner. 1979. *Women and World Religions*. Nashville, Tenn.: Abingdon Press.

Cassell, Joan. 1977. *A Group Called Women*. New York: David McKay.

Cavendish, Richard. 1979. *A History of Magic*. New York: Taplinger Publishing Co.

Chafe, William. 1977. *Women and Equality*. New York: Oxford University Press.

Chafetz, Janet Saltzman. 1978. *Masculine/Feminine or Human?* Itasca, Ill.: F. E. Peacock.

———. 1980. "Conflict resolution in marriage: Toward a theory of spousal strategies and marital dissolution rates." *Journal of Family Issues* 1:397–421.

———. 1984. *Sex and Advantage: A Comparative, Macro-Structural Theory of Sex Stratification*. Totowa, N.J.: Rowman & Allanheld.

Chafetz, Janet Saltzman, P. Beck, P. Sampson, J. West, and B. Jones. 1976. *Who's Queer? A Study of Homo and Heterosexual Women*. Sarasota, Fla.: Omni Press.

Chafetz, Janet Saltzman, and Anthony Gary Dworkin. 1983. "Macro and micro processes in the emergence of feminist movements: Toward a unified theory." *Western Sociological Review* 14:27–45.

Chafetz, Janet Saltzman, Rosalind J. Dworkin, and Anthony Gary Dworkin. 1976. "New migrants to the rat race: A model of rates of labor force participation and patterns of occupational deployment by gender, race, and ethnicity" (Unpublished). Sections appear in J. S. Chafetz, 1978. *A Primer on the Construction and Testing of Theories in Sociology*, Itasca, Ill.: F. E. Peacock, and A. G. Dworkin and R. J. Dworkin. 1976. *The Minority Report*. New York: Praeger Publishers.

Chaney, Elsa M. 1979. *Supermadre: Women in Politics in Latin America*. Austin: University of Texas Press.

Chesler, Phyllis. 1972. *Women and Madness*. Garden City, N.Y.: Doubleday.

Chesney-Lind, Meda. 1974. "Juvenile delinquency: The sexualization of female crime." *Psychology Today* (July):43–46.

———. 1978. "Young women in the arms of the law." In L. H. Bowker, ed., *Women, Crime, and the Criminal Justice System*. Lexington, Mass.: D. C. Heath.

Chincilla, Norma. 1977. "Industrialization, monopoly capitalism, and women's work in Guatemala." *Signs* 3:38–56.

Clements, Barbara Evans. 1979. *Bolshevik Feminist: The Life of Aleksandra Kollontai*. Bloomington: Indiana University Press.

Cleverdon, Catherine Lyle. 1950. *The Woman Suffrage Movement in Canada*. Toronto: University of Toronto Press.

Cohen, E. A. 1953. *Human Behavior in the Concentration Camp*. New York: W. W. Norton.

Cohn, Samuel Ross. 1985. "Clerical labor intensity and the feminization of clerical labor in Great Britain, 1857–1937." *Social Forces* 63:1060–68.

Colombo, Daniela. 1981. "The Italian feminist movement." *Women's Studies International Quarterly* 4:461–69.

Conrad, Peter, and Joseph W. Schneider. 1980. *Deviance and Medicalization: From Badness to Sickness.* St. Louis: C. V. Mosby.

Cortera, Marta. 1980. "Feminism: The Chicana and the Anglo versions." Pp. 217–34 in Margarita B. Melville, ed., *Twice a Minority: Mexican American Women.* St. Louis: Mosby.

Croll, Elisabeth. 1978. *Feminism and Socialism in China.* London: Routledge and Kegan Paul.

Currell, Melville. 1974. *Political Woman.* London: Croom Helm.

Currie, Elliott P. 1968. "Crimes without criminals: Witchcraft and its control in Renaissance Europe." *Law and Society Review* 3(August):7–32.

Dahrendorf, Ralf. 1959. *Class and Class Conflict in Industrial Society.* Palo Alto, Calif.: Stanford University Press.

Dannenbaum, Jed. 1984. *Drink and Disorder.* Urbana: University of Illinois Press.

Davies, James C. 1962. "Toward a theory of revolution." *American Sociological Review* 27:5–19.

———. 1969. "The j-curve of rising and declining satisfactions as a cause of some great revolutions and a contained rebellion." Pp. 690–730 in H. D. Graham and Ted R. Gurr, eds., *The History of Violence in America.* New York: Praeger Publishers.

Deacon, Desley. (forthcoming). "Political arithmetic: The nineteenth century Australian census and the construction of the dependent woman." *Signs.*

Deckard, Barbara Sinclair. 1983. *The Women's Movement.* New York: Harper & Row. 3rd. ed.

Department of Commerce and Labor. 1909. *Statistical Abstract of the United States.* Washington, D.C.: Government Printing Office.

———. 1920. *Statistical Abstract of the United States.* Washington, D.C.: Government Printing Office.

Desai, A. R. 1966. *Social Background of Indian Nationalism.* Bombay, India: Popular Prakashan.

Desroche, Henri. 1971. *The American Shakers.* Amherst: University of Massachusetts Press.

De Vries, Petra. 1981. "Feminism in the Netherlands." *Women's Studies International Quarterly* 4:389–407.

Dodds, Dinah. 1982. "Extra-parliamentary feminism and social change in Italy, 1971–1980." *International Journal of Women's Studies* 5:148–60.

Donald, David. 1970. "Toward a reconsideration of abolitionists." Pp. 13–29 in Joseph Gusfield, ed., *Protest, Reform and Revolt.* New York: John Wiley & Sons.

DuBois, Ellen. 1975. "The radicalism of the women suffrage movement: Notes toward the reconstruction of nineteenth-century feminism." *Feminist Studies* 3(Fall):63–71.

———. 1978. *Feminism and Suffrage.* Ithaca, N.Y.: Cornell University Press.

———. 1979. "Women's rights and abolition: The nature of the connection." Pp. 238–51 in L. Perry and M. Fellman, eds., *Anti-Slavery Reconsidered: New Perspectives on the Abolitionists.* Baton Rouge: Louisiana State University Press.

Dumond, Dwight Lowell. 1966. *Antislavery: The Crusade for Freedom in America.* New

York: The Norton Library.

Durkheim, Emile. 1951. *Suicide: A Study in Sociology*, trans. John A. Spaulding and George Simpson. Glencoe, Ill.: The Free Press of Glencoe.

———. 1953. *Sociology and Philosophy*, trans. D. F. Pocock. Glencoe, Ill.: The Free Press of Glencoe.

———. 1964. *The Division of Labor in Society*, trans. George Simpson. New York: The Free Press.

Dworkin, Anthony Gary. 1965. "Stereotypes and self-images held by native-born and foreign-born Mexican Americans." *Sociology and Social Research* 49:214–24.

———. 1968. "*No siesta mañana*: The Mexican Americans in Los Angeles." Pp. 387–440 in R. W. Mack, ed., *Our Children's Burden*. New York: Random House.

———. 1971. "National origin and ghetto experience as variables in Mexican-American stereotypes." Pp. 80–84 in Nathaniel N. Wagner and Marsha J. Haug, eds., *Chicanos: Social and Psychological Perspectives*. St. Louis, Mo.: C. V. Mosby.

———. 1972. "The peoples of *la raza*: The Mexican Americans of Los Angeles." Pp. 167–90 in N. P. Gist and A. G. Dworkin, eds., *The Blending of Races: Marginality and Identity in World Perspective*. New York: Wiley-Interscience.

———. 1980. "The changing demography of public school teachers: Some implications for faculty turnover in urban areas." *Sociology of Education* 53:65–73.

Dworkin, Anthony Gary, and Rosalind J. Dworkin. 1976. *The Minority Report: Introduction to Race, Ethnic, and Gender Relations*. New York: Praeger Publishers.

———. 1982. *The Minority Report: Introduction to Race, Ethnic, and Gender Relations*. 2nd ed. New York: Holt, Rinehart & Winston.

Dworkin, Anthony Gary, Janet Saltzman Chafetz, and Rosalind J. Dworkin. (forthcoming). "The effects of tokenism on work alienation among urban public school teachers." *Work and Occupations*.

Dworkin, Rosalind J. 1974. "The female American: Social structure, awareness, and ideology." Ph.D. dissertation, Northwestern University.

———. 1979. "Ideology formation: A linear structural model of the influence on feminist ideology." *The Sociological Quarterly* 20:345–58.

———. 1982. "A woman's report: Numbers are not enough." Pp. 375–400 in A. G. Dworkin and R. J. Dworkin, eds., *The Minority Report*. 2nd ed. New York: Holt, Rinehart and Winston.

Edmondson, Linda Harriet. 1984. *Feminism in Russia, 1900–17*. Stanford, Calif.: Stanford University Press.

Edwards, Alba M. 1943. *Comparative Occupation Statistics for the United States: 1870 to 1940*. Washington, D.C.: Government Printing Office.

Ehrenreich, Barbara, and Deirdre English. 1973. *Witches, Midwives, and Nurses: A History of Women Healers*. Old Westbury, N.Y.: The Feminist Press.

Ehrlich, Howard J. 1973. *The Social Psychology of Prejudice*. New York: Wiley-Interscience.

Elkins, Stanley. 1959. *Slavery: A Problem in American Institutional and Intellectual Life*. Chicago: University of Chicago Press.

Encyclopedia of Associations. 1984. 19th ed., Detroit: Gale Research Co.

Engel, Barbara Alpern. 1977. "The emergence of women revolutionaries in Russia." *Frontiers* 2(Spring):92–105.

———. 1978. "From separatism to socialism: Women in the Russian revolutionary movement of the 1870's." Pp. 51–74 in M. Boxer and J. Quataert, eds., *Socialist Women: Euro-*

pean Socialist Feminism in the Nineteenth and Early Twentieth Centuries. New York: Elsevier North-Holland.

_____. 1980. "Women revolutionaries: The personal and the political." Pp. 31–43 in T. Yedlin, ed., *Women in Eastern Europe and the Soviet Union.* New York: Praeger Publishers.

Epstein, Barbara Leslie. 1981. *The Politics of Domesticity.* Middletown, Conn.: Wesleyan University Press.

Estrada, Leobardo, F. Chris García, Reynaldo Flores Macías, and Lionel Maldonado. 1981. "Chicanos in the United States: A history of exploitation and resistance." *Daedalus* 110:103–32.

Evans, Richard J. 1976. *The Feminist Movement in Germany, 1894–1933.* London: Sage Publications.

_____. 1977. *The Feminists: Women's Emancipation Movements in Europe, America and Australia 1840–1920.* New York: Barnes & Noble Books.

Everett, Jana Matson. 1979. *Women and Social Change in India.* New York: St. Martin's Press.

_____. 1983. "The upsurge of women's activism in India." *Frontiers* 7(2):18–26.

Fanon, Frantz. 1968. *The Wretched of the Earth*, trans. Constance Farrington. New York: Grove Press.

Ferrer, Norma Valle. 1979. "Feminism and its influence on women's organizations in Puerto Rico." Pp. 38–50 in E. Acosta-Belén with E. H. Christensen, eds., *The Puerto Rican Woman.* New York: Praeger Publishers.

Feuer, Lewis. 1969. *The Conflict of Generations.* New York: Basic Books.

Finkler, Kaja. 1981. "Dissident religious movements in the service of women's power." *Sex Roles* 7(5):481–95.

Firestone, Shulamith. 1971. "On American feminism." Pp. 665–86 in V. Gornick and B. Moran, eds., *Women in Sexist Society.* New York City: Basic Books.

Flacks, Richard W. 1967. "The liberated generation: An exploration of the roots of student protest." *Journal of Social Issues* 23:52–75.

Flexner, Eleanor. 1975. *Century of Struggle.* Rev. ed. Cambridge: Harvard University Press. (orig. pub. 1959).

Fogelson, Robert, and Robert Hill. 1970. "Who riots? A study of participation in the 1967 riots." Pp. 375–87 in Marcel Goldschmid, ed., *Black Americans and White Racism.* New York: Holt, Rinehart and Winston.

Forbes, Geraldine. 1979. "Votes for women: The demand for women's franchise in India 1917–1937." Pp. 3–23 in V. Muzumbar, ed., *Symbols of Power.* New Delhi, India: Allied Pub.

_____. 1982. "Caged tigers: 'First wave' feminism in India." *Women's Studies International Forum* 5(6):525–36.

Forbes, Thomas Rogers. 1966. *The Midwife and the Witch.* New Haven: Yale University Press.

Foreman, Ann. 1977. *Femininity as Alienation: Women and the Family in Marxism and Psychoanalysis.* London: Pluto Press.

Forward, John, and Jay Williams. 1970. "Internal-external control and black militancy." *Journal of Social Issues* 26:75–92.

Foster, Lawrence. 1981. *Religion and Sexuality: Three American Communal Experiments of the Nineteenth Century.* New York: Oxford University Press.

Fox, Margery. 1978. "Protest in piety: Christian Science revisited." *International Journal of Women's Studies* 1(4):401–16.

Francis, Roy G. 1963. "The anti-model as a theoretical concept." *The Sociological Quarterly* 4:197–205.

Frank, Miriam. 1978. "Feminist publications in West Germany today." *New German Critique* 13:181–94.

Freeman, Jo. 1975. *The Politics of Women's Liberation*. New York: David McKay.

Friedman, Lawrence J. 1982. *Gregarious Saints*. Cambridge, Mass.: Cambridge University Press.

Gamson, William. 1975. *The Strategy of Social Protest*. Homewood, Ill.: Dorsey.

Garrett, Clarke. 1977. "Women and witches: Patterns of analysis." *Signs* 3(Winter):461–70.

Gelb, Joyce, and Marian Lief Palley. 1982. *Women and Public Policies*. Princeton, N.J.: Princeton University Press.

Gelder, Lindsy Van. 1981. "A 1960s rebel reviews the new protesters." *Ms.* Magazine (Nov.):66.

Gerhard, Ute. 1982. "A hidden and complex heritage: Reflections on the history of Germany's Women's movements." *Women's Studies International Forum* 5(6):561–67.

Geschwender, James A. 1964. "Social structure and the Negro revolt: An examination of some hypotheses." *Social Forces* 42:248–56.

Goffman, Erving. 1972. *Relations in Public*. New York: Harper Colophon Books.

Gonzales, Sylvia. 1978. "The white feminist movement: The Chicana perspective." Pp. 65–74 in K. O'Connor Blumhagen and W. D. Johnson, eds., *Women's Studies: An Interdisciplinary Collection*. Westport, Conn.: Greenwood Press.

Gordon, David M. 1972. *Theories of Poverty and Unemployment*. Lexington, Mass.: Lexington Books.

Gorham, Deborah. 1976. "The Canadian suffragists." Pp. 23–55 in G. Matheson, ed., *Women in the Canadian Mosaic*. Toronto: Peter Martin Associates.

Granovetter, Mark. 1978. "Threshold models of collective behavior." *American Journal of Sociology* 83:1420–43.

Gray, J. Patrick. 1979. "The universality of the female witch." *International Journal of Women's Studies* 2(Nov.-Dec.):541–50.

Grebler, Leo, Joan W. Moore, and Ralph C. Guzmán. 1970. *The Mexican-American People: The Nation's Second Largest Minority*. New York: Free Press.

Greenblatt, Susan L., and Charles V. Willie. 1980. "The serendipitous effects of school desegregation." Pp. 51–68 in Walter G. Stephan and Joe R. Feagin, eds., *School Desegregation: Past, Present, and Future*. New York: Plenum Press.

Grier, William H., and Price M. Cobbs. 1968. *Black Rage*. New York: Basic Books.

Grimshaw, Patricia. 1972. *Women's Suffrage in New Zealand*. Wellington, New Zealand: Consolidated Press.

Gross, Edward. 1964. "Industrial relations." Pp. 619–79 in Robert E. L. Faris, ed., *Handbook of Modern Sociology*. Chicago: Rand McNally.

Gurr, Ted Robert. 1970. *Why Men Revolt*. Princeton, N.J.: Princeton University Press.

Gusfield, Joseph R. 1963. *Symbolic Crusade: Status Politics and the American Temperance Movement*. Urbana: University of Illinois Press.

Guttentag, Marcia, and Paul Secord. 1983. *Too Many Women? The Sex Ratio Question*. Beverly Hills, Calif.: Sage Publications.

Hahner, June E. 1978. "The nineteenth-century feminist press and women's rights in Brazil." Pp. 254–85 in A. Lavrin, ed., *Latin American Women: Historical Perspectives.* Westport, Conn.: Greenwood Press.

_____. 1980. "Feminism, women's rights, and the suffrage movement in Brazil, 1850–1932." *Latin American Research Review* 15:65–111.

Haines, Herbert H. 1984. "Black radicalization and the funding of civil rights: 1957–1970." *Social Problems* 32:31–43.

Hare, Nathan, and Julia Hare. 1970. "Black women 1970." *Transaction* 8 (Nov.-Dec.):65–68, 90.

Harrison, Brian. 1978. *Separate Spheres: The Opposition to Women's Suffrage in Britain.* London: Croom Helm.

Hazelton, Lesley. 1977. *Israeli Women: The Reality Behind the Myths.* New York: Simon & Schuster.

Heath, Louis. 1976. *Mutiny does not Happen Lightly: The Literature of the American Resistance to the Vietnam War.* Metuchen, N.J.: Scarecrow Press.

Heitlinger, Alena. 1979. *Women and State Socialism: Sex Inequality in the Soviet Union and Czechoslovakia.* Montreal: McGill-Queen's University Press.

Hernández, Isabel Picó de. 1979. "The history of women's struggle for equality in Puerto Rico." Pp. 25–37 in E. Acosta-Belén with E. H. Christensen, eds., *The Puerto Rican Woman.* New York: Praeger Publishers.

Hersh, Blanche Glassman. 1978. *The Slavery of Sex: Feminist-Abolitionists in America.* Urbana: University of Illinois Press.

_____. 1979. " 'Am I not a woman and a sister?' Abolitionist beginnings of nineteenth-century feminism." Pp. 252–83 in L. Perry and M. Fellman, eds., *Anti-Slavery Reconsidered: New Perspectives on the Abolitionists.* Baton Rouge: Louisiana State University Press.

Hewitt, Nancy A. 1984. *Women's Activism and Social Change: Rochester, New York, 1822-1872.* Ithaca, N.Y.: Cornell University Press.

Hield, Melissa. 1979. " 'Union-minded': Women in the Texas ILGWU, 1933–50." *Frontiers* 4(2):59–70.

Hoch-Smith, Judith. 1978. "Radical Yoruba female sexuality: The witch and the prostitute." Pp. 245–67 in J. Hoch-Smith and A. Spring, eds., *Women in Ritual and Symbolic Roles.* New York: Plenum Press.

Hoerder, Dirk. 1977. *Crowd Action in Revolutionary Massachusetts, 1765-1780.* New York: Academic Press.

Hole, Judith, and Ellen Levine. 1984. "The first feminists." Pp. 533–42 in Jo Freeman, ed., *Women: A Feminist Perspective.* Palo Alto, Calif.: Mayfield Publishing Co.

Holton, Sandra. 1979a. "The ideas of the Women's Suffrage Movement in the twentieth century." (Unpublished). Cited in C. Bacchi " 'First wave' feminism in Canada: The ideas of the English-Canadian suffragists, 1877–1918." *Women's Studies International Forum* 5(1982):575–83.

_____. 1979b. "The common cause: A lost dimension in women's suffrage history" (unpublished). Cited in C. Bacchi, " 'First wave' feminism in Canada: The ideas of the English-Canadian suffragists, 1877–1918." *Women's Studies International Forum* 5(1982):575–83.

Honeycutt, Karen. 1979. "Socialism and feminism in Imperial Germany." *Signs* 5(Autumn):30–41.

Horne, Alistar. 1977. *A Savage War of Peace: Algeria 1954–1962*. London: Macmillan & Co.

Howard, John R. 1974. *The Cutting Edge: Social Movements and Social Change in America.* Philadelphia: J. B. Lippincott.

Huber, Joan. 1976. "Toward a sociotechnological theory of the women's movement." *Social Problems* 23(Apr.):371–88.

Huber, Joan, and Glenna Spitze. 1983. *Sex Stratification: Children, Housework, and Jobs.* New York: Academic Press.

Hufton, Oliver. 1971. "Women in revolution 1789–1796." *Past and Present* 53:90–108.

———. 1976. "Women in revolution, 1789–96," in D. Johnson, ed., *French Society and the Revolution*, Cambridge, England: Cambridge University Press.

Hughes, Everett C. 1945. "Dilemmas and contradictions of status." *American Journal of Sociology* 50:353–59.

Hyman, Herbert H. 1942. "The psychology of status." *Archives of Psychology* 269 (complete issue).

Izraeli, Dafna N. 1981. "The Zionist women's movement in Palestine 1911–1927: A sociological analysis." *Signs* 7(1):87–114.

Jackson, Elton. 1962. "Status consistency and symptoms of stress." *American Sociological Review* 27:469–80.

Jacobs, Monica. 1978. "Civil rights and women's rights in the Federal Republic of Germany today." *New German Critique* 13:165–74.

Jacoby, Robin Miller. 1975. "The Women's Trade Union League and American feminism." *Feminist Studies* 3(Fall):126–40.

Jancar, Barbara Wolfe. 1978. *Women under Communism*. Baltimore: The Johns Hopkins University Press.

Janeway, Elizabeth. 1971. *Man's World, Woman's Place*. New York: William Morrow.

Jeffrey, Julie Roy. 1975. "Women in the Southern Farmer's Alliance: A reconsideration of the role and status of women in the late nineteenth-century South." *Feminist Studies* 3(Fall):72–91.

Jenkins, J. Craig. 1983. "Resource mobilization theory and the study of social movements." *Annual Review of Sociology* 9:527–53.

Jenkins, J. Craig, and Charles Perrow. 1977. "Insurgency of the powerless: Farm worker movements (1946–1972)." *American Sociological Review* 42:292–304.

Jensen, Joan. 1983. "All pink sisters: The War Department and the feminist movement in the 1920s." Pp. 199–222 In L. Scharf and J. Jensen, eds., *Decades of Discontent: The Women's Movement, 1920–1940*. Westport, Conn.: Greenwood Press.

Johnson, Kay Ann. 1978. *Women, the Family and Peasant Revolution in China*. Chicago: University of Chicago Press.

Jones, Dawn E., and Rodney W. Jones. 1976. "Urban upheavals in India: The 1974 Nav Nirman riots in Gujarat." *Asian Survey* 16(11):1012–33.

Juusola-Halonen, Elina. 1981. "The Women's Liberation Movement – Finland." *Women's Studies International Quarterly* 4:453–60.

Kahne, Hilda. 1976. "Women's role in the economy: Economic investigation and research needs." Pp. 39–76 in Jane Chapman, ed., *Economic Independence for Women*. Beverly Hills, Calif.: Sage Publications.

Kanter, Rosabeth Moss. 1977. *Men and Women of the Corporation*. New York: Basic Books.

Katz, Elihu, and Paul F. Lazarsfeld. 1964. *Personal Influence*. New York: The Free Press.

Kaufmann-McCall, Dorothy. 1983. "Politics of difference: The women's movement in France from May 1968 to Mitterand." *Signs* 9(2):282–93.

Kawan, Hildegard, and Barbara Weber. 1981. "Reflections on a theme: The German women's movement then and now." *Women's Studies International Quarterly* 4:421–33.

Kelley, Harold H. 1952. "Two functions of reference groups." Pp. 410–14 in Guy E. Swanson, T. M. Newcomb, and E. L. Hartley, eds., *Readings in Social Psycology.* New York: Holt, Rinehart and Winston.

Kelley, K. D., and W. J. Chambliss. 1966. "Status consistency and political attitudes." *American Sociological Review* 31:375–84.

Keniston, Kenneth. 1968. *Young Radicals.* New York: Harcourt, Brace, & World.

Kern, Louis J. 1981. *An Ordered Love: Sex Roles and Sexuality in Victorian Utopias – The Shakers, the Mormons, and the Oneida Community.* Chapel Hill: University of North Carolina Press.

Kerpelman, Larry C. 1972. *Activists and Nonactivities.* New York: Behavioral Publications.

Kessler-Harris, Alice. 1975. "Where are the organized women workers?" *Feminist Studies* 3(Fall):92–109.

Klandermans, Bert. 1984. "Mobilization and participation: Social-psychological expansions of resource mobilization theory." *American Sociological Review* 49:583–600.

Klein, Viola. 1984. "The historical background." Pp. 519–32 in Jo Freeman, ed., *Women: A Feminist Perspective.* Palo Alto, Calif.: Mayfield Publishing Co.

Koehler, Lyle. 1980. *A Search for Power: The "Weaker Sex" in Seventeenth Century New England.* Urbana: University of Illinois Press.

Kontopoulos, Kyriakos. 1972. "Women's liberation as a social movement." Pp. 354–61 in Constantina Safilios-Rothschild, ed., *Toward a Sociology of Women.* Lexington, Mass.: Xerox College Pub.

Kornhauser, William. 1959. *The Politics of Mass Society.* New York: The Free Press.

Kraditor, Aileen. 1965. *The Ideas of the Woman Suffrage Movement, 1890–1920.* New York: Columbia University Press.

Lafleur, Ingrum. 1978. "Five socialist women: Traditionalist conflicts and socialist visions in Austria, 1893–1934." Pp. 215–48 in M. Boxer and J. Quataert, eds., *Socialist Women: European Socialist Feminism in the Nineteenth and Early Twentieth Centuries.* New York: Elsevier North-Holland.

Lance, Keith Curry. 1979. "Strategy choices of the British Women's Social and Political Union, 1903–18." *Social Science Quarterly* 60 (June): 51–61.

Lang, Kurt, and Gladys Lang. 1961. *Collective Dynamics.* New York: Thomas Y. Crowell Co.

Lapidus, Gail Warshofsky. 1976. "Occupational segregation and public policy: A comparative analysis of American and Soviet patterns." *Signs* 2: 119–36.

———. 1977. "Sexual equality in Soviet policy: A developmental perspective." Pp. 115–38 in D. Atkinson, A. Dallin, and G. W. Lapidus, eds., *Women in Russia,* Stanford, Calif.: Stanford University Press.

———. 1978. *Women in Soviet Society.* Berkeley: University of California Press.

La Rue, Linda J. M. 1970. "Black liberation and women's lib." *Trans-Action* 8 (Dec.): 59–64.

Latin American and Caribbean Women's Collective. 1977. *Slaves of Slaves: The Challenge of Latin American Women,* trans. M. Pollis. London: Zed Press.

La Vigna, Claire. 1978. "The Marxist ambivalence toward women: Between socialism and feminism in the Italian Socialist Party." Pp. 146–81 in M. Boxer and J. Quataert, eds., *Socialist Women: European Socialist Feminism in the Nineteenth and Early Twentieth Centuries.* New York: Elsevier North-Holland.

Le Bon, Gustave. 1960. *The Crowd: A Study of the Popular Mind.* New York: Viking Press.

Lederer, Wolfgang. 1968. *The Fear of Women.* New York: Grune & Stratton.

Leff, Gordon. 1967. *Heresy in the Later Middle Ages.* Manchester, England: Manchester University Press.

Lenski, Gerhard E. 1954. "Status crystallization: A nonvertical dimension of status." *American Sociological Review* 19:405–13.

Lerner, Robert E. 1972. *The Heresy of the Free Spirit in the Later Middle Ages.* Berkeley: University of California Press.

Liddington, Jill, and Jill Norris. 1978. *One Hand Tied Behind Us: The Rise of the Women's Suffrage Movement.* London: Virago.

Lipman-Blumen, Jean. 1984. *Gender Roles and Power.* Englewood Cliffs, N.J.: Prentice-Hall.

Little, Cynthia Jeffress. 1975. "Moral reform and feminism: A case study." *Journal of Interamerican Studies and World Affairs* 17:386–97.

―――. 1978. "Education, philanthropy, and feminism: Components of Argentine womanhood, 1860–1926." Pp. 235–53 in A. Lavrin, ed., *Latin American Women: Historical Perspectives.* Westport, Conn.: Greenwood Press.

Loomis, Charles P., and Anthony Gary Dworkin. 1976. "The Mexican American community." Pp. 344–408 in C. P. Loomis and E. D. Dyer, eds., *Social Systems: The Study of Sociology.* Cambridge, Mass.: Schenkman Publishing Co.

Lopata, Helena Z. 1971. *Occupation Housewife.* New York: Oxford University Press.

Lorence, Jon. forthcoming. "Gender differences in occupational labor market structures." *Journal of Work and Occupations.*

Lortie, Dan C. 1975. *School-Teacher: A Sociological Study.* Chicago: University of Chicago Press.

Loukes, Harold. 1965. *The Quaker Contribution.* New York: Macmillan Co.

Lutz, Alma. 1968. *Crusade for Freedom: Women of the Antislavery Movement.* Boston: Beacon Press.

Macías, Anna. 1978. "Felipe Carrillo Puerto and women's liberation in Mexico." Pp. 286–301 in A. Lavrin, ed., *Latin American Women.* Westport, Conn.: Greenwood Press.

Mack, Raymond W. 1954. "Ecological patterns in an industrial shop." *Social Forces* 32:351–56.

Maldonado, Lionel A. 1982. "Mexican-Americans: The emergence of a minority." Pp. 168–95 in A. G. Dworkin and R. J. Dworkin, eds., *The Minority Report.* 2nd ed. New York: Holt, Rinehart and Winston.

Mandle, Joan D. 1978. *Women and Social Change in America.* Princeton, N.J.: Princeton Book Co.

Marks, Elaine, and Isabell de Courtivron. 1980. *New French Feminisms: An Anthology.* Amherst: The University of Massachusetts Press.

Marshall, T. H. 1965. *Class, Citizenship, and Social Development.* Garden City, N.Y.: Doubleday/Anchor Press.

Marsot, Afaf Lutfi al-Sayyid. 1978. "The revolutionary gentlewomen in Egypt." Pp. 261–75 in L. Beck and N. Keddie, eds., *Women in the Muslim World.* Cambridge: Harvard University Press.

Martin, M. Kay, and Barbara Voorhies. 1975. *Female of the Species*. New York: Columbia University Press.

Marx, Gary T. 1967. *Protest and Prejudice*. New York: Harper & Row.

———. 1974. "Thoughts on a neglected category of social movement participant: The agent provocateur and the informant." *American Journal of Sociology* 80:402–42.

Marx, Gary T., and J. L. Wood. 1975. "Strands of theory and research in collective behavior." *Annual Review of Sociology* 1:363–428.

Marx, Karl. 1959. "The eighteenth Brumaire of Louis Bonaparte." Pp. 318–48 in Lewis S. Feuer, ed., *Marx and Engles: Basic Writings in Politics and Philosophy*. Garden City: N.Y.: Doubleday/Anchor Press.

May, Dean L. 1983. "A demographic portrait of the Mormons, 1830–1980." Pp. 37–69 in T. G. Alexander and J. L. Embry, eds., *After 150 Years: The Latter-Day Saints in Sesquicentennial Perspective*. Midvale, Utah: Signature Books.

Maykovich, Minako Kurokawa. 1972. "Reciprocity in racial stereotypes: White, black, and yellow." *American Journal of Sociology* 77:876–97.

Mazumdar, Vina. 1979. *Symbols of Power*. New Delhi, India: Allied Publishers.

McCarthy, John D., and M. N. Zald. 1973. *The Trends of Social Movements in America: Professionalization and Resource Mobilization*. Morristown, N.J.: General Learning Press.

———. 1977. "Resource mobilization in social movements: A partial theory." *American Journal of Sociology* 82(May):1212–39.

McDonnell, Ernest W. 1969. *The Beguines and Beghards in Medieval Culture*. New York: Octagon Books.

McWilliams, Carey. 1949. *North from Mexico*. New York: J. B. Lippincott Co.

Meier, August, and E. Rudwick. 1973. *C.O.R.E.*. New York: Oxford University Press.

Melder, Keith E. 1977. *Beginnings of Sisterhood: The American Woman's Rights Movement, 1800–1850*. New York: Schocken Books.

Melville, Margarita B. 1980. "Introduction." Pp. 1–9 in Margarita B. Melville, ed., *Twice a Minority: Mexican American Women*. St. Louis: C. V. Mosby.

Mernissi, Fatima. 1975. *Beyond the Veil: Male-Female Dynamics in a Modern Muslim Society*. Cambridge, Mass.: Schenkman Publishing Co.

Merton, Robert K. 1968. *Social Theory and Social Structure*. Rev. ed. New York: Macmillan Co.

Merton, Robert K., and Alice S. Kitt (Rossi). 1950. "Contributions to the theory of reference group behavior." Pp. 40–105 in R. K. Merton and P. F. Lazarsfeld, eds., *Continuities in Social Research: Studies in the Scope and Method of "The American Soldier."* New York: The Free Press.

Miller, Casey, and Kate Swift. 1977. *Words and Women: New Language in New Times*. Garden City, N.Y.: Doubleday/Anchor Books.

Mitchell, B. R. 1975. *European Historical Statistics: 1750–1975*. New York: Facts on File.

Mitchinson, Wendy. 1981. "The Woman's Christian Temperance Union: A study in organization." *International Journal of Women's Studies* 4(2):143–56.

Monter, E. William. 1976. *Witchcraft in France and Switzerland*. Ithaca, N.Y.: Cornell University Press.

Morgan, David. 1975. *Suffragists and Liberals: The Politics of Woman Suffrage in England*. Totowa, N.J.: Rowman and Littlefield.

Morrison, Denton E. 1971. "Some notes toward theory on relative deprivation." *American Behavorial Scientist* 14:675–90.

Morton, Ward. 1962. *Woman Suffrage in Mexico*. Gainesville: University of Florida Press.

Mota, Vivian. 1976. "Politics and feminism in the Dominican Republic: 1931–45 and 1966–74." Pp. 265–78 in J. Nash and H. I. Safa, eds., *Sex and Class in Latin America*. New York: Praeger Publishers.

Myrdal, Gunnar. 1944. *An American Dilemma: The Negro Problem and Modern Democracy*. New York: Harper and Brothers.

Nashat, Guity. 1983. *Women and Revolution in Iran*. Boulder, Colo.: Westview Press.

National Advisory Commission on Civil Disorders (Kerner Commission). 1968. *Report of the National Advisory Commission on Civil Disorders*. New York: Bantam Books.

Nielsen, Joyce. 1978. *Sex in Society: Perspectives on Stratification*. Belmont, Calif.: Wadsworth Publishing Co.

Oakley, Ann. 1974. *The Sociology of Housework*. New York: Pantheon Books.

Oberschall, Anthony. 1973. *Social Conflict and Social Movements*. Englewood Cliffs, N.J.: Prentice-Hall.

O'Kelly, Charlotte G. 1980. *Women and Men in Society*. New York: D. Van Nostrand.

Oliver, Melvin L., and Mark A. Glick. 1982. "An analysis of the new orthodoxy of black mobility." *Social Problems* 29:511–23.

Olsen, Marvin E. 1970. "Social and political participation of blacks." *American Sociological Review* 35:682–97.

Olson, Mancur. 1968. *The Logic of Collective Action*. New York: Schocken Books.

Omvedt, Gail. 1980. *We Will Smash This Prison! Indian Women in Struggle*. London: Zed Press.

O'Neill, William. 1969a. *The Woman Movement: Feminism in the United States and England*. Chicago: Quadrangle Books.

_____. 1969b. *Everyone Was Brave: The Rise and Fall of Feminism in America*. Chicago: Quadrangle Books.

Oppenheimer, Valerie K. 1970. *The Female Labor Force in the United States*. Berkeley: University of California Press.

Pagels, Elaine. 1976. "What became of God the mother? Conflicting images of God in early Christianity." *Signs* 2:293–315.

Paige, Jeffery M. 1971. "Political orientation and riot participation." *American Sociological Review* 36:810–20.

Parrinder, Geoffrey. 1963. *Witchcraft: European and African*. London: Faber and Faber.

Patterson, Cynthia M. 1982. "New directions in the political history of women: A case study of the National Woman's Party's campaign for the Equal Rights Amendment, 1920–1927." *Women's Studies International Forum* 5(6):585–97.

Paulson, Ross Evans. 1973. *Women's Suffrage and Prohibition: A Comparative Study of Equality and Social Control*. Glenview, Ill.: Scott, Foresman & Co.

Pettigrew, Thomas F. 1964. *A Profile of the Negro American*. Princeton, N.J.: D. Van Nostrand.

_____. 1971. *Racially Separate on Together?* New York: McGraw-Hill.

Philipp, Thomas. 1978. "Feminism and nationalist politics in Egypt." Pp. 277–94 in L. Beck and N. Keddie, eds., *Women in the Muslim World*. Cambridge: Harvard University Press.

Pinkney, Alphonso. 1975. *Black Americans*. 2nd ed. Englewood Cliffs, N.J.: Prentice-Hall.

Pitch, Tamar. 1979. "Notes from within the Italian women's movement: How we talk of Marxism and feminism." *Contemporary Crisis* 3:1–16.

Pitts, James P. 1982. "The Afro-American experience: Changing modes of integration and race consciousness." Pp. 141–67 in A. G. Dworkin and R. J. Dworkin, eds., *The Minority Report*. 2nd ed. New York: Holt, Rinehart and Winston.

Polanyi, Karl. 1957. *The Great Transformation*. Boston: Beacon Press.

Pollock, Mordeca Jane. 1972. "Changing the role of women." Pp. 10–20 in H. Wortis and C. Rabinowitz, eds., *The Women's Movement*. New York: John Wiley & Sons.

Ponse, Barbara. 1978. *Identities in the Lesbian World*. Westport, Conn.: Greenwood Press.

Quataert, Jean. 1978. "Unequal partners in an uneasy alliance: Women and the working class in Imperial Germany." Pp. 112–45 in M. Boxer and J. Quataert, eds., *Socialist Women: European Socialist Feminism in the Nineteenth and Early Twentieth Centuries*. New York: Elsevier North-Holland.

_____. 1979. *Reluctant Feminists in German Social Democracy, 1885–1917*. Princeton, N.J.: Princeton University Press.

Rague-Arias, Maria-Jose. 1981. "Spain: Feminism in our time." *Women's Studies International Quarterly* 4:470–76.

Ransford, H. Edward. 1968. "Isolation, powerlessness, and violence: A study of attitudes and participation in the Watts riot." *American Journal of Sociology* 73:581–91.

Rasmussen, Janet E. 1982. "Sisters across the sea: Early Norwegian feminists and their American connections." *Women's Studies International Forum* 5(6):647–54.

Richards, Eric. 1982. *Past and Present, A Journal of Historical Studies: The Last Scottish Food Riots*. Kendal, Cumbria: Past and Present Society.

Richter, Maurice N., Jr. 1956. "The conceptual mechanism of stereotyping." *American Sociological Review* 21:568–71.

Riger, Stephanie. 1977. "Locus of control, belief, and female activism." *Psychological Reports* 41:1043–46.

Robertson, Priscilla. 1982. *An Experience of Women*. Philadelphia: Temple University Press.

Robins-Mowry, Dorothy. 1983. *The Hidden Sun: Women of Modern Japan*. Boulder, Colo.: Westview Press.

Rogers, Mary F. 1974. "Instrumental and infra-resources: The bases of power." *American Journal of Sociology* 79:1418–33.

Roodkowsky, Mary. 1979. "Feminism, peace, and power." Pp. 254–65 in Severyn Bruyn and Paula Rayman, eds., *Nonviolent Action and Social Change*. New York: Irvington Publishers.

Rosen, Andrew. 1974. *Rise Up Women! The Militant Campaign of the Women's Social and Political Union 1903–1914*. London: Routledge and Kegan Paul.

Rosenthal, Bernice Glatzer. 1977. "Love on the tractor: Women in the Russian Revolution and after." Pp. 372–99 in Renate Bridenthal and Claudia Koonz, eds., *Becoming Visible: Women in European History*. Boston: Houghton Mifflin.

Rossi, Alice. 1964. "Equality between the sexes: An immodest proposal." Pp. 98–143 in Robert J. Lifton, ed., *The Woman in America*. Boston: Beacon Press.

Rotter, Julian B. 1966. "Generalized expectancies for internal versus external control of reinforcement." *Psychological Monographs* 80 (complete no. 609).

Rowbotham, Sheila. 1972. *Women, Resistance and Revolution*. New York: Pantheon Books.

_____. 1976. *Hidden From History: Rediscovering Women in History from the 17th Century to the Present*. New York: Vintage Books (orig. pub. London, 1973).

_____. 1983. *Dreams and Dilemmas*. London: Virago Press.

Rudé, George. 1959. *The Crowd in the French Revolution*. Oxford, England: Oxford University Press.

_____. 1970. "The pre-industrial crowd." Pp. 108–20 in Joseph Gusfield, ed., *Protest, Reform, and Revolt*. New York: John Wiley & Sons.

Ruether, Rosemary. 1973. *Religion and Sexism: Images of Woman in Jewish and Christian Traditions*. New York: Simon & Schuster.

Russell, Jeffrey B. 1972. *Witchcraft in the Middle Ages*. Ithaca, N.Y.: Cornell University Press.

Ruthchild, Rochelle. 1983. "Sisterhood and socialism: The Soviet feminist movement." *Frontiers* 7(2):4–12.

Saffioti, Helerith. 1978. *Women in Class Society*, trans. M. Vale. New York: Monthly Review Press.

Sargent, Lydia. 1981. *Women and Revolution: A Discussion of the Unhappy Marriage of Marxism and Feminism*. Boston: South End Press.

Sarri, Rosemary. 1976. "Juvenile Law: How it penalizes females." In L. Crites, ed., *The Female Offender*. Lexington, Mass.: D. C. Heath.

Sauter-Bailliet, Theresia. 1981. "The feminist movement in France." *Women's Studies International Quarterly* 4:409–20.

Sayles, Marnieh. 1984. "Relative deprivation and collective protest: An impoverished theory." *Sociological Inquiry* 54:449–65.

Scharf, Lois, and Joan M. Jensen. 1983. *Decades of Discontent: The Women's Movement, 1920–1940*. Westport, Conn.: Greenwood Press.

Schlager, Hilke. 1978. "The West German women's movement." *New German Critique* 13:59–68.

Schmink, Marianne. 1981. "Women in Brazilian *Abertura* politics." *Signs* 7:115–34.

Schur, Edwin M. 1984. *Labeling Women Deviant: Gender, Stigma, and Social Control*. New York: Random House.

Schwartz, Janet. 1979. "Women under socialism: Role definitions of Soviet women." *Social Forces* 58(Sept.):67–88.

Sebald, Hans. 1978. *Witchcraft: The Heritage of Heresy*. New York: Elsevier-North Holland.

Sharp, Buchanan. 1980. *In Contempt of All Authority: Rural Artisans and Riot in the West of England, 1586–1660*. Berkeley: University of California Press.

Shaw, Marvin E., and Philip R. Constanzo. 1970. *Theories of Social Psychology*. New York: McGraw-Hill.

Shibutani, Tamotsu. 1955. "Reference groups as perspectives." *American Journal of Sociology* 60:562–69.

Sievers, Sharon L. 1983. *Flowers in Salt: The Beginnings of Feminist Consciousness in Modern Japan*. Stanford, Calif.: Stanford University Press.

Sinclair, Andrew. 1965. *The Emancipation of the American Woman*. New York: Harper & Row.

Skocpol, Theda. 1979. *States and Social Revolution*. New York: Cambridge University Press.

Slaughter, M. Jane. 1978. "Women and socialism: The case of Angelica Balabanoff." Pp. 55–63 in K. O'Conner Blumhagen and W. D. Johnson, eds., *Women's Studies: An Interdisciplinary Collection*, Westport, Conn.: Greenwood Press.

Smelser, Neil J. 1959. *Social Change and the Industrial Revolution: An Application of Theory to the British Cotton Industry.* Chicago: University of Chicago Press.

———. 1963. *Theory of Collective Behavior.* New York: The Free Press.

Smith, Dorothy E. 1975. "Women and Psychiatry." In D. Smith and S. David, eds., *Women Look at Psychiatry.* Vancouver, B.C.: Press Gang Publishers.

Snyder, D., M. Hayward, and P. Hudis. 1978. "Locations of change in the sexual structure of occupations 1950–1970: Insights from labor market segmentation theory." *American Journal of Sociology* 84:706–17.

Snyder, David, and Charles Tilly. 1972. "Hardship and collective violence in France, 1830 to 1960." *American Sociological Review* 37:520–32.

Sochen, June. 1973. *Movers and Shakers: American Women Thinkers and Activists 1900–1970.* New York: Quadrangle/New York Times Book Co.

Sorokin, Pitirim. 1963. *A Long Journey.* New Haven, Conn.: College and University Press.

Speizman, Milton D., and Jane C. Kronick. 1975. "A seventeenth-century Quaker Women's Declaration." *Signs* 1(Autumn):231–45.

Stampp, Kenneth M. 1956. *The Peculiar Institution: Slavery in the Ante-Bellum South.* New York: Alfred A. Knopf.

Staples, Robert. 1973. *The Black Woman in America.* Chicago: Nelson-Hall Publishers.

Steinson, Barbara J. 1982. *American Women's Activism in World War I.* New York: Garland Publishers.

Stephenson, Jill. 1975. *Women in Nazi Society.* New York: Harper & Row.

Stevenson, John. 1979. *Popular Disturbances in England; 1700–1870.* New York: Longman, Inc.

Stites, Richard. 1977. "Women and the Russian intelligentsia: Three perspectives." Pp. 39–62 in D. Atkinson, A. Dallin, and G. W. Lapidus, eds., *Women in Russia.* Stanford, Calif.: Stanford University Press.

———. 1978. *The Women's Liberation Movement in Russia.* Princeton, N.J.: Princeton University Press.

———. 1980. "The women's liberation issue in nineteenth century Russia." Pp. 21–30 in T. Yedlin, ed., *Women in Eastern Europe and the Soviet Union.* New York: Praeger Publishers.

Stouffer, Samuel A., E. A. Suchman, L. C. Devinney, S. A. Star, A. A. Lumsdaine, R. M. Williams, Jr., M. B. Smith, I. L. Janis, and L. S. Cottrell, Jr. 1949. *The American Soldier,* vols. I, II. Princeton, N.J.: Princeton University Press.

Strachey, Ray. 1968. *"The Cause." A Short History of the Women's Movement in Great Britain.* Port Washington, N.Y.: Kennikut Press (orig. pub. 1928).

Strayer, Joseph R. 1971. *The Albigensian Crusades.* New York: The Dial Press.

Streijffert, Helena. 1974. "The women's movement—A theoretical discussion." *Acta Sociologia* 17(4):344–66.

Stryker, Sheldon, and Anne Statham Macke. 1978. "Status inconsistency and role conflict." *Annual Review of Sociology* 4:47–90.

Summers, Anne. 1975. *Damned Whores and God's Police: The Colonization of Women in Australia.* Ringwood, Australia: Allen Lane.

Swerdlow, Amy. 1982. "Ladies day at the capital: Women Strike for Peace versus HUAC." *Feminist Studies* 8(3):498–520.

Szasz, Thomas S. 1961. *The Myth of Mental Illness.* New York: Harper & Row.

Taeuber, Karl E., and Alma F. Taeuber. 1965. *Negroes in Cities.* Chicago: Aldine Publishing Co.

Taylor, John M. 1974. *The Witchcraft Delusion in Colonial Connecticut.* Williamstown, Mass.: Corner House Publishers.

Teather, Lynne. 1976. "The feminist mosaic." Pp. 301–46 in G. Matheson, ed., *Women in the Canadian Mosaic.* Toronto: Peter Martin Associates.

Thomas, P. 1964. *Indian Women Through the Ages.* Bombay, India: Asia Publishing House.

Thomis, Malcolm I., and Jennifer Grimmett. 1982. *Women in Protest 1800–1850.* New York: St. Martin's Press.

Thompson, Daniel C. 1963. *The Negro Leadership Class.* Englewood Cliffs, N.J.: Prentice-Hall, Spectrum Books.

Thönnessen, Werner. 1973. *The Emancipation of Women: The Rise and Decline of the Women's Movement in Social Democracy 1863–1933.* Bristol, England: Pluto Press.

Tilly, Charles L. 1974. "The chaos of the living city." Pp. 86–108 in Charles Tilly, ed., *An Urban World.* Boston: Little, Brown.

———. 1978. *From Mobilization to Revolution.* Reading, Mass.: Addison-Wesley.

Tilly, Charles, Louise Tilly, and Richard Tilly. 1975. *The Rebellious Century 1830–1930.* Cambridge: Harvard University Press.

Toch, Hans. 1965. *The Social Psychology of Social Movements.* Indianapolis, Ind.: The Bobbs-Merrill Co.

Tolchin, Susan, and Martin Tolchin. 1976. *Clout: Womanpower and Politics.* New York: G. P. Putnam, Capricorn Books.

Trieman, Donald J. 1966. "Status discrepancy and prejudice." *American Journal of Sociology* 71:651–54.

Turner, Ralph, and Lewis Killian. 1972. *Collective Behavior.* Englewood Cliffs, N.J.: Prentice-Hall.

Useem, Bert. 1980. "Solidarity model, breakdown model, and the Boston anti-busing movement." *American Sociological Review* 45:357–69.

van den Berghe, Pierre. 1967. *Race and Racism: A Comparative Perspective.* New York: John Wiley & Sons.

Veevers, J. E. 1974. "Voluntary childless wives." In A. Skolnick and J. Skolnick, eds., *Intimacy, Family and Society.* Boston: Little, Brown.

Vogel, Lise. 1983. *Marxism and the Oppression of Women.* New Brunswick, N.J.: Rutgers University Press.

Von Eschen, Donald; Jerome Kirk; and Maurice Pinard. 1976. "The disintegration of the Negro non-violent movement." Pp. 203–26 in Robert H. Lauer, ed., *Social Movements and Social Change.* Carbondale: Southern Illinois University Press.

Vreede de Stuers, Cora. 1960. *The Indonesian Woman.* The Hague: Mouton.

Wakefield, Walter L. 1974. *Heresy, Crusade and Inquisition in Southern France, 1100–1250.* Berkeley: University of California Press.

Wall, Naomi. 1982. "The last ten years: A personal/political view." Pp. 15–27 in M. Fitzgerald, C. Guberman, and M. Wolfe, eds., *Still Ain't Satisfied: Canadian Feminism Today.* Toronto: The Women's Press.

Ware, Susan. 1981. *Beyond Suffrage: Women in the New Deal.* Cambridge: Harvard University Press.

Welch, Finis. 1975. "Human capital theory." *American Economic Review* 65:63–73.

Westie, Frank. 1964. "Race and ethnic relations." Pp. 576–618 in Robert E. L. Faris, ed., *Handbook of Modern Sociology.* Chicago: Rand McNally.

Whitehurst, Carol A. 1977. *Women in America: The Oppressed Majority.* Santa Monica, Calif.: Goodyear Publishing Co.

Whitworth, John McKelvie. 1975. *God's Blueprints: A Sociological Study of Three Utopian Sects.* London: Routledge and Kegan Paul.

Wilensky, Harold, and Charles N. Lebeaux. 1965. *Industrial Society and Social Welfare.* New York: The Free Press.

Williams, Raymond. 1960. *Culture and Society, 1780–1950.* Garden City, N.Y.: Doubleday/Anchor.

Wilson, Bryan R. 1961. *Sects and Society.* Berkeley: University of California Press.

Wilson, John. 1973. *Introduction to Social Movements.* New York: Basic Books.

Wilson, William J. 1980. *The Declining Significance of Race.* 2nd ed. Chicago: University of Chicago Press.

Wood, James L. 1974. *The Sources of American Student Activism.* Lexington, Mass.: Lexington Books, D. C. Heath.

Wood, James L., and Maurice Jackson. 1982. *Social Movements: Development, Participation and Dynamics.* Belmont, Calif.: Wadsworth Publishing Co.

Yates, Gayle Graham. 1975. *What Women Want: The Ideas of the Movement.* Cambridge: Harvard University Press.

Youssef, Nadia H., and Shirley Foster Hartley. 1979. "Demographic indicators of the status of women in various societies." Pp. 83–112 in Jean Lipman-Blumen and Jessie Bernard, eds., *Sex Roles and Social Policy.* Beverly Hills, Calif.: Sage Publications.

Zald, Mayer N., and Roberta Ash. 1966. "Social movement organizations: Growth, decay, and change." *Social Forces* 44:327–41.

Zald, Mayer, and John D. McCarthy. 1979. *The Dynamics of Social Movements.* Cambridge, Mass.: Winthrop Publishers.

Zwemer, Samuel M., and Mrs. S. Zwemer. 1926. *Moslem Women.* Brattleboro: The Vermont Printing Co.

Index